THE MOUNTAIN BIKER'S GUIDE

TO CENTRAL APPALACHIA

Dennis Coello's America by Mountain Bike Series

THE MOUNTAIN BIKER'S GUIDE TO CENTRAL APPALACHIA

Dennis Coello's America by Mountain Bike Series

West Virginia
Western Maryland
Pennsylvania
New York

Joe Surkiewicz

Foreword and Introduction
by Dennis Coello, Series Editor

MENASHA RIDGE PRESS

FALCON PRESS®

Published by Menasha Ridge Press and Falcon Press
First edition, first printing

Library of Congress Cataloging-in-Publication Data: 92-055132

ISBN: 1-56044-198-4

Maps by Julie and David Taff
Cover photo by Dennis Coello

Menasha Ridge Press
3169 Cahaba Heights Road
Birmingham, Alabama 35243

Falcon Press
P.O. Box 1718
Helena, Montana 59624

I thought all the wilderness of America was in the West till the ghost of the Susquehanna showed me different. No, there is a wilderness in the East; it's the same wilderness Ben Franklin plodded in the oxcart days when he was postmaster, the same as it was when George Washington was a wildbuck Indian-fighter, when Daniel Boone told stories by Pennsylvania lamps and promised to find the Gap, when Bradford built his road and men whooped her up in log cabins. There were not great Arizona spaces for the little man, just the bushy wilderness of eastern Pennsylvania, Maryland, and Virginia, the backroads, the black-tar roads that curve among the mournful rivers like Susquehanna, Monongahela, old Potomac and Monocacy.

From *On the Road*, Jack Kerouac

Table of Contents

List of Maps

MAP LEGEND

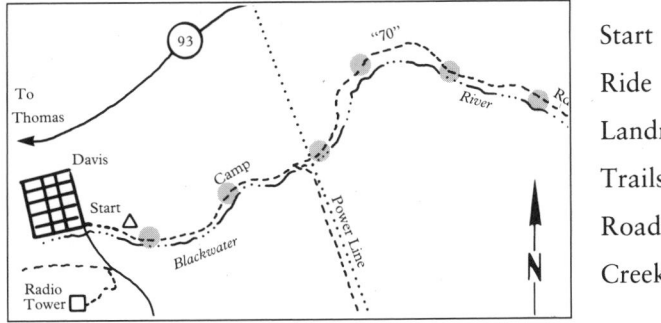

Foreword

Welcome to *America by Mountain Bike*, a twenty-book series designed to provide all-terrain bikers with the information necessary to find and ride the very best trails everywhere in the mainland United States. Whether you're new to the sport and don't know where to pedal, or an experienced mountain biker who wants to learn the classic trails in another region, this series is for you. Drop a few bucks for the book, spend an hour with the detailed maps and route descriptions, and you're prepared for the finest in off-road cycling.

My role as editor of this series was simple: First, find a mountain biker who knows the area and loves to ride. Second, ask that person to spend a year researching the most popular and very best rides around. And third, have that rider describe each trail in terms of difficulty, scenery, condition, elevation change, and all other categories of information which are important to trail riders. "Pretend you've just completed a ride and met up with fellow mountain bikers at the trailhead," I told each author. "Imagine their questions, be clear in your answers."

As I said, the *editorial* process—that of sending out riders and reading the submitted chapters—is a snap. But the work involved in finding, riding, and writing about each trail is enormous. In some instances our authors' tasks are made easier by the information contributed by local bike shops or cycling clubs, or even by the writers of local "where-to" guides. Credit for these contributions is provided in each chapter, and our sincere thanks go to all who have helped.

But the overwhelming majority of trails are discovered and pedaled by our authors themselves, then compared with dozens of other routes to determine if they qualify as "classic"—that area's best in scenery and cycling fun. If you've ever had the experience of pioneering a route from outdated topographic maps, or entering a bike shop to request information from local riders who would much prefer to keep their favorite trails secret, or know how it is to double- and triple-check data to be positive your trail info is correct, then you have an idea of how each of our authors has labored to bring about these books. You and I, and all the mountain bikers of America, are the richer for their efforts.

Dennis Coello
Salt Lake City

P.S. You'll get more out of this book if you take a moment to read the next few pages explaining the "Trail Description Outline." Newcomers to mountain biking might want to spend a minute as well with the Glossary, so that terms like *hardpack, single-track,* and *windfall* won't throw you when you come across them in the text. "Topographic Maps" will help you understand a biker's need for topos, and tell you where to find them. And the section titled "Land-Use Controversy" might help us all enjoy the trails a little more. Finally, though this is a "where-to," not a "how-to" guide, those of you who have not traveled the backcountry might find "Hitting the Trail" of particular value. All the best.

Preface

For the first 200 years after the Eastern Seaboard was settled, the central Appalachian Mountains formed a natural barrier that deterred pioneers from moving west. But the population of youthful America grew steadily. Around 1800 that barrier finally burst, and thousands of settlers surged west through the mountain passes into the Ohio Valley and beyond.

During the tumultuous years that followed, the West was won. And most people began to think of the East as a tame, settled world, inhabited by big-city slickers and sedentary bankers in bowler hats.

According to the myth, the *real* outdoor action had moved West, to the rugged frontier where the intrepid explorer could vanish at will into wild mountain terrain that promised both exhilarating opportunities and no small amount of physical risk.

That was the myth, anyway.

But this antiquated view has been shattered in recent years by a hardy new breed of recreational pioneers—mountain bikers—and their rediscovery of America's eastern wilderness.

Outfitted with the latest in lightweight, high-tech equipment, this new generation of cyclists can be found cruising along wooded ridges and plunging through mountain hollows from the Potomac Highlands of West Virginia to New York's Catskills.

As they climb old forest roads and descend on twisting single-track trails, mountain bikers are discovering that Jack Kerouac was right when he suggested that the mountains of the East contained wilderness aplenty for adventurers who know where to look.

This book is designed to help mountain bikers in their search for exciting wilderness rides. The trails it describes range in difficulty from easy rambles along rivers and canals to all-day treks through rugged mountains.

My survey of Central Appalachia's best rides begins in the high mountains of southeastern West Virginia and follows the ridges northeast through western Maryland and central Pennsylvania and into upstate New York. The terrain varies from Canadian-like tundra on the Allegheny Front in West Virginia to gentle paths along old railway routes in Pennsylvania's Poconos.

The southernmost rides, in Pocahontas County, West Virginia, are the highest, most rugged and remote—nearly six hours by car from any major city. Continuing northeast, the mountains get a little lower, and a lot closer to major highways. Davis, West Virginia, an increasingly popular destination for mid-Atlantic mountain bikers, is four hours from Washington, DC.

Who says biking in the mountains has to be hard? As this West Virginia rail trail shows, there's lots of easy riding in the Central Appalachians. *Photo by Steve Shaluta, Jr.*

In western Maryland the Appalachians are only a couple of hours from Washington, Baltimore, and Pittsburgh, while the trailheads are often only minutes from Interstate 68. Traveling farther to the northeast into Pennsylvania, you'll find highways that provide good access to state forests and gamelands which offer virtually unlimited opportunities for mountain biking.

Huge river valleys near Olean and Corning in western New York evoke images of Vermont, while in the Finger Lakes region of central New York state forests offer challenging mountain biking opportunities. Only a few hours north of New York City, the Shawangunk Mountains and Catskill Park are earning a national reputation among fat-tired cyclists. Some say the scenery rivals that of Colorado. And in Adirondack Park there are thousands of square miles of wilderness to explore.

And now a few words about riding in the Appalachians. These ancient, heavily forested mountains are often wet, especially in spring. Riding through creeks and wading small rivers with your bike hoisted on your shoulder is a common experience. Sinking in bogs up to your hubs is, alas, another.

Steep uphill climbs are a reality that can't be ignored. Many of the roads and trails were laid out by hardy pioneers with oxen-pulled carts who denied themselves the luxury of switchbacks. The short, steep, straight-to-the-top climbs can be a bear.

While mountain biking in the Appalachians is often challenging, the rewards are almost always worth the effort. In spring and summer the forests are green and explode with life. The sounds of birds fill the air, and it's not unusual to surprise a browsing deer, or a young black bear ambling up the trail ahead of you.

In winter, bare trees change the views dramatically. Trails along ridges, which in summer are often just narrow green tunnels through trees, open up to reveal dramatic views of neighboring mountains and valleys.

Yet many local riders say the best time to mountain bike the Appalachians is in fall. The leaves turn from dull green to brilliant red, orange, and yellow, and the air is crisp and cool. Fall is also the driest season of the year, making the roads and trails hard-packed and fast.

This book, however, is more than a collection of top-notch bike rides. It also contains numerous tributes to a great American institution—the bike shop.

As I did my research, it was bike shop owners and the people who work in them who took their time and drew on their love of cycling to show me their favorite rides, trace routes on maps, and at times even fix my bike. In many ways, therefore, this book is as much about America's dedicated bike shop professionals as it is about wilderness riding.

For most of us mountain biking is more than just a way to spin the cranks and get a good workout—it's our *favorite* way of exploring the backcountry.

And as we cruise these mountains day after day, we're confronted with some intriguing questions: What's on the other side of that ridge? Where does that single-track go? What's the view from the summit?

Armed with this guide, a knobby-tired bike, and a sense of adventure, you're ready to begin finding the answers.

Joe Surkiewicz

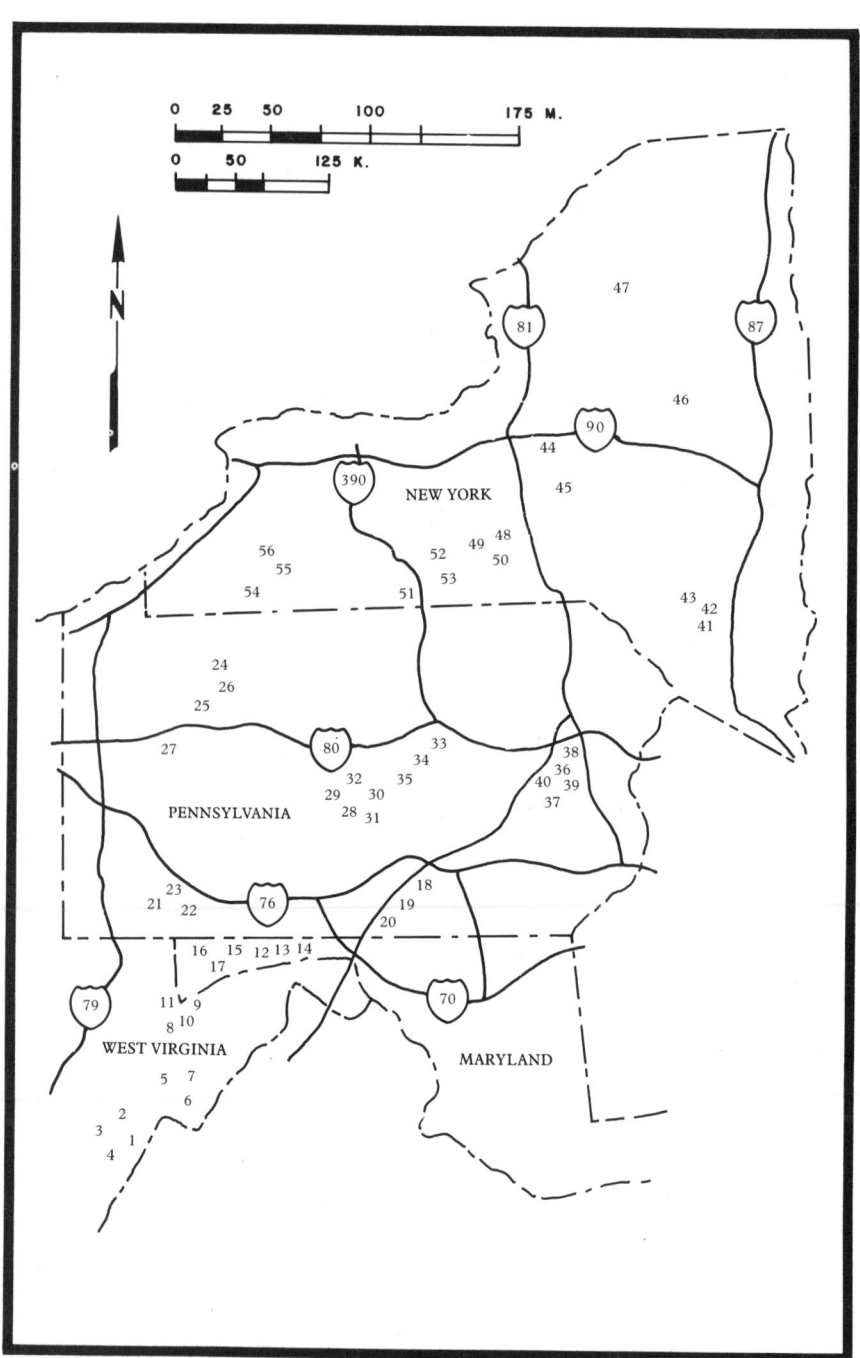

RIDE LOCATIONS

Introduction

TRAIL DESCRIPTION OUTLINE

Information on each trail in this book begins with a general description which includes length, configuration, scenery, highlights, trail conditions, and difficulty. Additional description is contained in eleven individual categories. The following will help you to understand all of the information provided.

Trail name: Trail names are as designated on USGS (United States Geological Survey) or Forest Service or other maps, and/or by local custom.

Length: The overall length of a trail is described in miles, unless stated otherwise.

Configuration: This is a description of the shape of each trail—whether the trail is a loop, out-and-back (that is, along the same route), figure-eight, trapezoid, isosceles triangle . . . , or if it connects with another trail described in the book.

Difficulty: This provides at a glance a description of the degree of physical exertion required to complete the ride, and the technical skill required to pedal it. Authors were asked to keep in mind the fact that all riders are not equal, and thus to gauge the trail in terms of how the middle-of-the-road rider—someone between the newcomer and Ned Overend—could handle the route. Comments about the trail's length, condition, and elevation change will also assist you in determining the difficulty of any trail relative to your own abilities.

Condition: Trails are described in terms of being paved, unpaved, sandy, hardpacked, washboarded, two- or four-wheel-drive, single-track or double-track. All terms that might be unfamiliar to the first-time mountain biker are defined in the Glossary.

Scenery: Here you will find a general description of the natural surroundings during the seasons most riders pedal the trail, and a suggestion of what is to be found at special times (like great fall foliage or cactus in bloom).

Highlights: Towns, major water crossings, historical sites, etc., are listed.

General location: This category describes where the trail is located in reference to a nearby town or other landmark.

Elevation change: Unless stated otherwise, the figure provided is the total gain and loss of elevation along the trail. In regions where the elevation variation is not extreme, the route is described in a more general manner of flat, rolling, or possessing short steep climbs or descents.

Season: This is the best time of year to pedal the route, taking into account trail condition (for example, when it will not be muddy), riding comfort (when the weather is too hot, cold, or wet), and local hunting seasons.

Note: Because the exact opening and closing dates of deer, elk, moose, and antelope seasons often change from year to year, it is suggested that riders check with the local Fish and Game department, or call a sporting goods store (or any place that sells hunting licenses) in a nearby town. Wear bright clothes in fall, and don't wear suede jackets while in the saddle. Hunter's-orange tape on the helmet is also a good idea.

Services: This category is of primary importance in guides for paved-road tourers, but is far less crucial to most mountain bike trail descriptions because there are usually no services whatsoever to be found. Authors have noted when water is available on desert or long mountain routes, and have listed the availability of food, lodging, campgrounds, and bike shops. If all these services are present, you will find only the words "All services available in...."

Hazards: Special hazards like steep cliffs, great amounts of deadfall, or barbed-wire fences very close to the trail are noted here.

Rescue index: Determining how far one is from help on any particular trail can be difficult due to the backcountry nature of most mountain bike rides. Authors therefore state the proximity of homes or Forest Service outposts, nearby roads where one might hitch a ride, or the likelihood of other bikers being encountered on the trail. Phone numbers of local sheriff departments or hospitals have not been provided because, again, phones are almost never available. Besides, if a phone is reached the local operator will connect you with emergency services.

Land status: This category provides information as to whether the trail crosses land operated by the Forest Service, Bureau of Land Management, a city, state, or national park, whether it crosses private land whose owner (at the time the author did the research) allowed mountain bikers right of passage, and so on.

Note: Authors have been extremely careful to offer only those routes that are open to bikers and are legal to ride. However, because land ownership changes over time, and because the land-use controversy created by mountain bikes still has not subsided totally, it is the duty of each cyclist to look for and to heed signs warning against trail use. Don't expect this book to get you off the hook when you're facing some small-town judge for pedaling past a "Biking Prohibited" sign erected the day before. Look for these signs, read them, and heed the advice. And remember there's always another trail.

Maps: The maps in this book have been produced with great care, and in conjunction with the trail-following suggestions will help you stay on course. But as every experienced mountain biker knows, things can get tricky in the backcountry. It is therefore strongly suggested that you avail yourself of the detailed information found in the 7.5 minute series USGS (United States Geological Survey) topographic maps. In some cases, authors have found that specific Forest Service or other maps may be more useful than the USGS quads, and tell how to obtain them.

Finding the trail: Detailed information on how to reach the trailhead, and where to park your car is provided here.

Sources of additional information: Here you will find the address and/or phone number of a bike shop, governmental agency, or other source from which trail information can be obtained.

Notes on the trail: This is where you are stepped carefully through any portions of the trail that are particularly difficult to follow. The author also may add information about the route that does not fit easily into the other categories.

ABBREVIATIONS

The following road-designation abbreviations are used in the *America by Mountain Bike* series:

CR	County Road
FR	Farm Route
FS	Forest Service road
I-	Interstate
IR	Indian Route
US	United States highway

State highways are designated with the appropriate two-letter state abbreviation, followed by the road number. *Example:* UT 6 = Utah State Highway 6.

Postal Service two-letter state code

AL	Alabama	MT	Montana
AK	Alaska	NE	Nebraska
AZ	Arizona	NV	Nevada
AR	Arkansas	NH	New Hampshire
CA	California	NJ	New Jersey
CO	Colorado	NM	New Mexico
CT	Connecticut	NY	New York
DE	Delaware	NC	North Carolina
DC	District of Columbia	ND	North Dakota
FL	Florida	OH	Ohio
GA	Georgia	OK	Oklahoma
HI	Hawaii	OR	Oregon

ID	Idaho	PA	Pennsylvania
IL	Illinois	RI	Rhode Island
IN	Indiana	SC	South Carolina
IA	Iowa	SD	South Dakota
KS	Kansas	TN	Tennessee
KY	Kentucky	TX	Texas
LA	Louisiana	UT	Utah
ME	Maine	VT	Vermont
MD	Maryland	VA	Virginia
MA	Massachusetts	WA	Washington
MI	Michigan	WV	West Virginia
MN	Minnesota	WI	Wisconsin
MS	Mississippi	WY	Wyoming
MO	Missouri		

TOPOGRAPHIC MAPS

The maps in this book, when used in conjunction with the route directions present in each chapter, will in most instances be sufficient to get you to the trail and keep you on it. However, these maps cannot begin to provide the detailed information found in the 7.5 minute series USGS (United States Geological Survey) topographic maps. Recognizing how indispensable these are to bikers and hikers alike, many bike shops and sporting goods stores now carry topos of the local area.

But if you're brand new to mountain biking you might be wondering "What's a topographic map?" In short, these differ from standard "flat" maps because they indicate not only linear distance, but elevation as well. One glance at a topo will show you the difference, for "contour lines" are spread across the map like dozens of intricate spider webs. Each contour line represents a particular elevation, and each topo has written at its base a particular "contour interval" designation. Yes, it sounds confusing if you're new to the lingo, but it truly is a simple and wonderfully helpful system. Keep reading.

Let's assume that the 7.5 minute series topo before us says "Contour Interval 40 feet." And that the short trail we'll be pedaling is two inches in length on the map, and crosses five contour lines between its beginning and end. What do we know? Well, because the linear scale of this series is two thousand feet to the inch (roughly 2¾ inches representing a mile), we know our trail is approximately four-fifths of a mile long (2" × 2,000'). But we also know we'll be climbing or descending two hundred vertical feet (5 contour lines × 40 feet each) over that distance. And the elevation designations written on occasional contour lines will tell us if we're heading up or down.

The authors of this series warn their readers of upcoming terrain, but only a detailed topo gives you the information that enables you to pinpoint your position exactly on a map, steer you toward optional trails and roads nearby, plus let you know at a glance if you'll be pedaling hard to take them. It's a lot of information for a very low cost. In fact, the only drawback with topos is their size—several feet square. I've tried rolling them into tubes, folding them carefully, even cutting them into blocks and photocopying the pieces. Any of these systems is a pain, but no matter how you pack the maps you'll be happy they're along (you'll want to take a compass, too).

Major universities and some public libraries also carry topos; you might try photocopying the ones you need to avoid the cost of buying them. But if you want your own and can't find them locally, write to:

USGS Map Sales
Box 25286
Denver, Colorado 80225

Ask for an index while you're at it, plus a price list and a copy of the booklet *Topographic Maps*. In minutes you'll be reading them like a pro.

A second excellent series of maps available to mountain bikers is that put out by the United States Forest Service. If your trail runs through an area designated as a national forest, look in the phone book (white pages) under the United States Government listings, find the Department of Agriculture heading, and then run your finger through that section until you find the Forest Service. Give them a call and they'll provide the address of the regional Forest Service office, from which you can obtain the appropriate map.

LAND-USE CONTROVERSY

A few years ago I wrote a long piece on this issue for *Sierra Magazine*, and called literally dozens of government land managers, game wardens, mountain bikers, and local officials, to get a feeling for how ATBs were being welcomed on the trails. All that I've seen personally since, and heard from my authors, indicates there hasn't been much change. Which means we're still considered the new kid on the block, that we have less right to the trails than horses and hikers, and that we're excluded from many areas including:

a) wilderness areas
b) national parks (except on roads, and those paths specifically marked "bike path")
c) national monuments (except on roads open to the public)
d) most state parks and monuments (except on roads, and those paths specifically marked "bike path")

e) an increasing number of urban and county parks, especially in California (except on roads, and those areas specifically marked "bike path")

Frankly, I have little difficulty with these exclusions, and would in fact restrict our presence from some trails I've ridden (one time) due to the environmental damage and chance of blind-siding the many walkers and hikers I met up with along the way. But these are my personal views. They should not be interpreted as those of the authors, and are mentioned here only as a way to introduce the land-use problem and the varying positions on it which even mountain bikers hold.

You can do your part in keeping us from being excluded from even more trails by riding responsibly. Many local and national off-road bicycle organizations have been formed with exactly this in mind, and one of the largest—NORBA, the National Off-Road Bicycle Association—offers the following code of behavior for mountain bikers:

1. I will yield the right of way to other non-motorized recreationists. I realize that people judge all cyclists by my actions.
2. I will slow down and use caution when approaching or overtaking another and will make my presence known well in advance.
3. I will maintain control of my speed at all times and will approach turns in anticipation of someone around the bend.
4. I will stay on designated trails to avoid trampling native vegetation and minimize potential erosion to trails by not using muddy trails or short-cutting switchbacks.
5. I will not disturb wildlife or livestock.
6. I will not litter. I will pack out what I pack in, and pack out more than my share whenever possible.
7. I will respect public and private property, including trail use signs, no trespassing signs, and I will leave gates as I have found them.
8. I will always be self-sufficient and my destination and travel speed will be determined by my ability, my equipment, the terrain, the present and potential weather conditions.
9. I will not travel solo when bikepacking in remote areas. I will leave word of my destination, and when I plan to return.
10. I will observe the practice of minimum impact bicycling by "taking only pictures and memories and leaving only waffle prints."
11. I will always wear a helmet whenever I ride.

Now, I have a problem with some of these—number nine, for instance. The most enjoyable mountain biking I've ever done has been solo. And as to leaving word of destination and time of return, I've enjoyed living in such a way as to say, "I'm off to pedal Colorado. See you in the fall." Of course it's senseless to take needless risks, and I plan a ride and pack my gear with this in mind. But for me number nine smacks too much of the "never-out-of-touch" mentality. And getting away from civilization, deep into the wilds, is for many people what mountain biking's all about.

All in all, however, theirs is a good list, and surely we mountain bikers would be liked more, and excluded less, if we followed the suggestions. But let me offer a "code of ethics" I much prefer, one given cyclists by Utah's Wasatch-Cache National Forest office.

Study a Forest Map Before You Ride
Currently, bicycles are permitted on roads and developed trails within the Wasatch-Cache National Forest except in designated Wilderness. If your route crosses private land, it is your responsibility to obtain right of way permission from the land owner.

Keep Groups Small
Riding in large groups degrades the outdoor experience for others, can disturb wildlife and usually leads to greater resource damage.

Avoid Riding on Wet Trails
Bicycle tires leave ruts in wet trails. These ruts concentrate runoff and accelerate erosion. Postponing a ride when the trails are wet will preserve the trails for future use.

Stay on Roads and Trails
Riding cross-country destroys vegetation and damages the soil.

Always Yield to Others
Trails are shared by hikers, horses and bicycles. Move off the trail to allow horses to pass and stop to allow hikers adequate room to share the trail. Simply yelling "Bicycle!" is not acceptable.

Control Your Speed
Excessive speed endangers yourself and other forest users.

Avoid Wheel Lock-up and Spin-out
Steep terrain is especially vulnerable to trail wear. Locking brakes on steep descents or when stopping needlessly damages trails. If a slope is steep enough to require locking wheels and skidding, dismount and walk your bicycle. Likewise, if an ascent is so steep your rear wheel slips and spins, dismount and walk your bicycle.

Protect Waterbars and Switchbacks
Waterbars, the rock and log drains built to direct water off trails, protect trails from erosion. When you encounter a waterbar, ride directly over the top or dismount and walk your bicycle. Riding around the ends of waterbars destroys them and speeds erosion. Skidding around switch-

back corners shortens trail life. Slow down for switchback corners and keep your wheels rolling.

If You Abuse It, You Lose It

Mountain bikes are relative newcomers to the forest and must prove themselves responsible trail users. By following the guidelines above, and by participating in trail maintenance service projects, bicyclists can help avoid closures which would prevent them from using trails.

I've never seen a better trail-etiquette list for mountain bikers. So have fun. Be careful. And don't screw up things for the next guy.

HITTING THE TRAIL

Once again, because this is a "where-to," not a "how-to" guide, the following will be brief. If you're a veteran trail rider these suggestions might serve to remind you of something you've forgotten to pack. If you're a newcomer, they might convince you to think twice before hitting the backcountry unprepared.

Water: I've heard the questions dozens of times. "How much is enough? One bottle? Two? Three?! But think of all that extra weight!" Well, one simple physiological fact should convince you to err on the side of excess when it comes to determining how much water to pack: a human working hard in ninety-degree temperature needs approximately ten quarts of fluids every day. Ten quarts. That's two and a half gallons—*twelve* large water bottles, or *sixteen* small ones. And with water weighing in at approximately eight pounds per gallon, a one-day supply comes to a whopping twenty pounds.

In other words, pack along two or three bottles even for short rides. And make sure you can purify the water found along the trail on longer routes. When writing of those routes where this could be of critical importance, each author has provided information on where water can be found near the trail—if it can be found at all. But drink it untreated and you run the risk of disease. [See *Giardia* in the Glossary.]

One sure way to kill both the bacteria and viruses in water is to boil it for ten minutes, plus one minute more for each one thousand feet of elevation above sea level. Right. That's just how you want to spend your time on a bike ride. Besides, who wants to carry a stove, or denude the countryside stoking bonfires to boil water?

Luckily, there is a better way. Many riders pack along the effective, inexpensive, and only slightly distasteful tetraglycine hydroperiodide tablets (sold under the names of Potable Aqua, Globaline, Coughlan's, and others). Some invest in portable, lightweight purifiers that filter out the crud. Yes, purifying water with tablets or filters is a bother. But catch a case of Giardia sometime and you'll understand why it's worth the trouble.

Tools: Ever since my first cross-country tour in '65 I've been kidded about the number of tools I pack on the trail. And so I will exit entirely from this discussion by providing a list compiled by two mechanic (and mountain biker) friends of mine. After all, since they make their livings fixing bikes, and get their kicks by riding them, who could be a better source?

The following is suggested as an absolute minimum:

tire levers
spare tube and patch kit
air pump
allen wrenches (3, 4, 5, and 6 mm)
six-inch crescent (adjustable-end) wrench
small flat-blade screwdriver
chain rivet tool
spoke wrench

But their personal tool pouches carried on the trail contain, in addition to the above:

channel locks (small)
air gauge
tire valve cap (the metal kind, with a valve-stem remover)
baling wire (ten or so inches, for temporary repairs)
duct tape (small roll for temporary repairs or tire boot)
boot material (small piece of old tire or a large tube patch)
spare chain link
rear derailleur pulley
spare nuts and bolts
paper towel and tube of waterless hand cleaner

First-aid kit: My personal kit contains the following, sealed inside double zip-lock bags:

sunshade
aspirin
butterfly closure bandages
band-aids
gauze compress pads (a half-dozen 4"×4")
gauze (one roll)
ace bandages or Spenco joint wraps
Benadryl (an antihistamine to guard against possible allergic reactions)
water purification tablets
moleskin/Spenco "Second Skin"

hydrogen peroxide/iodine/Mercurochrome (some kind of antiseptic)
snakebite kit

Final considerations: The authors of this series have done a good job in suggesting that specific items be packed for certain trails—like raingear in particular seasons, a hat and gloves for mountain passes, or shades for desert jaunts. Heed their warnings, and think ahead. Good luck.

Dennis Coello
Salt Lake City

WEST VIRGINIA

Pocahontas County

For mountain bikers who like riding in wilderness—and lots of it—Pocahontas County is arguably the best mountain biking destination in the East. Consider: This county in southeastern West Virginia boasts a major chunk of the 830,000-acre Monongahela National Forest, where the rugged Allegheny Mountains soar toward 5,000 feet. Here too are the headwaters of eight rivers: the Greenbrier, Cherry, Elk, Cheat, Gauley, Tygart Valley, Williams, and Cranberry. With 330,000 acres of state and national forests to explore in Pocahontas County alone, it's not stretching the point to call this place "Mountain Bike Heaven."

Additional high-quality wilderness attractions include the Cranberry Glades Wilderness Area (closed to mountain bikes, but open to mountain *bikers* who don't mind hiking for a while), which features 35,000 acres of bogs and forests that evoke visions of Alaskan tundra. Underground erosion created over 96 significant caverns in the county. The Cass Scenic Railroad, a steam locomotive–pulled train that climbs Bald Knob (the state's second-highest peak), is a spectacular trip that should not be missed. The Highland Scenic Highway extends 22 miles at altitudes reaching over 4,000 feet, and has views of wilderness stretching in all directions to the horizon.

So what's the mountain biking like in Pocahontas County? The answer is scenic, varied, and virtually unlimited. While many trails are surprisingly easy (the Greenbrier River Trail, for example, is 75 miles long and virtually flat), the region is renowned for its steep and rugged trails. Be warned: Mountain biking on foot trails in the mountains often means negotiating wet, steep, rocky, boggy, and root-tangled obstacle courses. If this isn't your idea of fun, stick to the many Forest Service roads that lace the mountains. But if mile after mile of technical single-track turns you on, this is the place.

A word of warning to intrepid backcountry trekkers: The weather in the high mountains of Pocahontas County matches the terrain for severity and unpredictability. Mountain bikers embarking on an all-day ride should carry rain gear and extra clothes, food, water, first-aid items, tools, a topo map, and compass.

Mountain bike headquarters in Pocahontas County is the Elk River Touring Center in Slatyfork, a small village about 20 miles north of Marlinton. Owners Gil and Mary Willis started guiding mountain bike tours in 1984 and are the resident mountain biking experts for this vast area. On your visit to Pocahontas County, be sure to visit Slatyfork for the latest information on trail conditions. Elk River also offers lodging, an excellent restaurant, a mountain bike shop and rentals, and touring services (both guided and self-guided). Gil and Mary want to help visiting mountain bikers have a good time, and thereby spread the word about "Mountain Bike Heaven."

RIDE 1   *GREENBRIER RIVER TRAIL / MARLINTON TO SHARP'S TUNNEL*

The Greenbrier River Trail winds through a remote mountain valley along a clean, fast-flowing river that has been involved in wild and scenic river studies. Old Appalachian farms, many of them deserted and overgrown, overlook the river. On this section of the trail you can explore the 511'-long Sharp's Tunnel. And if the weather's warm, check out the swimming hole at the base of the trestle leading to the tunnel. The wildflower blossoms in late May and early June are spectacular.

This 8.5-mile (one-way), out-and-back ride takes you along some of the best scenery in Pocahontas County. And being virtually flat, it's a perfect introductory ride to the area. The trail, formerly a railroad right-of-way, is mostly hard-packed gravel. There are short sections of loose gravel, and washouts occasionally occur where streams and creeks empty into the river.

General location: The ride starts in Marlinton, West Virginia, located on US 219 between Lewisburg and Elkins.

Elevation change: With a virtually flat grade, the change in elevation along the trail is nominal.

Season: The trail can be ridden from late March through late October. Spring can be muddy and cold, and expect snow from November through March. Avoid riding in deer hunting season, in the late fall.

Services: All services are available in Marlinton. Water is available at the restored railroad depot in town. Two primitive camping areas ideal for cyclists are located above and below Sharp's Tunnel. Elk River Touring Center, 20 miles north of Marlinton in Slatyfork, has a mountain bike shop.

Hazards: Sharp's Tunnel is littered with rocks; carrying a flashlight is a good idea, although not absolutely necessary. Watch for washouts along the trail where creeks flow into the river.

Rescue index: The trail runs through isolated country. While there are farms in the area, many are remote and hard to reach.

Land status: West Virginia state park.

Maps: A map of the Greenbrier River Trail is available at the restored railroad depot in Marlinton. The USGS 7.5 minute topo maps for this section of the Greenbrier River Trail are Marlinton and Edray.

Finding the trail: Marlinton is located at the intersection of WV 39 and US 219, between Lewisburg and Elkins, West Virginia. Park at the Old Train

GREENBRIER RIVER TRAIL/
MARLINTON TO SHARP'S TUNNEL

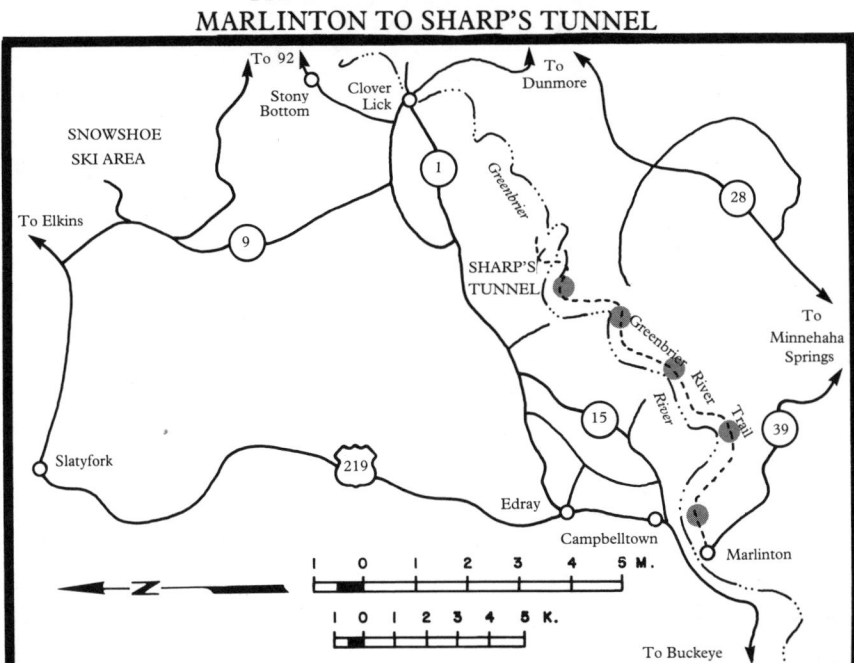

Depot on Main Street (WV 39), which serves as Marlinton's Visitor Center. The trail starts behind the building.

Sources of additional information:

Superintendent
Greenbrier River Trail
Star Route
Box 125
Caldwell, West Virginia 24925
(304) 536-1944

Pocahontas County Tourism Commission
P.O. Box 275
Marlinton, West Virginia 24954
(800) 336-7009

Elk River Touring Center
Slatyfork, West Virginia 26291
(304) 572-3771

Easy pedaling along the Greenbrier River. *Photo by Ron Snow*

Notes on the trail: From the Old Train Depot, pedal out 4th Avenue for a half mile to the sign for the trail on the left. This stretch of the Greenbrier River Trail north of Marlinton is probably the most scenic and remote on the trail's 75-mile length. As it winds its way through the river valley, the trail passes through many villages and traverses 35 bridges and 2 tunnels.

RIDE 2   *PROP'S RUN*

Here's a ride for the serious off-road enthusiast that shows what West Virginia mountain biking is all about. Strictly for experienced, well-conditioned cyclists, Prop's Run is a 16-mile loop that climbs for 2,000′ on a well-main-

PROP'S RUN

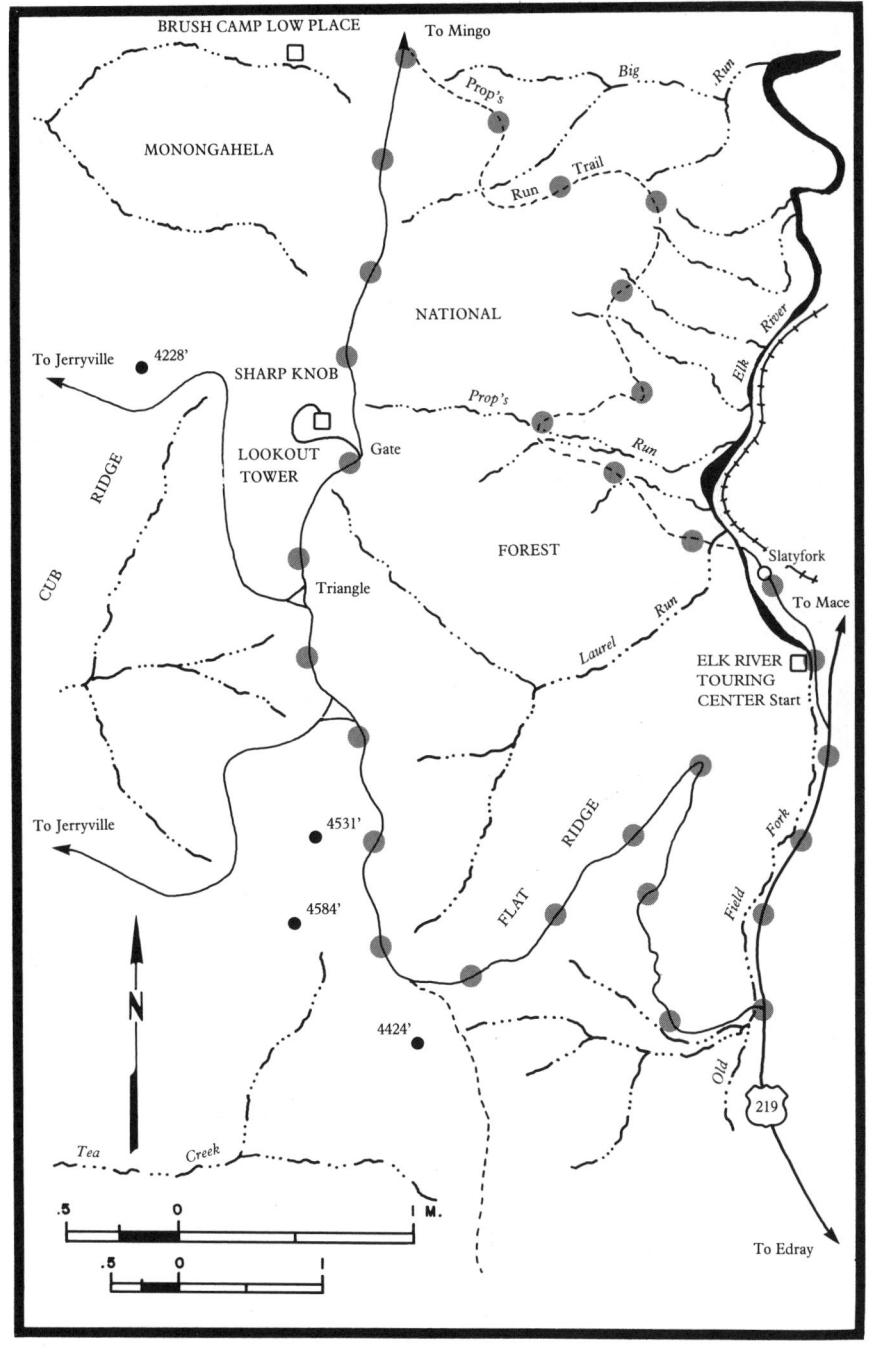

tained Forest Service road, followed by 6 miles of steep, wet, and rocky downhill single-track that only expert riders will "clean."

From the lookout tower on Sharp Knob, spectacular wilderness views in all directions are your reward for the long climb. But for the truly hard-core, it's the 6 intense miles of downhill single-track on Prop's Run that make this ride memorable. After the hammering descent, the final spin along the Elk River is quiet and peaceful, and affords a nice place to wash off your bike. It'll need it.

General location: Monongahela National Forest, near the village of Slatyfork, 20 miles north of Marlinton, West Virginia.

Elevation change: The ride starts at 2,735' of elevation in Slatyfork and climbs to 4,532' at the lookout tower on Sharp Knob. Next comes approximately 2 miles of roller-coaster Forest Service road. At the trailhead to Prop's Run, the elevation is 4,216' and drops to 2,671'. The total elevation gain is around 2,000'.

Season: The best riding is from mid-May through early October. Spring is wet and usually cold. Expect snow from late October through April. Avoid riding in deer hunting season, in the late fall.

Services: Water, bicycle equipment and repairs, a restaurant and lodging are available at Elk River Touring Center. All other services are available in Marlinton to the south and in Linwood to the north. Camping is available at Tea Creek Campground and Handley Public Hunting and Fishing Area.

Hazards: You can get seriously lost in this wilderness, so be sure to carry a topo map and compass. The weather in these mountains can change dramatically. Carry raingear, extra clothing, food, water, first-aid items, and tools. The single-track is intense; don't exceed your abilities.

Rescue index: Mountain bikers won't see a soul on this ride. There are no residences, very little traffic on the Forest Service road, no farms, no *nothing*.

Land status: Monongahela National Forest.

Maps: The USGS 7.5 minute topo is Sharp Knob.

Finding the trail: The ride starts at Elk River Touring Center on US 219 in Slatyfork, about 20 miles north of Marlinton. Park in the lot past the wooden bridge.

Sources of additional information:

District Ranger
Monongahela National Forest
Cemetery Road
Marlinton, West Virginia 24954
(304) 799-4334

Elk River Touring Center
Slatyfork, West Virginia 26291
(304) 572-3771

Notes on the trail: Riding from the Touring Center in Slatyfork, turn right on US 219 and go 1.5 miles to Forest Service Road 24; turn right. Stay on this road, climbing past several trailheads and roads on the left, to the big intersection with the triangle in the middle of the road (look for pine trees growing inside the triangle) and bear right. Pass through a gate past the lookout tower on Sharp Knob, then look for the Prop's Run Trail sign on the right.

At the end of the trail, cross Laurel Run, a small stream. Ride 50 yards to a "T" intersection and turn left to reach the Elk River. Wade through the river; the old ford turns into a double-track trail. Follow it across the railroad tracks, bear right and pedal about .2 miles to US 219, which is paved. Turn right for the short return spin to Elk River Touring Center.

RIDE 3 *RED RUN*

While only a 7-mile loop ride, this stretch of single-track is demanding. Though fairly level, the technical riding requirements make up for the lack of climbing. Most of the trail surfaces are spongy and mossy—and wet. Rocks, wet roots, bogs, deep mud, and stream crossings make for low-speed, technical riding. The trails are frequently littered with deadfalls. Yet intermediate- and advanced-level riders will be delighted by the challenges of the trails and the natural beauty of the area.

The ride starts in lush hardwood forests, progresses through red spruce groves, and then ends in a mixed hardwood and spruce forest. From the overlook at the start, the view is of cranberry bogs and the headwaters of the Williams River. Hawks soar at eye level. This is subtle, beautiful, rugged West Virginia at its best.

General location: Monongahela National Forest, off the Highland Scenic Highway, about 10 miles from Marlinton, West Virginia.

Elevation change: The ride starts at 4,200' of elevation and varies only a few hundred feet or so over its length.

Season: The trail is usually rideable from mid-May through early October. Avoid riding in deer hunting season, in the late fall. Expect snow from late October through March.

Services: Most services are available in Marlinton, about 10 miles from the intersection of US 219 and the Scenic Highway. Bike supplies, repairs, a restaurant and lodging are available at Elk River Touring Center in Slatyfork, about 9 miles north on US 219.

Hazards: The single-track is technical, with lots of slick rocks and tree roots. The weather at this altitude changes fast, so carry raingear, extra clothes, food, water, first-aid items, and tools.

RED RUN

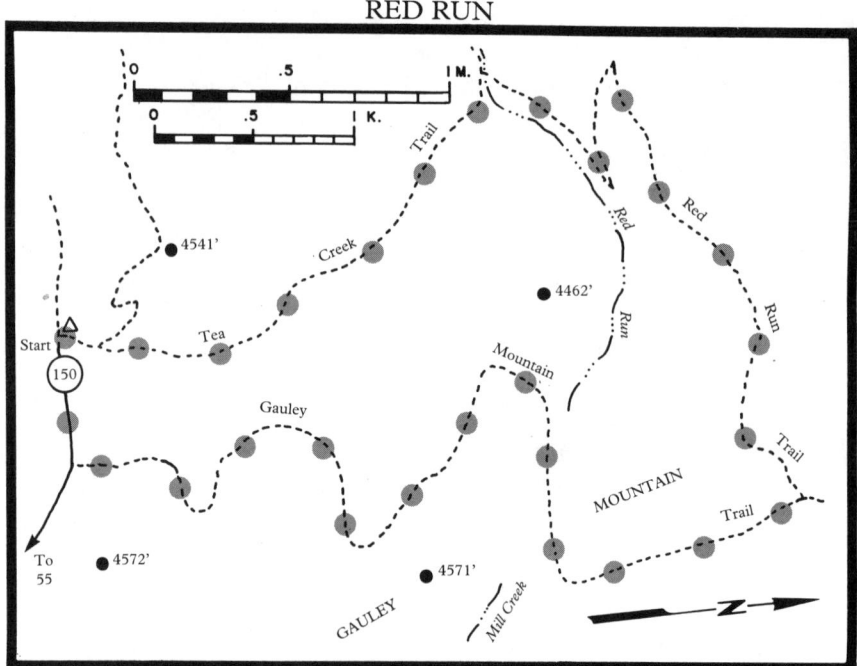

Rescue index: This ride goes deep into the national forest; there are no farms or residences on the loop. Cars can be flagged down on the Scenic Highway where the ride starts.

Land status: Monongahela National Forest.

Maps: The USGS 7.5 minute topo is Woodrow.

Finding the trail: From Marlinton, drive north on US 219 to the intersection with WV 150, the Highland Scenic Highway. Drive 4 miles to the second overlook (Little Laurel Overlook), and park. The trailhead is across the road and through the large field.

Sources of additional information:

District Ranger
Monongahela National Forest
Cemetery Road
Marlinton, West Virginia 24954
(304) 799-4334

Elk River Touring Center
Slatyfork, West Virginia 26291
(304) 572-3771

Riders cross an open field to begin the Red Run—a demanding 7-mile stretch of single track. *Photo by Ron Snow*

Notes on the trail: To start the loop, turn right out of the overlook parking lot and ride down the Scenic Highway a short distance to the Gauley Mountain Trail on the left.

Red Run Trail is significantly more gnarly than Gauley Mountain Trail; if it gets too intense, turn back and continue on Gauley Mountain Trail to do an easier out-and-back ride. All the trails in this area are signed, so it's an easy area to explore.

RIDE 4   *WILLIAMS RIVER LOOP*

While this 12-mile loop begins and ends at the same location as the Red Run ride, it's completely different in character. Technically, it's easy, but requires good endurance for the long climbs. The loop begins on the paved Highland Scenic Highway, then changes to a gravel road, then to a dirt road, and then

WILLIAMS RIVER LOOP

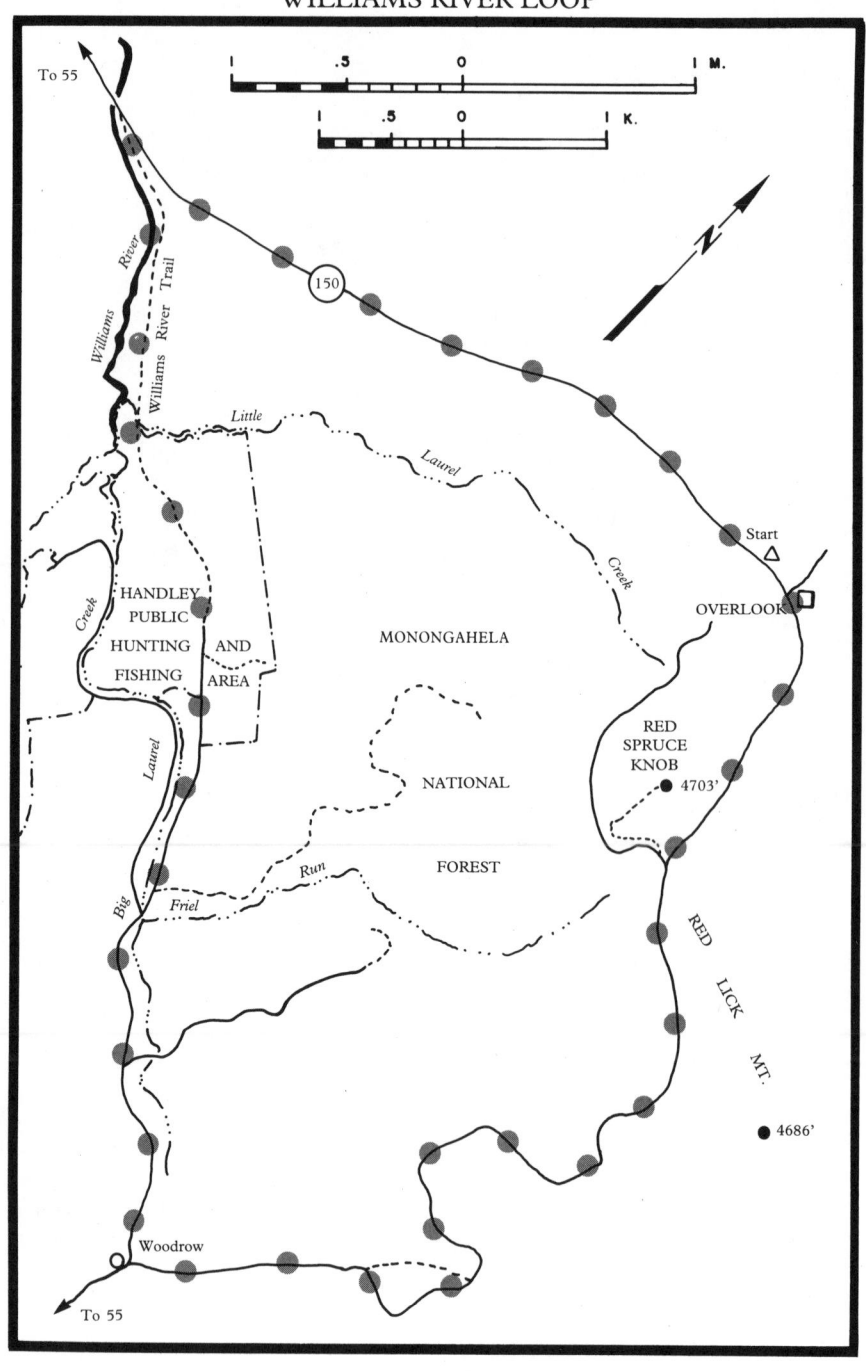

to a wide, grassy single-track. The ride finishes with a long climb on the paved Scenic Highway.

This ride is an energetic blast through huge mountains and isolated alpine valleys. At the beginning of the loop, the descent on the gravel road into Woodrow seems like it goes forever. Then it continues through the Handley Public Hunting and Fishing Area, with views of ponds and lakes, ducks and geese, and the Williams River. On the climb back to the start the vista gets better and better, which helps take your mind off your legs.

At the beginning of the ride there are majestic views from the Highland Scenic Highway. After the descent into the Williams River Valley the loop winds through sheep farms, old homesteads, meadows, and forests with a backdrop of 5,000' mountains. Along the headwaters of the Williams River, the views from the trail look down through mixed pine and hardwood forests to the river below.

General location: Monongahela National Forest and Handley Public Hunting and Fishing Area, off the Highland Scenic Highway near Marlinton, West Virginia.

Elevation change: The ride starts at 4,200' of elevation and drops to 3,200' at Woodrow. This is followed by some roller coaster riding that drops to 3,022'. The ride ends with a 1,200' climb back to the overlook on the Scenic Highway. The total elevation gain is around 1,400'.

Season: This route is rideable from late May through early October. Expect snow from late October through April. Avoid riding in deer hunting season, in late November.

Services: Most services are available in Marlinton, about 10 miles from the intersection of US 219 and the Highland Scenic Highway. Bike supplies, repairs, a restaurant and lodging are available at Elk River Touring Center in Slatyfork, about 9 miles north on US 219.

Hazards: The descent on the gravel road from the overlook is long and steep; watch for metal cattle grates, which should be crossed at right-angles.

Rescue index: There is light traffic on all the roads on this loop. You will find a forest ranger residence at the Handley Public Hunting and Fishing Area.

Land status: Monongahela National Forest, state game lands, state and county roads.

Maps: The USGS 7.5 minute topo is Woodrow.

Finding the trail: From Marlinton, drive north on US 219 to the intersection with WV 150, the Highland Scenic Highway. Drive 4 miles to the second pulloff (Little Laurel Overlook), and park.

Sources of additional information:

District Ranger
Monongahela National Forest
Cemetery Road

Marlinton, West Virginia 24954
(304) 799-4334

Elk River Touring Center
Slatyfork, West Virginia 26291
(304) 572-3771

Notes on the trail: From the overlook, turn right and continue on the Scenic Highway past the head of the Gauley Mountain Trail on the left. At the next intersection turn right, ride about 60 yards, and turn left onto Williams River Road (a gravel road that starts to drop rapidly). The gravel road ends at a "T" intersection; turn right onto the paved road and ride into Woodrow. Follow the signs into the Handley Public Hunting and Fishing Area. At the lake, the road turns to gravel. Ride toward the houses and through the gate; the road will begin to narrow into single-track (the Williams River Trail). Turn right onto a small footpath that leads to a parking lot at the Scenic Highway; if you reach a cement highway overpass, you've gone too far. Turn right at the Scenic Highway and climb back to the overlook.

Gil Willis of Elk River Touring Center calls this ride "a confidence builder": a ride so scenic—yet non-technical—that it converts novice mountain bikers into fanatics.

Spruce Knob / Monongahela National Forest

God knows it's a long drive. This mountain bike destination is about six hours from Washington, and the last 12-mile segment snakes up a mountain on a narrow dirt road. But it seems only natural that some of the best mountain biking in West Virginia is in the middle of nowhere.

"Nowhere," in this case, happens to be Spruce Knob (the highest point in West Virginia—elevation 4,861 feet), and the mountains surrounding it. Located near the center of Monongahela National Forest, the Spruce Knob area has a well-earned reputation for ruggedness. Don't be put off by that, however, if you're a strong rider. For mountain bikers the area really isn't too formidable, since the terrain around Spruce Knob features meadows, open woods uncluttered by underbrush, and easy-to-follow streams and ridges.

But this is still West Virginia. Much of the single-track is incredibly technical, with long obstacle courses full of rocks, roots, mud, and flowing water. Yet the area contains enough Forest Service roads, off-road-vehicle trails, and well-graded hiking paths to make Spruce Knob attractive to all mountain bikers, regardless of their skill level.

Spruce Knob rates four stars in backcountry ambience. The area's remoteness, high altitude, and mature forests create a pristine wilderness setting. After all, these remote mountains contain the headwaters of three major river systems—the Cheat, Potomac, and Greenbrier Rivers. The wildlife species range from the shy black bear to wild turkey. Mosses and ferns grow in great variety on the forest floor. Rhododendron and mountain laurel add their waxy green beauty to the scene. Because of a wide variety of trees, the fall foliage is particularly riotous in these mountains.

The mountain biking possibilities around Spruce Knob are nearly endless. The Seneca Creek Trail System, just north of Spruce Knob, contains more than 60 miles of hiking trails. Using Spruce Knob Lake Campground as a base, it would take weeks to explore all the trails and Forest Service roads in the area. For multi-day treks, ride west to Middle Mountain (west of Spruce Knob), to link up with Canaan Valley and Dolly Sods to the north and Shavers Fork and the Williams River region to the south. It's no exaggeration to say that Monongahela National Forest represents a lifetime of mountain biking opportunities.

But if you can't quit your job to spend a few weeks exploring this fascinating area, at least plan a long weekend. The three rides that follow are an excellent introduction to the mountain biking around Spruce Knob. Set up a base camp at Spruce Knob Campground, and get ready for one of the best mountain biking experiences this side of Colorado.

RIDE 5 *GRANTS BRANCH TO GANDY CREEK LOOP*

Mountain biking doesn't get easier than this fun ride in the mountains around Spruce Knob. This 5-mile loop starts with a gentle descent on an abandoned railroad grade that's been converted to a wide, grassy off-road-vehicle trail. The return follows a well-maintained dirt Forest Service road with a gentle uphill grade.

It's a loop with a little of everything. The descent on Grants Branch Trail is through a mature hardwood forest. At WV 29 the ride is along Gandy Branch, a fast-moving mountain stream. On Forest Service Road 1, the trail leaves the stream and begins a gentle ascent. On the climb, the views of the mountains just get better and better.

General location: Spruce Knob, located in Monongahela National Forest, is about 40 miles southwest of Petersburg, West Virginia.

Elevation change: The loop starts at Spruce Knob campground at an elevation around 3,800', and descends to about 3,400' at Gandy Creek. The altitude is recovered on the return leg along Narrow Ridge. The total elevation gain is around 400'.

Season: Mid-summer through fall are the best seasons to ride around Spruce Knob. Spring and early summer can be cold and wet. Expect snow from November through March. Avoid riding in deer hunting season, in the late fall.

Services: The nearest town is Petersburg. Limited services—motels, small grocery stores, and gas—are available in the villages of Seneca Rocks and Riverton. The nearest bike shop is Blackwater Bikes in Davis.

Hazards: On this easy ride, the biggest hazard is the weather. It can change rapidly, so carry raingear and extra clothes.

Rescue index: This is an isolated area, so the closest help is at Spruce Knob Lake Campground. Cars can be flagged down on WV 29, but traffic is very light.

Land status: National forest.

Maps: The USGS 7.5 minute topo is Spruce Knob. In addition, the Seneca Creek Trail System, Spruce Knob Unit map complements the topo by showing more trail details.

Finding the trail: From WV 28, turn onto FS 112, 3 miles south of Riverton. (There is a sign for Spruce Knob.) Follow the road about 13 miles to the camp-

GRANTS BRANCH TO
GANDY CREEK LOOP

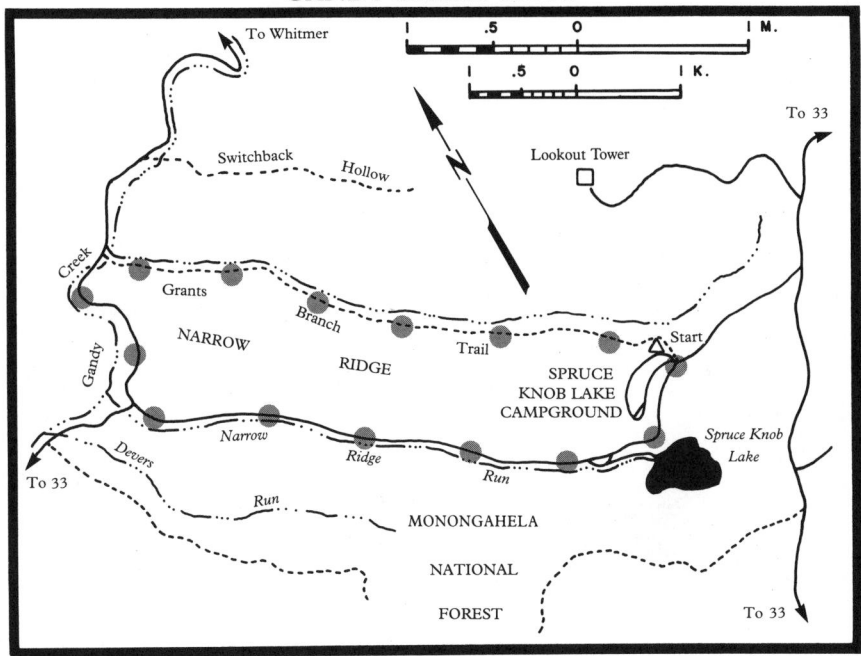

ground or to Spruce Knob Lake and park. The Grants Branch trailhead is at the entrance to the campground.

Sources of additional information:

U.S. Forest Service
Monongahela National Forest
Route 3 Box 240
Petersburg, West Virginia 26847
(304) 257-4488

Blackwater Bikes
West Virginia Highway 32
Davis, West Virginia 26260
(304) 259-5286

Photo by Ron Snow

RIDE 6 *BIG RUN LOOP*

This ride is for dedicated hammerheads. While most of the riding is on Forest Service roads, the route's technical single-track (featuring rocks, wet roots, bogs, mud, and streams) requires good bike handling skills and endurance. But without a lot of steep climbing to wear you down, this ride is considered moderate by rugged West Virginia standards. The high elevation, remoteness, and varied terrain make Big Run Loop challenging and beautiful.

The 8-mile loop features excellent views of Spruce Knob (at 4,861 feet, the highest point in West Virginia) to the east and into Big Run Valley. Much of the trail passes through huge, grassy meadows on the ridges. Big Run is an excellent trout-fishing stream and is lined with beaver ponds. The single-track near the beginning of the ride is intense, with an amazing tangle of tree roots along a line of spruce trees that will challenge expert riders. More railroad grade follows, leading you through open meadows and over a couple of high fences. The last half of the ride follows a dirt Forest Service (FS) road.

BIG RUN LOOP

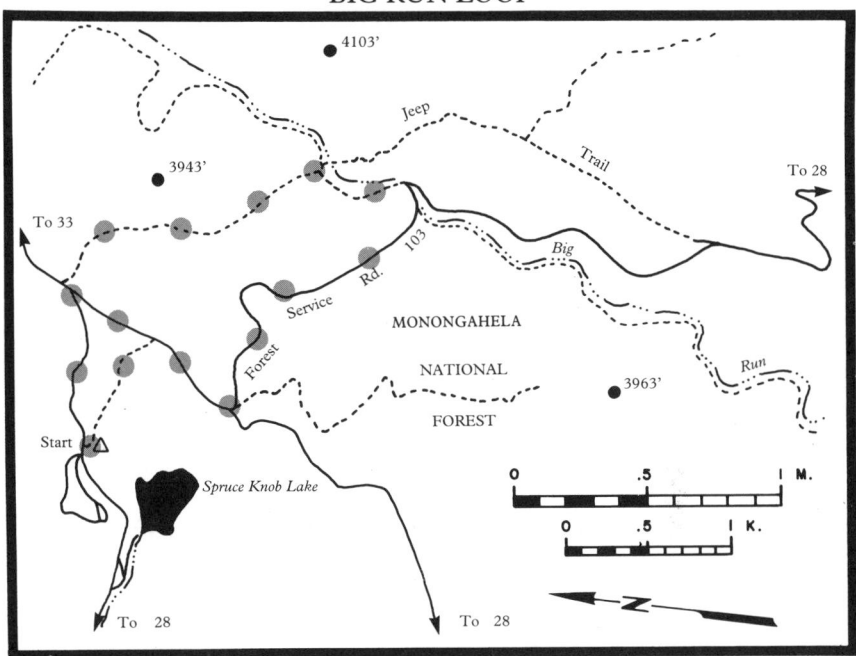

General location: Spruce Knob, located in Monongahela National Forest, is about 40 miles southwest of Petersburg, West Virginia.

Elevation change: The ride starts around 4,000' of elevation, descends to about 3,700', and then slowly returns to 4,000' at the end of the ride.

Season: The best riding is from mid-summer through the fall. Spring and early summer tend to be wet and cool. Expect snow from November through March. Avoid riding in deer hunting season, in the late fall.

Services: The nearest town is Petersburg. Limited services—motels, small grocery stores, and gas—are available in the villages of Seneca Rocks and Riverton. The nearest bike shop is Blackwater Bikes in Davis.

Hazards: This is remote country, so carry a topo map and a compass. Be prepared for severe weather and carry extra food, water, and bike tools.

Rescue index: Mountain bikers venturing into this wilderness rarely meet other people. A vehicle could be flagged down on lightly traveled FS 103.

Land status: National forest.

Maps: The USGS 7.5 minute topo is Spruce Knob. In addition, the Seneca Creek Trail System, Spruce Knob Unit map complements the topo by showing more trail details.

Finding the trail: From WV 28, turn onto FS 112, 3 miles south of Riverton. (There is a sign for Spruce Knob.) Follow the road about 13 miles to the campground or to Spruce Knob Lake and park.

Sources of additional information:

U.S. Forest Service
Monongahela National Forest
Route 3 Box 240
Petersburg, West Virginia 26847
(304) 257-4488

Blackwater Bikes
West Virginia Highway 32
Davis, West Virginia 26260
(304) 259-5286

Notes on the trail: Start the ride on the Short Trail, a narrow, technical single-track that begins near the campground entrance. Turn left at FS 103 and ride a short distance to the hiking trail on the right at the intersection with FS 1.

This loop can be tricky to follow. Good map and compass skills are a must. Often the trail is obscured, especially when crossing fields and meadows. Check the map and compass regularly.

RIDE 7   *ALLEGHENY MOUNTAIN / SENECA CREEK LOOP*

For a great variety of terrain and views, this 15-mile loop can't be beat. It starts with the Allegheny Trail, a wide, grassy double-track that's an easy ramble along a forested mountain ridge. Bear Hunter Trail, a challenging single-track, drops through a mature forest along a small stream. Next, the loop follows Seneca Creek on a gentle path through a forest that is rapidly returning to wilderness after being logged at the turn of the century. The ride ends on well-maintained, dirt Forest Service roads.

The single-track on Bear Hunter Trail is white-knuckle all the way, so good bike handling skills are a must. Also, this is a long ride requiring good endurance. But most of the trails are well-maintained, wide and smooth, and are a joy to ride.

General location: Spruce Knob, located in Monongahela National Forest, is about 40 miles southwest of Petersburg, West Virginia.

Elevation change: The ride starts at 3,900' of elevation and follows the Allegheny Trail along a mountain ridge. The steep descent on Bear Hunter Trail

ALLEGHENY MOUNTAIN/
SENECA CREEK LOOP

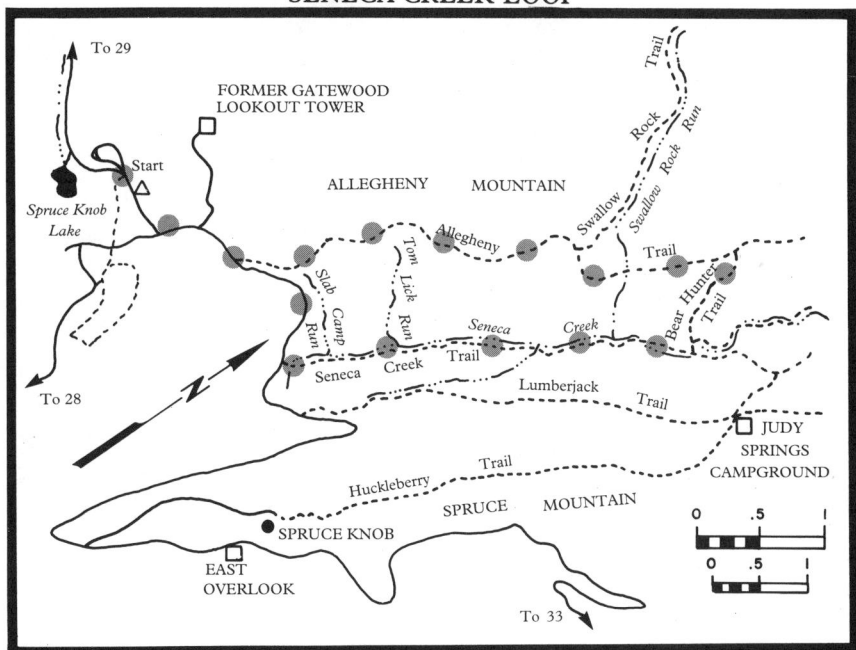

drops over 500' in just over 1 mile. The elevation is regained slowly on the return along Seneca Creek Trail.

Season: The best riding is from mid-summer through fall. Spring and early summer tend to be wet and cool. Expect snow from November through March. Avoid riding in deer hunting season, in the late fall.

Services: The nearest town is Petersburg. Limited services—motels, small grocery stores, and gas—are available in the villages of Seneca Rocks and Riverton. The nearest bike shop is Blackwater Bikes in Davis.

Hazards: Bear Hunter Trail, with its steep and rocky descent, offers a high potential for "unscheduled dismounts" (crashes). Also, be prepared for rapid changes in the weather.

Rescue index: Judy Springs Campground, on Seneca Creek Trail, is a camping area that is popular in the summer months. There is light traffic on FS 112.

Land status: National forest.

Maps: The USGS 7.5 minute topo maps are Spruce Knob and Whitmer. In addition, the Seneca Creek Trail System, Spruce Knob Unit map complements the topo maps by showing more trail details.

Finding the trail: From WV 28, turn onto FS 112, 3 miles south of River-

Photo by Ron Snow

ton. (There is a sign for Spruce Knob.) Follow the road about 13 miles to the campground or to Spruce Knob Lake and park. The entrance to the Allegheny Trail is on the left-hand side of FS 112, past the entrance to the Gatewood Lookout Tower.

Sources of additional information:

U.S. Forest Service
Monongahela National Forest
Route 3 Box 240
Petersburg, West Virginia 26847
(304) 257-4488

Blackwater Bikes
West Virginia Highway 32
Davis, West Virginia 26260
(304) 259-5286

Davis

While most of West Virginia was settled by pioneers in the late eighteenth and early nineteenth centuries, the region around the Allegheny Front—a huge geologic fault that runs north and south through Pennsylvania, Maryland, and West Virginia—wasn't settled until the 1840s and later. Pioneers avoided this region of rugged mountains, dense forests, and severe weather as they surged west into Ohio, Indiana, Illinois and beyond. The early explorers saw the neighborhood as dark and forbidding, and originally named the upper plateaus along the Allegheny Front "Canada."

Two unique geological features in this part of northeastern West Virginia are Dolly Sods and Canaan (k'NANE) Valley. Wedged between the Allegheny Front to the east and Canaan Valley to the west, Dolly Sods is a high plateau of spruce and hemlock stands, sphagnum moss bogs, and beaver ponds. Renowned for its harsh weather—snow in July, and a lowest recorded winter temperature of −48 degrees—the region is the unique result of heavy deforestation in the late nineteenth and early twentieth centuries, followed by fires that burned away the topsoil. What remains is a unique blend of second-growth forests, open spaces dominated by bogs and beaver ponds, and gently rolling ridges.

Canaan Valley, too, was heavily deforested and is now a mixture of small farms, second-growth forests, and vacation homes. At 3,200 feet of elevation, this is the highest alpine valley of its size east of the Mississippi River. Surrounded by 4,300-foot ridges, the valley is considered to be "a bit of Canada gone astray." The climate and plant life are more common to northern regions than to the southern Appalachians.

The northern end of Canaan Valley is 6,000 acres of wetlands, a wildlife habitat for an abundance of animals: white-tailed deer, black bear, bobcat, fisher, fox, mink, beaver, and cottontail rabbit. Over 160 species of birds and waterfowl have been identified here, including great blue heron, Canada goose, black duck, woodcock, turkey, and grouse. The goshawk and common snipe have their southernmost nesting sites in the valley.

Geographic anomalies and ruggedly beautiful, Dolly Sods and Canaan Valley are popular destinations for hikers, backpackers, birders, skiers, and, increasingly, mountain bikers. Davis, an old logging town located over the mountain from Canaan Valley, is well situated for mountain biking. Off-road cyclists can ride in virtually any direction from town to the best mountain biking in the state: flat or mountainous, single-track or Forest Service road, old strip mines or bogs, and, for the energetic, all of the above. As a result, Davis is one of the most popular mountain biking destinations in the East.

The Canaan Mountain Series of mountain bike races, held every summer in Davis, is the oldest race series in the United States and has introduced thousands of cyclists to the area. The ramshackle old town even boasts its own mountain bike shop, Blackwater Bikes. When visiting Davis, stop in and ask owners Gary and Matt for the latest trail information. The shop also sells maps and the latest in bike components, offers expert repairs, and sells and rents mountain bikes.

The trail descriptions that follow, written with the help of former Blackwater Bikes employee Mary Morningstar, are the most popular rides around Canaan Valley. Yet they represent only a fraction of the riding in this large and fascinating section of West Virginia. Let the experts at Blackwater Bikes turn you on to other great rides in this beautiful and rugged region.

RIDE 8   *PLANTATION TRAIL*

The Plantation Trail got its name in the 1930s when clear-cut Canaan Mountain was replanted with spruce trees. Rhododendron thickets grow rampant throughout this area, creating a glorious sight on a spring day when the bushes are in bloom and dripping with moisture from a rain shower. That's one reason why this 12-mile loop, which has a shorter 9-mile option, is legendary among knowledgeable East Coast mountain bikers. As the trails wind through these forests, the trees drop suddenly away and the trail crosses through the peat bogs that Canaan is so famous for. Just as quickly, the trail dives back into the thick underbrush and wooded canopy of the spruce forest. When riding around corners keep a sharp lookout for the mother bear and cubs seen often in these parts.

The majority of this ride is on rugged hiking trails, and good technical riding skill is required. Expect to encounter wet roots, windfall, mountain streams, short steep hills, and peat bogs. Canaan Loop Road is a graded Forest Service road of hard-packed rock and gravel. Warning: Don't be deceived by the low mileages. Only highly skilled mountain bikers will be able to ride all the single-track without dismounting. This is a low-speed, *very* technical ride.

General location: Monongahela National Forest, near Davis, West Virginia.

Elevation change: The ride starts in Davis at 3,080' of elevation and climbs 2.5 miles on the paved road to 3,600', a climb of 520'. Plantation Trail rolls along the ridge of Canaan Mountain through creeks and ravines, creating short, steep climbs and descents but losing only 300' in elevation over 5 miles. Davis Trail drops 400' in elevation over 1.5 miles. Lindy Trail drops 300' in elevation in about a mile.

Season: The best riding conditions are from mid-summer through fall. Fall has the best surface conditions and inspiring foliage. Late May through early

PLANTATION TRAIL

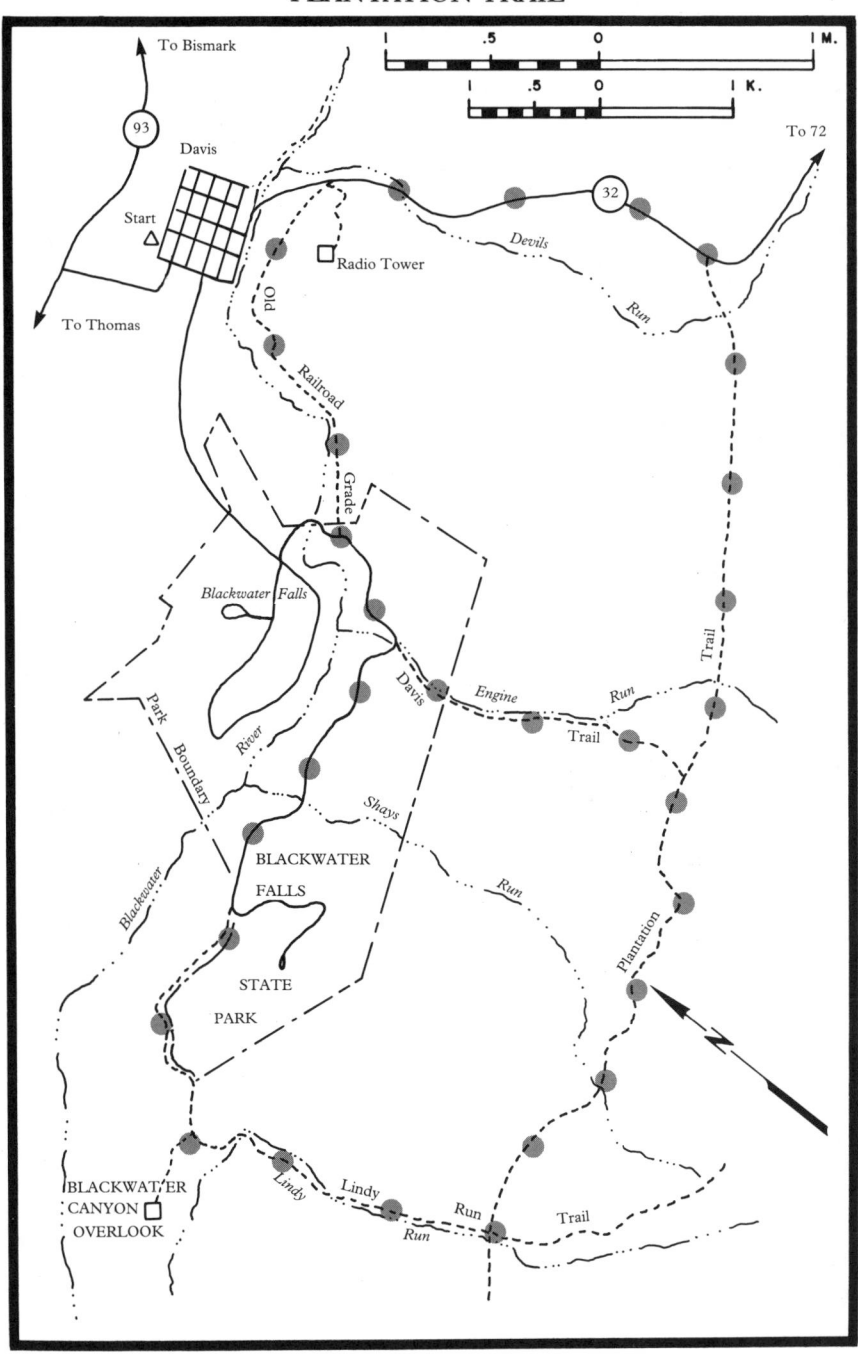

June, although wet and often cold, offer huge thickets of rhododendrons in bloom.

Services: All services are available in Davis, West Virginia. Additional lodging and restaurants are available over the mountain in Canaan Valley. Camping is available at Blackwater Falls State Park from spring through fall and at Canaan Valley State Park year-round.

Hazards: This is rugged terrain over rocks, roots, and bogs. There are steep and unexpected dropoffs and descents. Water crossings can be waist-deep when high and the water is always cold.

Rescue index: Blackwater Falls State Park is staffed and has phones. It is unusual to encounter anyone on the trails; occasionally four-wheel-drive vehicles can be spotted on Canaan Loop Road.

Land status: Monongahela National Forest and Blackwater Falls State Park.

Maps: The USGS 7.5 minute topos for this ride are Mozark Mountain and Blackwater Falls. A detailed mileage guide and maps are available at Blackwater Bikes in Davis. A small map of the hiking trails is available at Blackwater Falls State Park.

Finding the trail: The ride starts in Davis, West Virginia. Blackwater Bikes on WV 32 is a good starting point, or park anywhere in town. Ride south on WV 32 and cross the Blue Bridge.

Sources of additional information:

U.S. Forest Service
Cheat Ranger District
Nursery Bottom
Parsons, West Virginia 26287
(304) 478-3183

Blackwater Bikes
West Virginia Highway 32
Davis, West Virginia 26260
(304) 259-5286

Blackwater Falls State Park
Davis, West Virginia 26260
(304) 259-5216 or
(800) CALL WVA

Notes on the trail: From Davis, ride south on WV 32 (Williams Avenue, the main street) and follow it as it bears right at the convenience store/motel. Cross over the Blue Bridge and continue on WV 32 up Canaan Mountain for about 2.5 miles. The trailhead is on the right and is well marked with a sign. After turning onto the Plantation Trail from WV 32, there are two options. The 9-mile ride turns right onto the Davis Trail (2.5 miles from the start of

Plantation Trail). It descends 1.5 miles into Blackwater Falls State Park. The other option (12 miles) is to continue another 2.5 miles to the intersection with the Lindy Run Trail and turn right. This is a tricky, technical trail with a steep, treacherous hill.

Both these trails end at Canaan Loop Road. Turn right and follow the dirt road into Blackwater Falls State Park. Turn left onto the paved road and ride about 2 miles to Falls View Gentle Trail (on the left). Turn right onto a maintenance road, then take an immediate left onto an old railroad grade. This leads to a settling pond on the left. Skirt around the edge of the pond and follow the railroad grade back to the Blue Bridge and into Davis.

RIDE 9 *CANAAN LOOP ROAD (FOREST SERVICE ROAD 13)*

While definitely not a technical ride—virtually the entire 25-mile loop follows a well-maintained Forest Service road and paved road—the Canaan Loop Road requires stamina. Although most of the route is along rolling hills, the last 7 miles are all up. But the rewards are worth the effort. The road passes through magnificent spruce and hardwood forests and accesses trails leading to breathtaking overlooks.

Look for spectacular rhododendron blooms in late May or early June. For a view of the Blackwater Canyon, take a short spur trail at about the 5.5-mile mark. (Look for a small wooden post, no sign.) Although technical, the trail is only a half-mile long and leads to a limestone outcropping overlooking the Blackwater River 860 feet below. A tougher option, but worth the effort, is the spur leading to Table Rock Overlook. There is a well-marked sign at about the 10.5-mile mark. It's a brutal 1.5-mile trail (all but the most advanced riders will portage most of it) leading to an overlook of the Dry Fork River 1,635 feet below.

General location: Blackwater Falls State Park and Monongahela National Forest, near Davis, West Virginia.

Elevation change: The ride starts at 3,080' in Davis and is fairly level for the first 4 miles. Then the Loop Road gradually climbs 280' in elevation with several roller-coaster dips and rises through creeks and ravines. It crosses the mountain ridge at 3,360'. Here, a fast 425' descent begins with a drop to the low point on the ride of 2,935'. A long uphill climb (7 miles) starts with a steep hill. It evens out and starts to roll along until reaching the high point of 3,800', ending an 825' elevation gain. The remainder of the ride is mostly downhill, a descent of 720' in elevation on pavement. The total elevation gain is around 1,100'.

CANAAN LOOP ROAD
(FOREST SERVICE ROAD 13)

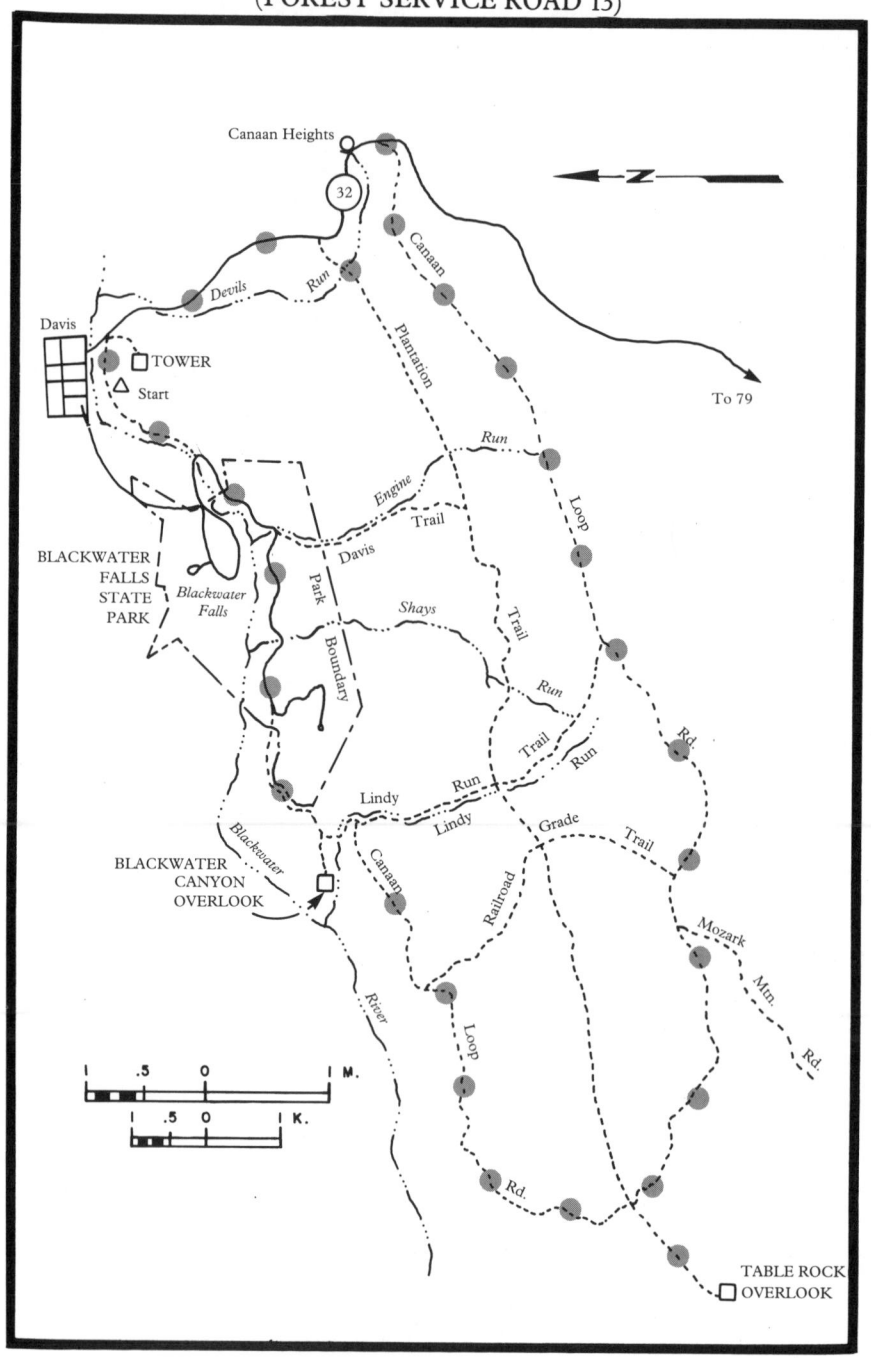

Photo by Larry Belcher

Season: The best seasons for riding this loop are from mid-summer through fall. The water crossings can be high in spring and winter. In all seasons, be prepared with raingear and warm clothes. The summer climate is typified by Canadian-like weather and cool temperatures.

Services: All services are available in Davis, West Virginia. Additional motels, restaurants, and camping are in nearby Canaan Valley.

Hazards: The biggest hazards are changes in the weather—which can be sudden and brutal—leading to hypothermia, wet feet, and darkness. Watch for traffic on the roads, especially WV 32.

Rescue index: The Loop Road is accessible to two-wheel-drive, high-clearance vehicles and is a popular camping spot, so traffic can be flagged down. Blackwater Falls State Park is fully staffed.

Land status: Monongahela National Forest and Blackwater Falls State Park.

Maps: The USGS 7.5 minute topos for this ride are Mozark Mountain and Blackwater Falls. A detailed mileage guide and maps are available at Blackwater Bikes in Davis. A small map of the Canaan Loop Road and interconnecting trails is available at Blackwater Falls State Park.

Finding the trail: The ride begins in Davis, West Virginia. Park near Blackwater Bikes on WV 32 or anywhere else in town. Ride south on WV 32, cross the Blue Bridge and immediately turn right onto an old dirt road to begin the loop.

Sources of additional information:

U.S. Forest Service
Cheat Ranger District
Nursery Bottom
Parsons, West Virginia 26287
(304) 478-3183

Blackwater Bikes
West Virginia Highway 32
Davis, West Virginia 26260
(304) 259-5286

Blackwater Falls State Park
Davis, West Virginia 26260
(304) 259-5216 or
(800) CALL WVA

Notes on the trail: To start the ride, pedal south on WV 32 (Williams Avenue, the main street in Davis) toward the convenience store/motel on the right. Bear right, cross the Blue Bridge, and take an immediate right onto a dirt road (an old railroad grade). This follows the river, then bears left; look for a settling pond on the right. Follow the railroad grade to the far end of the pond, where the road forks. Turn right onto a rocky double-track that follows the fence line of the pond. The railroad grade will continue through a stream crossing and will end at the intersection of a maintenance road and a paved road.

Turn left onto the paved road and continue about 2.5 miles. When the road bears left, turn right onto the dirt road marked with a wooden sign for Sled Run. This is the beginning of Canaan Loop Road. Canaan Loop Road ends at WV 32, a paved road with heavy traffic. Turn left and descend into Davis.

RIDE 10 CAMP 70 ROAD TO CANAAN VALLEY OVERLOOK

Camp 70 Road is a virtually flat dirt road that starts in Davis, follows the Blackwater River, and then heads out into the northern end of Canaan Valley. At the start of this very easy 9.5-mile, out-and-back ride, Northern hardwoods line the road. Expect to see cherry, beech, birch, and sugar maple, making this

CAMP 70 ROAD TO
CANAAN VALLEY OVERLOOK

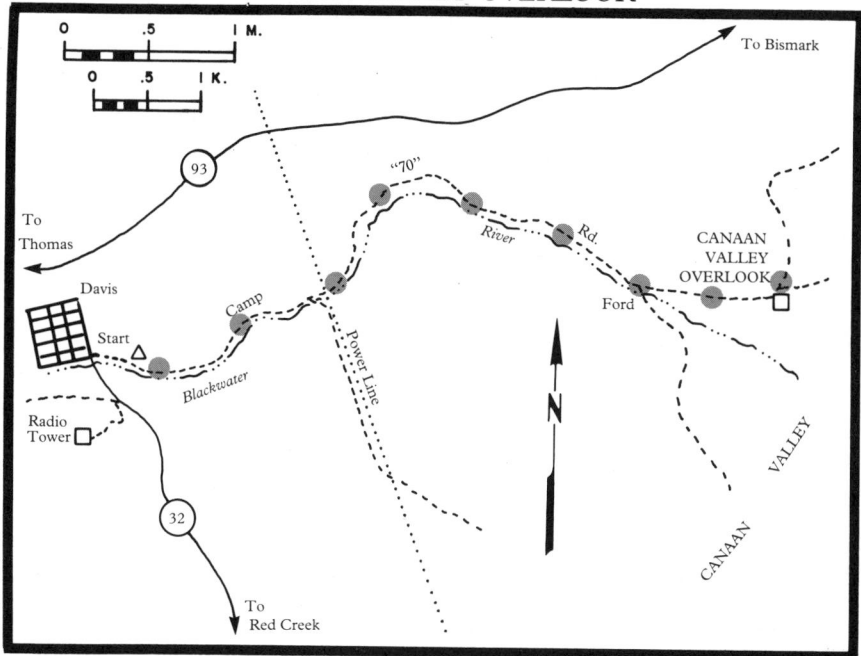

an especially enjoyable trip in the fall. Interspersed among the hardwoods are aspen groves, hemlock, spruce, and balsam fir stands. Look for blueberries, blackberries, and the unusual and delicious service (sarvis) tree berries that ripen in the summer sun.

About .75 miles from Davis on the right are the remains of an old dam, a great place to swim and sun. At the 3.5-mile mark, look for a spring on the left side of the road surrounded by blueberries. At the 4-mile mark, bear left at a fork in the road to ride out into Canaan Valley. The road will begin to deteriorate and become rocky and increasingly narrow, but still easy to ride.

To reach a swinging bridge over the Blackwater River that leads out into a beautiful section of Canaan Valley, look for all-terrain-vehicle tracks going to the right from a point less than a quarter mile past the fork. Follow these tracks down a gully (toward the river), bear right through a hemlock grove and follow the river about 150 yards to the bridge. Cross the bridge, turn left, and follow an old railroad grade that leads out across the valley floor. On all sides look for peat bogs, shrub swamps, and beaver ponds. The railroad grade may be muddy and there are always puddles. In a couple of spots, the beaver dams have flooded the trail. But it's one of the most unique places in all of West Virginia.

General location: Davis, West Virginia.

Elevation change: The road starts at 3,079' of elevation and then winds its way along the banks of the Blackwater River. It never climbs more than 40' in any one spot. The total elevation gain is 80'.

Season: The road can be ridden year-round. Mid-summer is best for berry picking. In winter and early spring, the road can get very muddy. Certain weekends during the year should be avoided because of the heavy influx of all-terrain vehicles to the area: Memorial Day, Father's Day and Labor Day.

Services: All services are available in Davis. Additional motels and restaurants are in nearby Canaan Valley.

Hazards: Look and listen for four-wheel-drive vehicles and four-wheel all-terrain vehicles. Avoid riding this road on popular weekends such as Memorial Day, Father's Day, and Labor Day.

Rescue index: Most of Camp 70 Road is accessible to high-clearance, two-wheel-drive vehicles, so it's easy to flag down traffic.

Land status: Private. Owned by Monongahela Power Company and open for recreational use.

Maps: The USGS 7.5 minute topo is Davis, West Virginia.

Finding the trail: The ride starts in Davis. Blackwater Bikes on WV 32 is a convenient place to begin. Park near the shop or anywhere else in town. With a high-clearance, two-wheel-drive or four-wheel-drive vehicle you can drive directly onto Camp 70 Road and park anywhere. Ride south on WV 32 (Williams Avenue, the main street in Davis). When the road bears right at the convenience store/motel continue straight onto a rough paved road, which quickly turns to dirt. Cross the bridge over Beaver Creek; this is the beginning of Camp 70 Road. It follows the Blackwater River on the right upstream.

Sources of additional information:

Tucker County Chamber of Commerce Visitor Center
West Virginia Highway 32
Davis, West Virginia 26260
(304) 259-5315

Blackwater Bikes
West Virginia Highway 32
Davis, West Virginia 26260
(304) 259-5286

RIDE 11 *OLSON FIRE TOWER*

For spectacular West Virginia scenery, this is a hard ride to beat. Simply pedal on a well-maintained fire road to the top of a mountain and you're rewarded with a 360-degree view of all the mountains surrounding Canaan Valley, the highest alpine valley in the East. On a clear day you can see as far away as Spruce Knob, the highest point in West Virginia.

This 18-mile, out-and-back ride doesn't require any technical riding skills —just the endurance to pedal 9 miles uphill to the top. The reward, of course, is that it's all downhill on the return.

Make sure to make some stops on the ascent. About 5 miles up the road, look for an overlook blazed with a yellow dot on a boulder on the left. From this point you can see the Blackwater Canyon to the left and Big Run heading down to the river on your right. The entire mountainside is covered with rhododendron, an amazing sight when in bloom. At the 6.5-mile mark, look carefully for a trail to the left that leads to high elevation marshlands and a bird sanctuary. An elevated boardwalk leads out to the middle of the wetlands, where there is a beaver pond and several bird houses.

General location: The ride starts near Thomas, West Virginia, about 4.5 miles from Davis.

Elevation change: The ride starts at an elevation of 2,820′ and climbs steadily along the rim of the Blackwater Canyon for 7.3 miles to an elevation of 3,355′ at the left turn onto Forest Service Road 717. Here the road becomes steeper for the short climb to the tower at an elevation of 3,736′. The total elevation gain is 920′.

Season: This ride is excellent all year. Each season has its special attractions. When the leaves are down in winter there are dramatic views of the canyon. In spring the road isn't as muddy as other areas, and the rhododendron are blooming. In summer the majority of the ride is in the shade. There are pockets of hemlock groves and cold mountain streams to cool off in. And in fall the colors are the best in all of Canaan.

Services: All services are available in Davis. There is a water pump near the fire tower.

Hazards: Avoid excessive speed on the return trip. Watch for blind corners, for the roads are open to traffic.

Rescue index: Canyon Rim Road is accessible to two-wheel-drive vehicles and is a popular spot in the summer months. But, as is the case with most of Canaan Valley, its remoteness can lead to problems when help is needed.

Land status: Monongahela National Forest.

OLSON FIRE TOWER

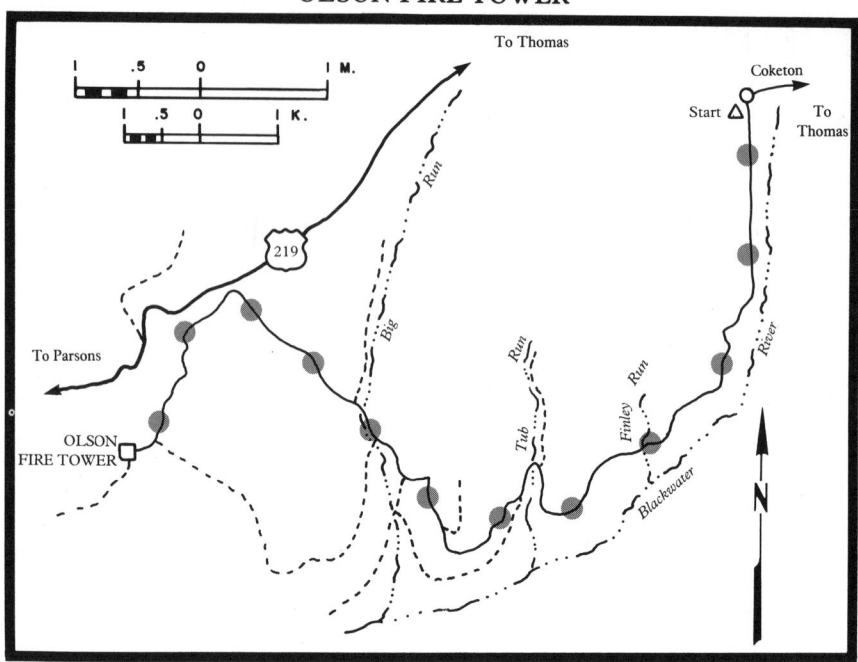

Maps: The USGS 7.5 minute topos are Lead Mine and Mozark Mountain. A detailed mileage log and trail guide are available at Blackwater Bikes in Davis. **Finding the trail:** The ride starts at Canyon Rim Road (FS 18). From Davis drive north on WV 32 toward the town of Thomas. A quarter mile past the Mountain Top Market on the left, turn left onto Douglas Road. Drive 2.5 miles, crossing over 2 bridges. Park on the right immediately after the second bridge. At this point Douglas Road turns to dirt and becomes Canyon Rim Road.

Sources of additional information:

Monongahela National Forest
Cheat River District
Nursery Bottom
Parsons, West Virginia 26287
(304) 478-3183

Blackwater Bikes
West Virginia Highway 32
Davis, West Virginia 26260
(304) 259-5286

Notes on the trail: The scenery on this ride is spectacular and shouldn't be missed. The view from Olson Fire Tower includes the entire western rim of Dolly Sods and its northern drainage.

This ride can be lengthened to 28.5 miles by riding from Davis. Check with Blackwater Bikes about the route that parallels WV 32 through the woods (and away from traffic).

MARYLAND

Green Ridge State Forest

Mountain bikers living in the Washington and Baltimore areas are lucky. When they get bored riding the same old trails over and over, relief is only two hours away.

A half hour west of Hancock, Maryland (where the state narrows down to a stone's throw between West Virginia and Pennsylvania), lies a series of mountain ridges running north and south. It's all state forest land, and it's Maryland's best-kept mountain biking secret.

Little-known and seldom visited, Green Ridge State Forest features 28,000 acres of mountain ridges and valleys. The forest is laced with dirt roads, jeep trails, and single-track hiking trails. It's also a crazy quilt of campsites, private hunting shacks, vacation homes, overlooks, power line cuts, and logging operations strewn over several low mountains that border the Paw Paw Bends of the Potomac River.

To be blunt: Colorado it ain't. These mountains have been heavily deforested in the past, and the poor soil doesn't yield the lush kind of scenery you associate with, say, Shenandoah National Park in Virginia. Yet in some respects this is an advantage to mountain bikers. The area doesn't draw crowds or traffic, and on a mountain bike the less scenic areas are quickly bypassed. But there are beautiful views of mountains, forests, and the Paw Paw Bends of the Potomac River.

Camping and mountain biking are a great combination at Green Ridge. Campsites are scattered throughout the forest, and many are secluded. Some are ideally located for the mountain biker bent on exploration, and the many circuit rides mean you won't have to move your car. Camping is free (register at the park headquarters) and the only major drawback is the lack of drinking water at campsites. Just bring lots of water jugs and a sun shower, and fill up at the park headquarters. Some campsites offer picnic tables (it's nice to have one on a multi-day visit), but otherwise they are completely primitive.

Getting to Green Ridge State Forest is easy, because it's interstate all the way from either Washington or Baltimore. Head out Interstate 70 (from Baltimore) or I-270 (from D.C.) to Hancock, Maryland, where you bear left onto the new I-68 (formerly US 40/48) toward Cumberland. From the top of Sideling Hill (where there is a Visitor Center and rest area) Green Ridge State Forest is visible to the left.

Continue on I-68 over Town Hill to the next ridge, Green Ridge Mountain, and take Exit 64 (M.V. Smith Road) to the park headquarters. Stop here to pick up a free map and, if you're camping, to register your campsite.

RIDE 12 *MERTENS AVENUE AREA*

The attractions of this area are low-key. There are miles and miles of roads twisting through mountain hollows and second-growth forest, the luxury of camping in one spot for days while mountain biking different trails every day, and solitude. This area is a maze of small roads and trails which are great for exploration by mountain bike; rides lasting from an hour to all day are possible. The roads are well-maintained, but watch out for the steep climbs that go up to the ridges. Switchbacks are rare.

Loop rides are easy to design. Here's some help. The easiest roads are Gordon, Railroad Hollow (an old railroad right-of-way), and Mertens Avenues (heading west, away from Green Ridge Mountain). More challenging roads are Jacobs, Twigg, Piclic, and Sugar Bottom. This area can be linked to the area north of I-68 by going out Fifteen Mile Creek Road. (Piclic Road is a good choice to reach it.) To get to the Stafford–East Valley Roads ride, take Fifteen Mile Creek Road over Green Ridge Mountain to Stafford Road.

The roads are well maintained for county residents who live on private land inside the boundaries of the state forest. Railroad Hollow is a single-track that requires some scrambling over small streams, but is virtually flat. Piclic Road has a steep and rocky drop as it approaches Fifteen Mile Creek Road. It has the best descent (fast, and verging on the technical) and Gordon Road is the prettiest ride in the area. Pedal Railroad Hollow in the late afternoon and you may see wild turkey.

General location: Fifteen miles west of Hancock, Maryland.

Elevation change: Your climb is up to 500′ if you decide to ride to the top of Green Ridge Mountain. Smaller climbs are still nasty since there's little or no switchbacking to ease your pain. The climbing can be minimized by staying inside the area defined by Gordon Road, Railroad Hollow, Jacobs Road, and Williams Road.

Season: Summers here are as hot, humid, and buggy as in the nearby cities, so try to start your ride early in the day to beat the worst heat. Spring, the wettest season of the year (and discouraging for all but the most intrepid mountain bikers), is a good time to visit this area, since the well-maintained roads are usually less muddy than the forest trails at home. Winter is good, too, if you like cold-weather riding; snow is rare. Fall is probably the best time to ride Green Ridge State Forest because of the cool weather and fall foliage. Stay out of the woods during deer hunting season, which starts the Saturday after Thanksgiving.

Services: There are small grocery stores on Orleans Road north of I-68 and

MERTENS AVENUE AREA

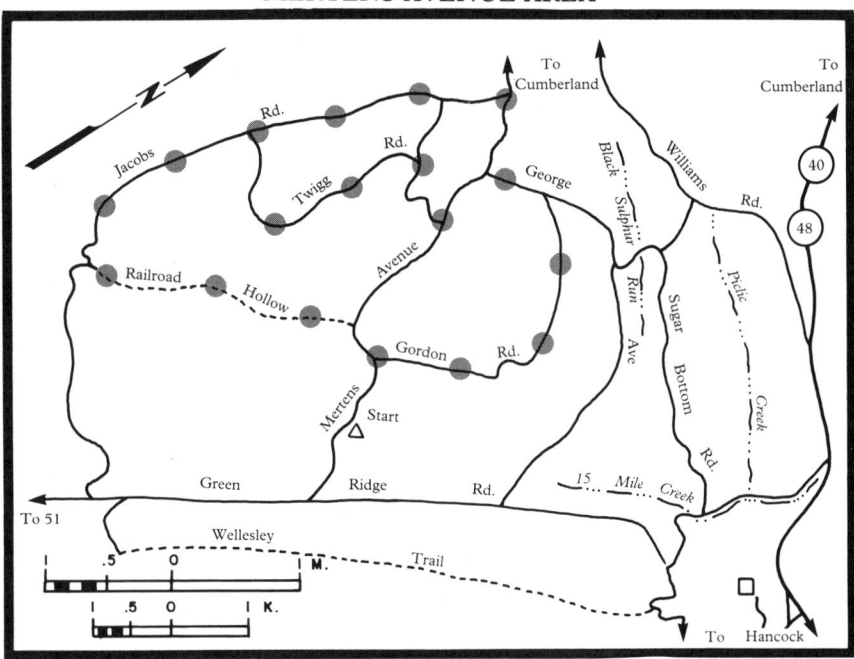

in Flintstone. The nearest bike shop is in Cumberland. All other services are available in Hancock and Cumberland.

Hazards: Water is scarce in these mountains, so be sure to carry enough. Watch out for traffic on the steep descents.

Rescue index: Farms and private residences are scattered throughout this part of the forest.

Land status: State forest.

Maps: A map of the roads and trails is free at Green Ridge State Forest headquarters on M.V. Smith Road (Exit 64 off I-68).

Finding the trail: From I-68 get off at Exit 62, Fifteen Mile Creek Road (1 mile west of M.V. Smith Road). Turn left at the stop sign, cross back over the highway and follow the road about a mile (it runs alongside its namesake on the left). After crossing Fifteen Mile Creek the road begins climbing up Green Ridge Mountain. Just before the top there's an intersection; continue straight (the road's name changes to Green Ridge Road). Go about 2 miles to the second right (Mertens Avenue), and turn. You'll begin to see campsites (where you can park your car) after the descent from the ridge.

Sources of additional information:

> Green Ridge State Forest
> Star Route
> Flintstone, Maryland 21530
> (301) 777-2345

Notes on the trail: While Green Ridge State Forest does have its drawbacks—it's a weird mix of forests, hunting shacks, power line cuts, logging operations, even a juvenile detention center—the area's pluses outweigh the minuses. It's close to major population centers, yet is located in a sparsely populated area and is largely ignored by everyone but hunters (and you'll only see them in the fall).

Stake out a campsite, set up a tent, and do a loop ride before lunch and another after. Or start with your lunch in the morning and ride all day, returning to your campsite before dinner. Come to Green Ridge for the kind of riding usually associated with the western United States—long rides over mountain ridges. The scenery's not the same, but your quads won't know the difference.

RIDE 13 NORTH OF I-68

This section of Green Ridge State Forest is less visited than the areas below I-68, so it's even more secluded. And with fewer campsites and private cabins (none on Treasure Road), it has more of a wilderness feel. The scenery is of low mountains and mixed hardwood forests, and some rolling farmland on Old Cumberland Road. The ride along Fifteen Mile Creek—a narrow dirt road that follows the falling mountain stream—is beautiful.

This 8-mile loop follows well-maintained dirt roads and requires no technical skills, except for a short, steep, rocky descent on Treasure Road. The challenges lie in the long climbs, especially on Old Cumberland Road. To connect with the other rides in the area, take Fifteen Mile Creek Road south into the main body of the forest. A left on Sugar Bottom Road (great name) is the easiest way to ride into the Mertens Avenue Area. To get to Stafford–East Valley Roads, stay on Fifteen Mile Creek Road, turning left as you approach the ridge on Green Ridge Mountain. Then, after passing the Wellesley Trail parking area, turn right onto Stafford Road.

General location: Fifteen miles west of Hancock, Maryland.

Elevation change: About 400' total. The ride starts with a stiff climb up Big Ridge Road, which is paved for a short stretch. Most of the elevation loss is on Old Cumberland Road as you descend to Fifteen Mile Creek Road.

Season: This trail is good riding year-round, with the exception of deer

NORTH OF I-68

hunting season (which starts the Saturday after Thanksgiving). Summers are usually hot, humid, and buggy, so plan your rides to start and finish early in the day. The area usually doesn't get much snow, so winter riding is good. Spring and fall are the best seasons. Spring offers relatively mud-free riding on these hard-packed roads, and fall provides cool weather and beautiful foliage when the leaves are changing.

Services: There are small grocery stores on Orleans Road north of I-68 and in Flintstone. The nearest bike shop is in Cumberland. All other services are available in Hancock and Cumberland.

Hazards: Be careful on the steep descents.

Rescue index: You're never more than a couple of miles from a private residence or farm.

Land status: State forest.

Maps: Free maps are available at Green Ridge State Forest headquarters off Exit 64 (M.V. Smith Road) on I-68.

Finding the trail: Leave I-68 at Exit 62 (Fifteen Mile Creek Road). Turn right at the stop sign and park your car at the pulloff a quarter of a mile on the right. Start the ride on Big Ridge Road, the paved road on the left. (It turns to dirt at the top of the hill.)

Sources of additional information:

> Green Ridge State Forest
> Star Route
> Flintstone, Maryland 21530
> (301) 777-2345

Notes on the trail: While this area isn't as easy to link up with other rides (you must cross over I-68 on Fifteen Mile Creek Road—hardly a wilderness experience), it's worth a visit on its own. The highway isolates it from the rest of the forest, and once you start your ride you probably won't see anyone else.

RIDE 14 *STAFFORD–EAST VALLEY ROADS*

The demands of this 9-mile loop ride are strictly cardiovascular, not technical. The ride starts with a stiff climb up Stafford Road to the ridge of Town Hill Mountain and ends with another steep climb just before you return to your car. Only really well-conditioned cyclists will be able to ride these; lesser mortals will push their bikes up the steep (but relatively short) hills. Stafford Road is a well-maintained dirt road; East Valley Road is a jeep road—essentially, a double-track—that's closed to motor traffic.

The rewards of this ride? No Name Overlook on Stafford Road and Banner's Overlook (at the intersection of Stafford and Mertens Avenue) offer grand views of the Paw Paw Bends, the Potomac River's meandering course between Maryland and West Virginia. The C&O Canal, stretching from Cumberland to Washington, follows the river on the Maryland side. And both Stafford and East Valley Roads are roller-coaster romps through hardwood forests.

General location: Twenty miles west of Hancock, Maryland.

Elevation change: From your car it's a stiff climb (a couple of hundred feet of elevation gain) to the top of Town Hill. There's a big descent on Mertens Avenue to East Valley Road, which ends with a steep climb back to your car. But most of this ride is along a ridge. The total elevation change is about 500′.

Season: Good year-round, with the exception of deer hunting season (which starts the Saturday after Thanksgiving). Summers are usually hot, humid, and buggy, so plan your rides to start and finish early in the day. Green Ridge usually doesn't get much snow, so winter riding is good. Spring and fall are the best seasons. Spring offers relatively mud-free riding on these hard-packed roads, and fall offers cool weather and beautiful foliage when the leaves are changing.

Services: There are small grocery stores on Orleans Road north of I-68 and

STAFFORD-EAST VALLEY ROADS

in Flintstone. The nearest bike shop is in Cumberland. All other services are available in Hancock and Cumberland.

Hazards: The descent from Banner's Overlook on Mertens Avenue is very steep; be on the lookout for traffic. The intersection with East Valley Road comes up very fast and it's easy to blow past it. (You want to turn right there.)

Rescue index: All of the route except East Valley Road carries light traffic.

Land status: State forest.

Maps: Free at Green Ridge State Forest headquarters on M.V. Smith Road (Exit 64 off I-68).

Finding the trail: From I-68 get off at Exit 62, Fifteen Mile Creek Road. Turn left at the stop sign, cross back over the highway, and follow the road about 2 miles. After crossing Fifteen Mile Creek the road ascends Green Ridge Mountain. Just before the top turn left at the intersection (straight becomes Green Ridge Road). Continue past the parking area for the Wellesley Trail, then turn right onto Stafford Road. Park at the intersection with East Valley Road (look for the gate on the right).

Sources of additional information:

Green Ridge State Forest
Star Route
Flintstone, Maryland 21530
(301) 777-2345

Notes on the trail: This part of Green Ridge State Forest has spectacular views of the Potomac River as it snakes between Maryland and West Virginia. Also, the rides along Stafford and East Valley Roads are a blast to ride—a series of undulating hills that let momentum do most of the hard work.

Garrett County / Savage River State Forest

Driving from the east, dramatic changes occur about a half hour west of Cumberland, Maryland, as you crest Big Savage Mountain on Interstate 68. In summer the temperature drops, and in winter the weather can turn near-Arctic in intensity. The character of the mountains changes here, too. They're higher, wetter, and not as steep as the ridges to the east. Wide, rolling valleys dominated by hemlock forests separate the mountains. You've reached the Appalachian Plateau.

Welcome to Garrett County, Maryland, the state's most isolated county. Located entirely on the Appalachian Plateau, Garrett County averages 2,300 feet in elevation. Although farming, coal mining and timbering dominate the county's economy, outdoor recreation is big business. Because of cool, bug-free summers and dependable snow (or at least snow-making) conditions for skiing, Garrett County draws vacationers from Pittsburgh, Washington, and Baltimore.

Deep Creek Lake, a 3,900-acre reservoir, is the major tourist hub, with many vacation homes littering its 65-mile shoreline. The county also has two major whitewater attractions, the Youghiogheny (Yock-uh-ganey) and Savage rivers, which draw paddlers and rafters literally from around the world. In 1989 the World Whitewater Canoe/Kayak Championships were held on the rapids of the Savage River.

As befits an isolated corner of the Appalachian Mountains, there are 70,000 acres of state forests and parks in Garrett County, creating a mecca for mountain bikers. The largest (and most accessible) tract of state-owned land is Savage River State Forest, which straddles Big Savage Mountain to the east and Meadow Mountain to the west. Its 53,000 acres contain two state parks (New Germany and Big Run), the 350-acre Savage River Reservoir, and many lakes, rivers, and streams. Camping, swimming, fishing, and even rental cabins make the forest an attractive destination for mountain bikers. And there are many miles of forest trails and woods roads to explore by bike.

New Germany State Park is a great place to set up a base camp for exploring the forest. The park is easy to reach (only five miles from I-68, the county's major highway), and all the rides in this chapter start there. It has the basic amenities—camping, hot showers, and a lake for swimming (perfect after a ride). *Après*-ride, nearby Frostburg is a college town with restaurants ranging from French and Italian to Greek. For breakfast drive to Grantsville, where you can stoke up on buckwheat pancakes at the Casselman Restaurant (circa 1824). For details on camping call New Germany State Park at (301) 895-5453.

RIDE 15 *MEADOW MOUNTAIN SNOWMOBILE / OFF-ROAD-VEHICLE TRAIL*

Meadow Mountain O.R.V. Trail, a 10-mile, out-and-back ride, follows the ridge of the mountain through beautiful mature hemlock and hardwood forest, interspersed with views of Big Savage Mountain, surrounding valleys, and small farms. This ride requires almost no technical skill, since most of the trail is along a well-maintained woods road. Yet the dirt road is punctuated by climbs, bogs, and rough sections that make the ride challenging. Flatlanders will breathe a little harder—and do some pushing—on the half-mile climb that starts the ride up Meadow Mountain. The rest of the trail follows the ridge of Meadow Mountain.

Starting from parking lot #5 in New Germany State Park, the first half mile is along paved road to the trailhead in the park maintenance area. (Or you can park in front of the park office and skip the paved road.) The trail is a well-maintained, 10-foot-wide forest road. However, plenty of boggy and rocky sections will keep your attention riveted to the 100 square inches in front of your wheel. The optional trail to the Meadow Mountain Overlook at the end of the O.R.V. Trail is narrower and littered with deadfalls. The reward for your efforts is a spectacular, down-the-throat view of Monroe Run with Big Savage Mountain in the background.

While riding, stay alert for wildlife. The mountains are home to a great diversity of animal species, ranging from black bear to brook trout, and great horned owls to long-tailed salamanders. Mammals include deer, bobcat, raccoon, squirrel, beaver, and bats. There are over 100 species of birds, including hawks, owls, turkey, grouse, and warblers. Snakes, turtles, salamanders, frogs, and fish complete the long list of animals you may encounter on your Meadow Mountain ramble.

General location: Savage River State Forest. The ride starts at New Germany State Park, 5 miles southeast of Grantsville, Maryland.

Elevation change: The narrow road climbs from 2,468' of elevation at New Germany to 2,900' on Meadow Mountain. The balance of the trail follows the ridge with little change in elevation. The overlook (an option at the end of the O.R.V. Trail) brings you to 2,959'.

Season: The best riding conditions are from June through October. The summer climate on the Appalachian Plateau is pleasant. It's much cooler than in big cities to the east and has no mosquitoes or ticks. Early spring can be very muddy. Snow is possible from October through April. Avoid riding

MEADOW MOUNTAIN SNOWMOBILE/
OFF-ROAD-VEHICLE TRAIL

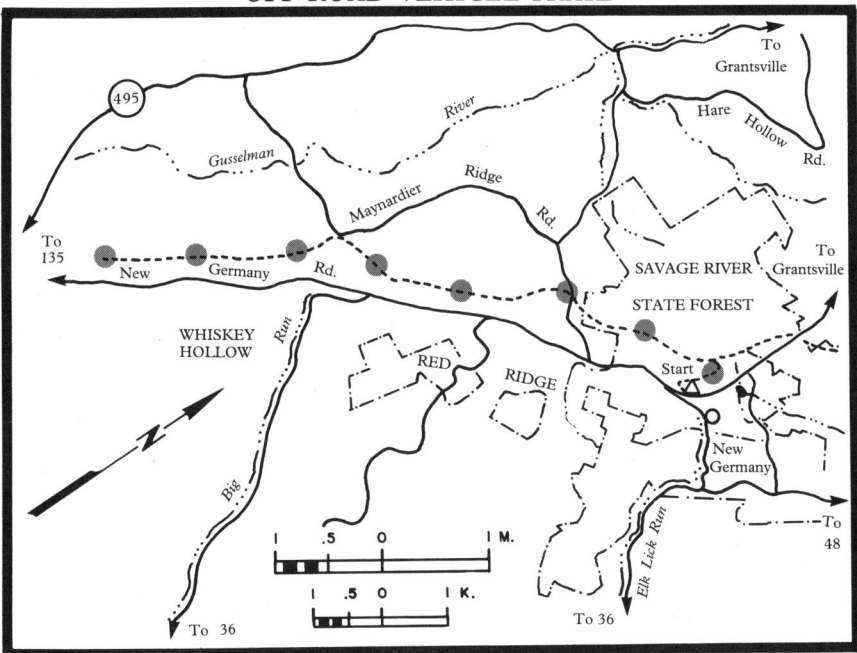

during deer hunting season (after Thanksgiving). In mid-June the mountain laurel along the ridge blooms. The spectacular fall foliage is at its best in late September and early October.

Services: The nearest restaurants, lodging, and grocery stores are in Grantsville, north of I-68. Frostburg, about a half-hour drive east of New Germany, has a great selection of restaurants and lodging. The nearest bike shop is in Cumberland.

Hazards: The woods road is well maintained. However, be alert for downed trees. Use caution at all road crossings. You may come across timber rattlesnakes, especially on the ridge—be alert and give them plenty of room.

Rescue index: The O.R.V. Trail parallels New Germany Road, which carries a fair amount of traffic. Residences can be reached from Otto Lane, Maynardier Ridge Road, and Frank Brenneman Road.

Land status: Maryland state forest and parks, and short sections of county road.

Maps: Maps of the trail are available at the State Forest Administrative Office on New Germany Road. The Grantsville and Bittinger quadrangles of the USGS topo series and the Garrett County topo map (available at the administrative office) are also good.

Finding the trail: Take Exit 24 from I-68; follow the signs for New Germany State Park/Savage River State Forest. The Administrative Office and the trailhead are located on the right side of New Germany Road, where you may park. Or turn left into New Germany State Park and park in lot #5 (across from the lake). Ride your bike back to the park entrance and cross New Germany Road to the trailhead, which is just past the park office. (No overnight parking is allowed.)

Sources of additional information:

Savage River State Forest
Route #2, Box 63-A
Grantsville, Maryland 21536
(301) 895-5759

Notes on the trail: The ride starts with a .7-mile climb to a "T" intersection; turn left. (To the right the O.R.V. Trail continues 4.5 miles north toward I-68.) After a couple of miles the trail reaches another "T" intersection. Turn left and ride a short distance to the intersection of 2 dirt roads (Otto Lane and West Shale Roads). From here you can see the O.R.V. Trail to the right.

When the trail ends at Frank Brenneman Road (the trail to Meadow Mountain Overlook is across the road), you have the option of creating a loop ride by returning to the park via New Germany Road (which is paved and has a wide shoulder). To ride the loop, turn left and descend to the intersection. Turn left for the 5-mile spin back to the park.

RIDE 16 *POPLAR LICK / ELK LICK LOOP*

Here's a great ride for the beginning mountain biker—just don't tell him or her that all mountain biking is this easy. It starts with 5 miles of gentle downhill through a gorgeous forest beside a fast-flowing mountain stream. While lacking spectacular views of the surrounding mountains, this ride shows off the intrinsic beauty of the Appalachian Plateau. Be on the lookout for wildlife—bear, deer, bobcat, raccoon, great horned owls, beaver, and bats are abundant here. Also, the rhododendrons along the streams bloom in early July, and the fall foliage peaks in late September or early October.

The ride begins in a hemlock forest and follows a beautiful mountain stream, Poplar Lick Run. The forest changes to second-growth hardwood as you descend. The O.R.V. Trail ends in a wide, grassy meadow where Poplar Lick Run flows into the Savage River. There are a few short stretches of easy

POPLAR LICK/ELK LICK LOOP

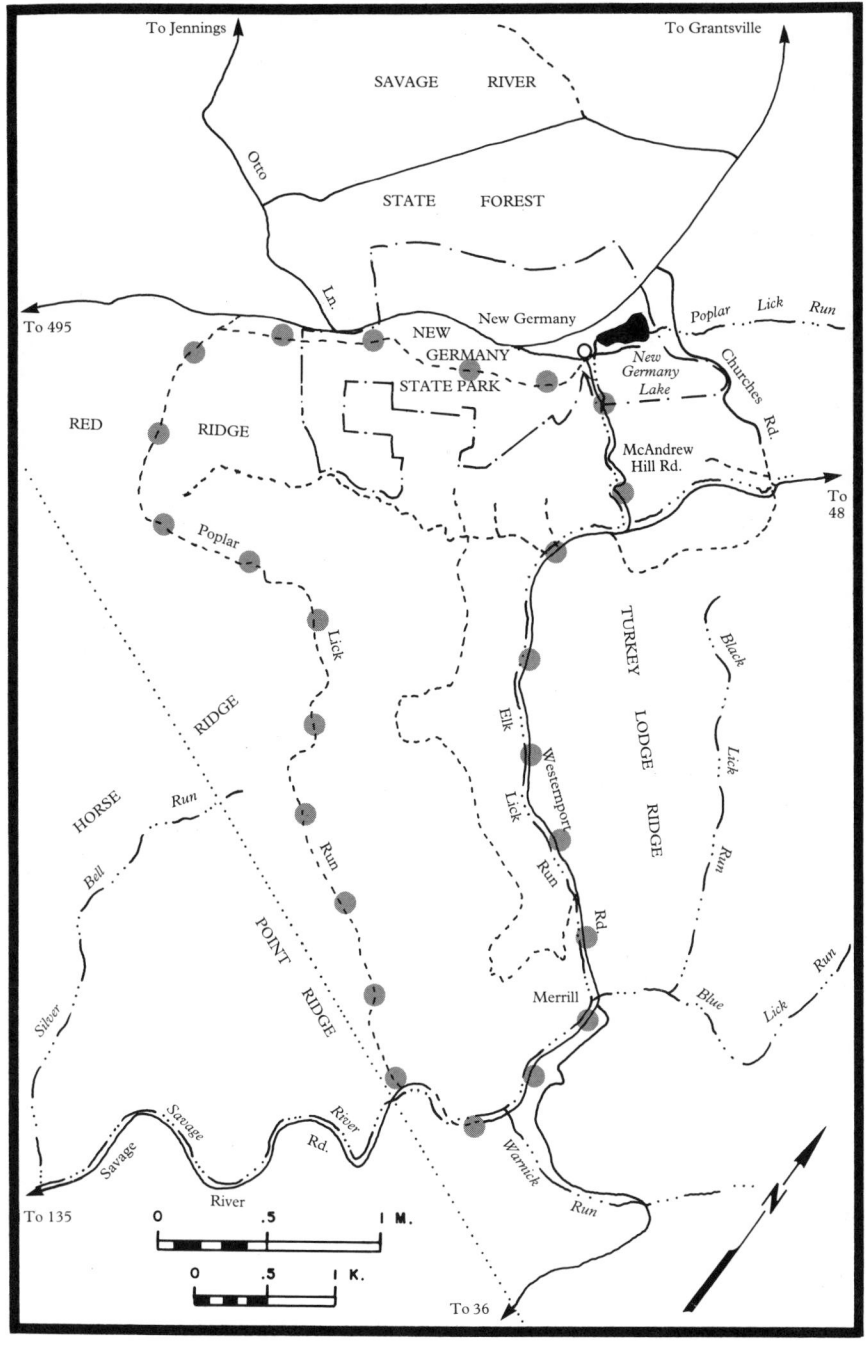

Photo by author

single-track. The return trip (on paved road) follows Elk Lick Run. A note to purists: Don't let the paved road put you off. This is a very pretty ride.

The trail requires no technical skills except for the five stream crossings along Poplar Lick (which can be walked). Expect to get your feet wet; in the spring or after rain you may have to carry your bike and wade through calf-deep water. Last but not least, there's a stiff climb on McAndrew Hill Road just before the finish.

General location: Savage River State Forest. The ride begins at New Germany State Park, 5 miles southeast of Grantsville, Maryland.

Elevation change: There's a gentle slope downstream along Poplar Lick dropping from 2,468' of elevation to 1,686', followed by a gentle rise along the Savage River and Elk Lick up to 2,300'. The short, steep climb on McAndrew Hill Road (about a 300' elevation gain) is followed by a short descent back to the start.

Season: The best biking conditions are from June through October. Earlier in the spring the dirt roads and trails can be extremely muddy, and the stream crossings deep. (This may not be the best choice for a cold-weather ride.)

Snow is possible from October through April. Avoid riding in deer hunting season (late fall).

Services: The nearest restaurants, lodging, and grocery stores are in Grantsville, north of I-68. Frostburg, about a half-hour drive distant, has a great selection of restaurants and lodging. The nearest bike shop is in Cumberland.

Hazards: Use caution on county roads and the O.R.V. Trail; traffic is minimal, but keep alert. Slippery rocks can make stream crossings hazardous. Extreme care should be exercised during periods of high water (usually in the spring).

Rescue index: You can flag down motorists on New Germany Road (follow the O.R.V. Trail uphill from the intersection of the 3 Bridges Trail) and other roads along the loop. There are residences along the paved and unpaved roads on the second half of the ride.

Land status: State forest and park; county roads.

Maps: Ask for a map of the Poplar Lick O.R.V. Trail and the New Germany Hiking Trails at the park office, which is across from the park entrance on New Germany Road. You can also purchase a Garrett County topo map there.

Finding the trail: Take Exit 24 from I-68 (Grantsville) and follow signs for New Germany State Park/Savage River State Forest. Park in lot #5 at New Germany State Park.

Sources of additional information:

Savage River State Forest
Route #2, Box 63-A
Grantsville, Maryland 21536
(301) 895-5759

Notes on the trail: The trailhead is near the end of parking lot #5. The key to reaching the Poplar Lick O.R.V. Trail is to stay with the stream. (Don't climb any hills.) Look for the gate that marks the entrance to the O.R.V. Trail and follow it downstream for about 5 miles. The O.R.V. Trail ends at the intersection with Savage River Road; turn left and go 1.5 miles to the stop sign. Turn left onto the paved Westernport Road where you cross a rail and concrete bridge over the Savage River. Follow this county road (traffic is light) for almost 3 miles along Elk Lick Run. After crossing the third wooden bridge, turn left onto the second road (McAndrew Hill Road). Follow this unpaved road back to New Germany State Park.

RIDE 17 MEADOW MOUNTAIN / MONROE RUN / POPLAR LICK LOOP

This is a ride for the well-conditioned cyclist, for it's a long and strenuous 20-mile loop. There are rough riding surfaces (mud, rocks, gravel, logs) and many stream crossings. Start early in the day and pack a lunch. Although the trails are well marked, it's a good idea to carry a topo map and compass.

The ride along Meadow Mountain is on a woods road featuring views of the surrounding mountains. The fast descent on Big Run Road is through beautiful forests and ends at Big Run State Park, with views of Savage River Reservoir—an uncluttered jewel ringed by cliffs and forested hills. The Poplar Lick O.R.V. Trail is a woods road about 5 miles long and has 5 stream crossings. The 3 Bridges Trail is a single-track that connects with the Green Trail, an easy woods road that returns you to New Germany State Park. Warning: This ride could induce sensory overload during peak fall foliage in late September or early October.

General location: Five miles southeast of Grantsville, Maryland.

Elevation change: The loop climbs from 2,468' at New Germany State Park to 2,900' on Meadow Mountain. There's little change in elevation along the ridge until the descent to Big Run Road (2,525'). A gentle descent along the Big Run Road drops you to 1,500' at Savage River Road, followed by a gentle rise up the Savage River and Poplar Lick Run to the starting point in New Germany State Park.

Season: June through October offer the best riding conditions. The summer climate is very pleasant, with no mosquitoes or ticks. Early spring can be extremely muddy. From October through April snow is possible. Avoid riding in deer hunting season (late fall). Mountain laurel blooms peak along the ridges in mid-June; rhododendron blooms peak along the streams in early July.

Services: The nearest restaurants, lodging, and grocery stores are in Grantsville, north of I-68. Frostburg, about a half-hour drive distant, has a good selection of restaurants and lodging. The nearest bike shop is in Cumberland.

Hazards: Use caution on county roads and the O.R.V. Trail; traffic is usually light, but keep alert. Slippery rocks make stream crossings hazardous—use care during periods of high water (usually in the spring.) And keep an eye peeled for rattlesnakes, especially along the ridges.

Rescue index: Meadow Mountain O.R.V. Trail parallels New Germany Road, which carries a lot of traffic. There is a phone at B.J.'s Store, a small grocery store on Savage River Road 1 mile upstream from Big Run State Park.

Land status: Maryland State Forest and Parks; county roads.

Maps: A hiking map of the loop is available at the New Germany Park office. A topo map of Garrett County is also available there.

MEADOW MOUNTAIN/MONROE RUN/
POPLAR LICK LOOP

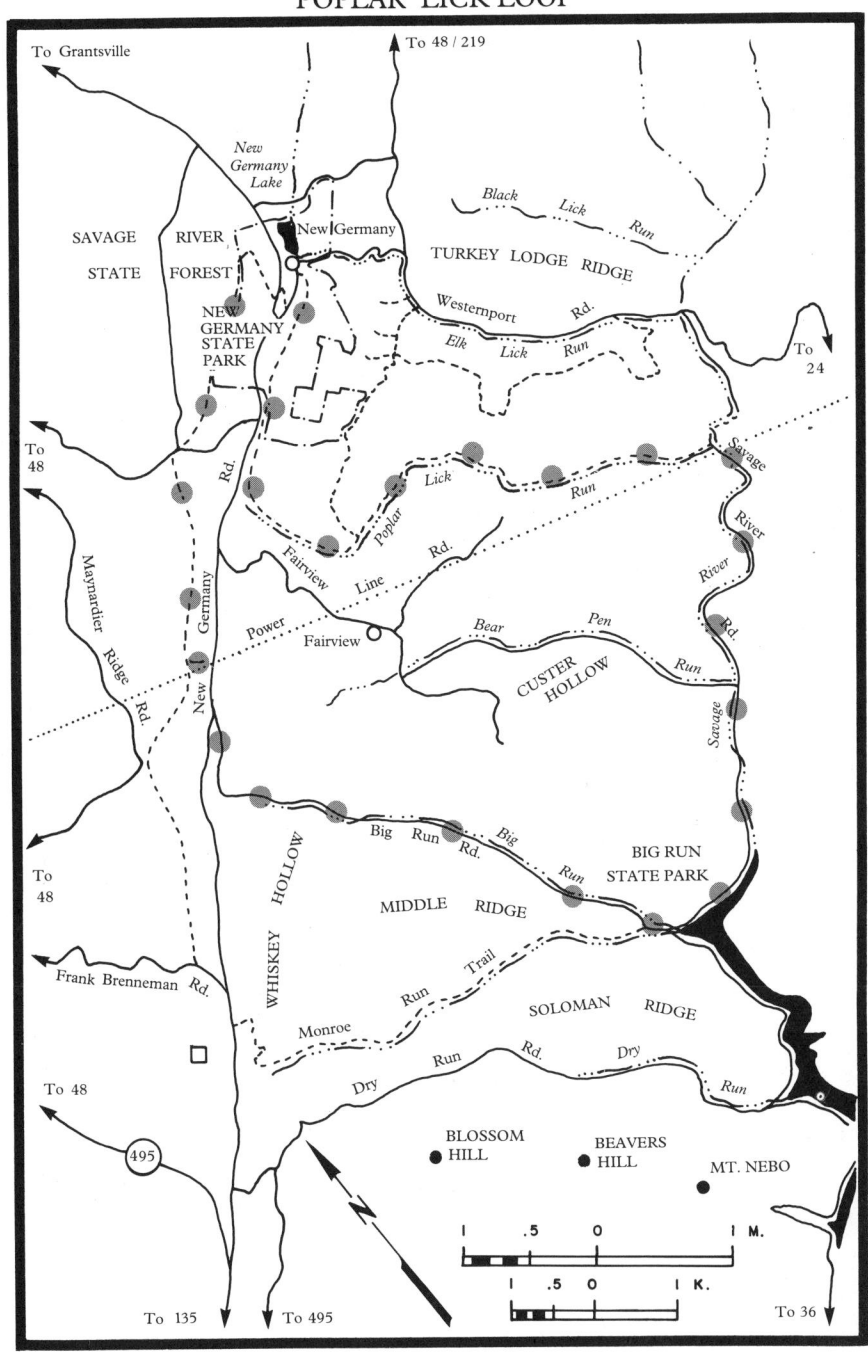

Finding the trail: Take Exit 24 from I-68 and follow the signs to New Germany State Park/Savage River State Forest. Turn left into the Park and park at lot #5, or turn right and park at the administrative office. The trailhead (Meadow Mountain O.R.V. Trail) is on the right, just past the office.

Sources of additional information:

> Savage River State Forest
> Route #2, Box 63-A
> Grantsville, Maryland 21536
> (301) 895-5759

Notes on the trail: On Meadow Mountain O.R.V. Trail, which starts this loop, look for an old woods road that makes a sharp left immediately before the power lines. This trail is marked with a sign that says "No Snowmobiling." Follow this steep woods road to a yellow-pole gate on New Germany Road; turn right for a quarter mile and turn left onto Big Run Road, which descends to Big Run State Park.

Turn left onto Savage River Road (which parallels its namesake) to the Poplar Lick O.R.V. Trail on the left (there's a sign). Follow this trail to the gate and pick up the blue-blazed 3 Bridges Trail, which continues upstream along Poplar Lick Run. Turn left at the end and follow the Green Trail (a woods road) back to New Germany State Park.

PENNSYLVANIA

Michaux State Forest

Located between Gettysburg to the east and Chambersburg to the west, Michaux State Forest encompasses over 82,000 acres of Pennsylvania forests and mountains. With a well-defined system of roads, snowmobile trails, and foot trails, Michaux (me-SHOW) is an increasingly popular destination for mountain bikers.

The prominent geographic feature in the forest is South Mountain, a long ridge that runs north out of nearby Maryland into Pennsylvania. Forty miles of the Appalachian Trail, the 2,000-mile foot trail running from Maine to Georgia, follow the ridge of South Mountain the length of the forest. The Appalachian Trail is closed to mountain bikes, as are most trails in the state parks located inside the forest.

Only a few hours away from large metropolitan areas such as Baltimore, Washington, and Philadelphia, Michaux is convenient to many mountain bikers hankering for a weekend of exploration. With its extensive trail and road system, Michaux offers a wide variety of interesting and scenic rides.

Jes Stith, owner of Gettysburg Schwinn bike shop, has raced mountain bikes for five years and trains in Michaux regularly. Michaux, he says, offers hard-core riders and racers looking for difficult training rides lots of technical single-track and numerous long climbs. Yet, Jes points out, there are also miles of moderate trails and roads for non-expert riders. "Plus," he adds, "it's so darned beautiful up there." With a knowledgeable staff dedicated to mountain biking, Gettysburg Schwinn is headquarters for off-road enthusiasts in south-central Pennsylvania. Be sure to stop by for information on other great places to ride.

RIDE 18   *SLATE ROAD, PINEY RIDGE ROAD TO POLE STEEPLE LOOP*

The geologic centerpiece of this 11-mile loop ride is Pole Steeple, a rock feature composed of 60- to 80-foot-high cliffs at the top of a ridge. Pole Steeple provides great views of nearby mountains. Without trees in the way the vista is impressive in any season. More attractions on this difficult ride include steep climbs and descents through dense forest, which provide plenty of opportunities to glimpse wildlife. Pine Grove Furnace Park, at the start of the loop, features hiking and nature trails, as well as some interesting historical features and two large lakes for swimming.

Most of the route is on all-terrain-vehicle trails covered with loose scree.

SLATE ROAD, PINEY RIDGE ROAD TO POLE STEEPLE LOOP

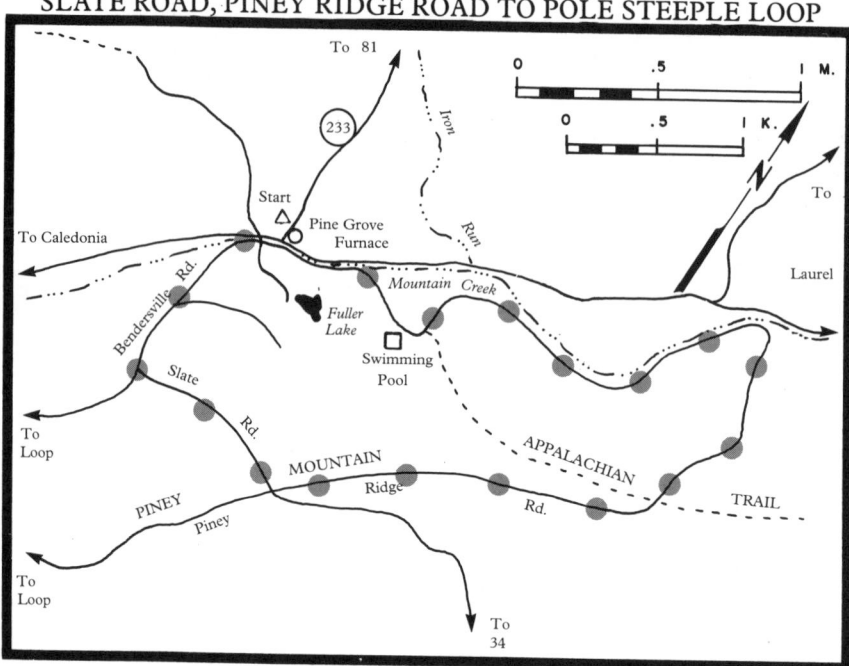

Good bike handling skills are a must for the descents. Some sections on Piney Ridge Road are fast descents on a loose, irregular surface. The final descent is on a deeply rutted trail that frequently has water flowing on it. A cinder trail completes the loop.

General location: Six miles east of Chambersburg, Pennsylvania.

Elevation change: The initial climb up Slate Road to the top of the ridge on Piney Ridge Road involves approximately 500' of vertical gain in under 3 miles. Piney Ridge Road to Pole Steeple undulates between 100' gains and losses. After Pole Steeple it's all downhill.

Season: The loop is usually rideable from late spring through the fall. Spring can be wet and summer is usually hot, humid, and buggy. Fall, with its foliage, is probably the best time of year to ride this loop. Avoid riding in deer hunting season, which starts in the late fall.

Services: Water and toilet facilities are available in Pine Grove Furnace State Park. The park has a general store, youth hostel, and overnight camping.

Hazards: The trails are used by all-terrain vehicles. Use caution if clambering on the boulders of Pole Steeple.

Rescue index: Return to Pine Grove Furnace or Bendersville Road, which is paved and carries light traffic.

Land status: Pennsylvania state forest and park. Trails are not open to moun-

tain bikes in the state park, so return through the park on the bike/hike trail.
Maps: The USGS topo is the Dickinson quad. The Pennsylvania State Park's
Pine Grove Furnace map features additional trail detail.
Finding the trail: From Interstate 81 take either US 30 or Route 94 to PA 233
and Pine Grove Furnace State Park. Park near the furnace.

Sources of additional information:

District Forester
Michaux State Forest
10099 Lincoln Way East
Fayetteville, Pennsylvania 17222
(717) 352-2211

Gettysburg Schwinn
100A Buford Avenue
Gettysburg, Pennsylvania 17325
(717) 334-7791

Notes on the trail: After parking, pedal south on Bendersville Road approximately a half mile to Slate Road and turn left. Climb to Piney Ridge Road and turn left. Cross the Appalachian Trail and pick up the blue-blazed trail to Pole Steeple. (The dead-end spur trail on the left leads to a cliff overlook.) Drop down the ravine to Laurel Forge Pond, then follow the cinder path to Pine Grove Furnace.

RIDE 19   *ALL-TERRAIN-VEHICLE TRAIL TO LOG SLED TRAIL VIA PINEY RIDGE ROAD*

This 12-mile loop follows a combination of paved roads, two-wheel-drive roads, hard-packed dirt roads, all-terrain-vehicle trails, and multiple-use trails. While there are some steep sections, this ride is not very technical. However, since the ride features some steep climbing and fast descents on loose rock and dirt, it requires a good fitness level and good bike handling skills.

The trail passes through second-growth mixed coniferous and deciduous forest. There are excellent views from Piney Ridge Road. The descent on Log Sled Trail is through a beautiful wooded hollow along a mountain stream. Pine Grove Furnace State Park features hiking and nature trails, and two large lakes for swimming.
General location: Six miles east of Chambersburg, Pennsylvania.
Elevation change: The ride starts at about 900' of elevation and climbs gradually to over 1,500' on Piney Mountain. The elevation drops sharply along Log Sled Trail to 1,049' and then gradually to around 900' along paved PA 233. The total elevation gain is about 800'.

ATV TRAIL TO LOG SLED TRAIL VIA PINEY RIDGE ROAD

Season: The best riding is between late spring and fall. Spring can be wet and summer can be hot, humid, and buggy. Fall is the best time to ride, but avoid riding in deer hunting season, which starts in the late fall.

Services: Water and toilet facilities are available in Pine Grove Furnace State Park. The park has a general store and youth hostel, and overnight camping is permitted.

Hazards: Watch out for hikers and all-terrain vehicles on the fast descent on Log Sled Trail.

Rescue index: For help, return to Pine Grove Furnace or wave down traffic on PA 233.

Land status: State forest and state park.

Maps: The USGS 7.5 minute topos are Pine Grove Furnace and Arentsville.

Finding the trail: From I-81, take either US 30 or Route 94 to PA 233 and Pine Grove Furnace State Park. Park near the furnace.

Sources of additional information:

District Forester
Michaux State Forest
10099 Lincoln Way East

Fayetteville, Pennsylvania 17222
(717) 352-2211

Gettysburg Schwinn
100A Buford Avenue
Gettysburg, Pennsylvania 17325
(717) 334-7791

Notes on the trail: Ride out Bendersville Road past Slate Road to the orange-signed all-terrain-vehicle trail on the left. At the end of the climb, turn right onto Piney Ridge Road. Ride for 4 miles to Log Sled Trail on the right. Descend to PA 233, turn right, and return to Pine Grove Furnace.

RIDE 20 *LONG PINE RESERVOIR LOOP*

The major attraction of this 12-mile loop ride is a chance to explore a vast, undeveloped forest. The geography features long ridges called "flats," due to their flat-top profiles. Another nice aspect to this ride is Long Pine Reservoir, a large, beautiful lake nestled in the hills that's also a popular destination for anglers. The hollows and valleys between the flats are heavily wooded, mostly with conifers. The views of the surrounding valleys and mountains from the ridges are striking in any season.

Steep climbs on loose rock and dirt require good fitness and bike-handling skills. However, this ride isn't very technical. The trail follows hard-packed dirt roads (some sections with washboarded surface), rough double-track covered with loose rock, and single-track that varies from packed dirt with a pine-humus surface to football-sized rock scree.

General location: Six miles east of Chambersburg, Pennsylvania.

Elevation change: The first 3 miles gain about 600' in elevation, followed by a ridge traverse with slight undulations. A single-track drops 300' in a half mile, which is followed by a 100' climb and a 300' drop on a dirt road. A 400' climb over 1 mile on a double-track is followed by a 400' drop over 1 mile, then a gradual descent and a final 200' climb over a quarter mile. The total elevation gain is around 1,500'.

Season: The best riding is between late spring and fall. Spring can be wet and summer can be hot, humid, and buggy. Fall is the best season to ride, but avoid riding in deer hunting season, which starts in the late fall.

Services: Water, rest rooms, and camping are available in Caledonia State Park on PA 233. All other services are available in Chambersburg, Pennsylvania.

Hazards: Aside from all-terrain vehicles and blind curves on single-track de-

LONG PINE RESERVOIR LOOP

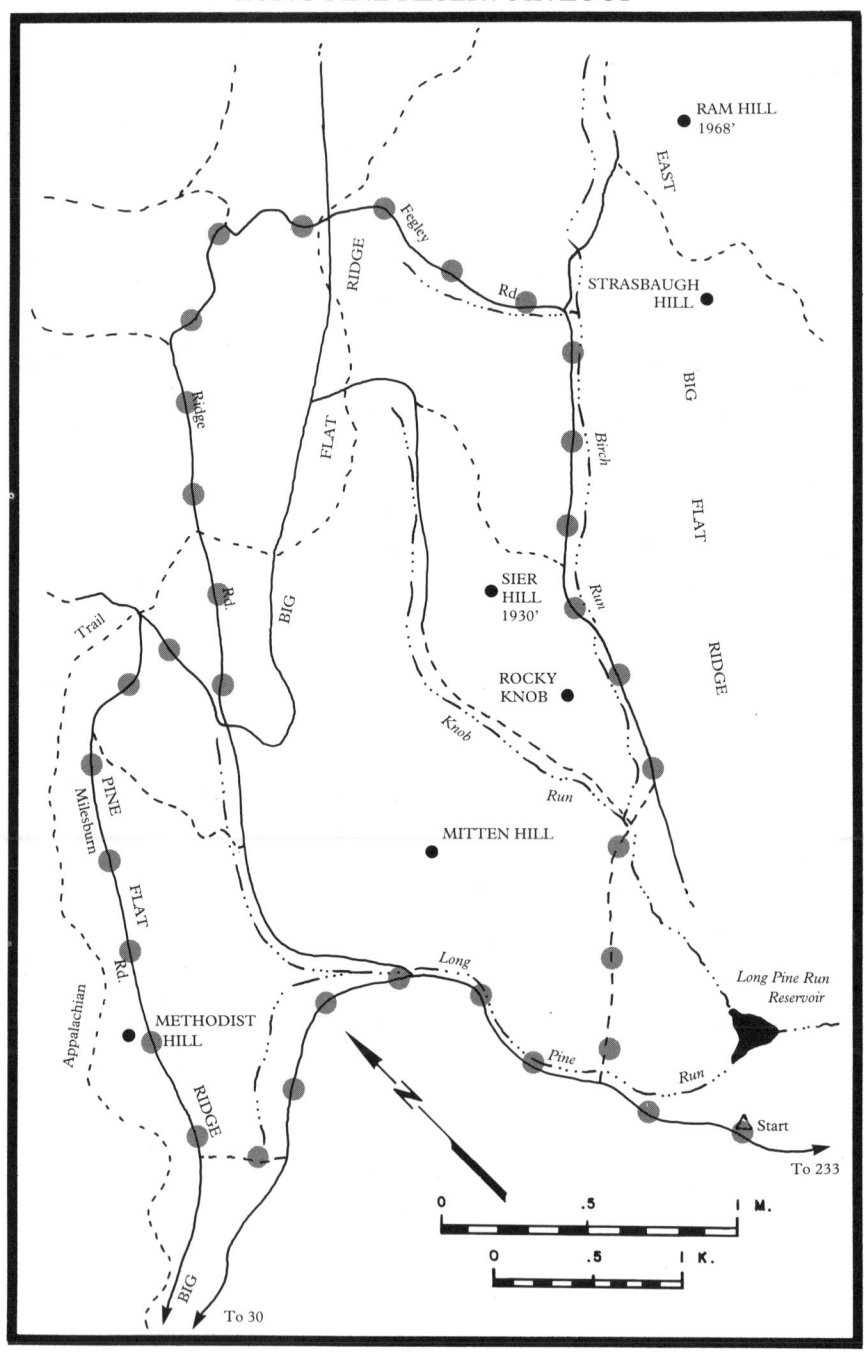

scents, the biggest hazard in the area is getting lost. There are many roads, unmarked trails, and a sameness to the topography, so it's easy to get confused. Carry a map and compass.

Rescue index: The area is closed to motorized vehicles; the closest help is traffic on PA 233.

Land status: State forest.

Maps: The USGS 7.5 minute topo is Caledonia Park.

Finding the trail: From I-81, take either US 30 or PA 94 to PA 233. Look for a dirt road on the north side of PA 233 at the Chambersburg Reservoir pull-out. Take this road approximately 3 miles to Long Pine Reservoir and park in the parking area.

Sources of additional information:

District Forester
Michaux State Forest
10099 Lincoln Way East
Fayetteville, Pennsylvania 17222
(717) 352-2211

Gettysburg Schwinn
100A Buford Avenue
Gettysburg, Pennsylvania 17325
(717) 334-7791

Notes on the trail: From the parking area, ride north on the dirt road and pass the first road on the right of the fork. At the next fork, bear left and climb to the top of Big Pine Flat. Turn right along the power line right-of-way and then turn right onto the dirt road. After 2 miles or so take the fourth trail on the right. (All 4 trails drop down the south side of the mountain to a road in the valley.) Turn right onto the road at the bottom of the descent and go straight at the next intersection. Take the rough dirt road a mile later and climb to a partially clear-cut meadow. Bear right at the next trail intersection. Continue to climb to the top of Big Flat. Cross the road and take the trail for the descent. At the dirt road turn right toward the reservoir. Bear right at the fork and then turn left at the dirt road and return to the parking area.

Confused? Even mountain bikers that ride the area regularly get disoriented on occasion. Carry a map and compass, and give yourself enough time so that you're not racing against a setting sun.

Laurel Highlands

Two hundred fifty miles west of Philadelphia, the Laurel Highlands of southwestern Pennsylvania stretch over a five-county region dominated by two large mountain ridges, the Laurel and the Chestnut, both carved by the Youghiogheny River and the Conemaugh Gorges. These mountains offer virtually unlimited possibilities for rugged, scenic mountain biking.

Historically, a lot happened in the hills, valleys, and deep forests located in the Laurel Highlands. Major skirmishes in the French and Indian War were fought here, and George Washington suffered his only military defeat at Fort Necessity. The Whiskey Rebellion, the United States' first constitutional crisis, was crushed here by federal troops under the command of General "Mad" Anthony Wayne. We've been paying taxes ever since.

The nineteenth century brought coal mining, steel making, and coke production into the Laurel Highlands. Railroads and canals linked the region with Pittsburgh to the west and Cumberland, Maryland, to the south. Following the decline of the steel industry, tourism became increasingly important to the region. The hills and mountains of the Laurel Highlands attract hikers, skiers, and whitewater enthusiasts. The Youghiogheny (YOCK-uh-ganey) River, which defines the southwest corner of the Highlands, is considered the best whitewater river east of the Mississippi.

Hikers can trek the Laurel Highlands Hiking Trail, which stretches for 70 miles between Ohiopyle and Youngstown. The Connellsville-Cumberland Trail, a proposed 70-mile hiking and biking route along the old Western Maryland Railroad right-of-way, will eventually link up with the C&O Canal (which extends to Washington, D.C.).

The Laurel Highlands are characterized by beautiful vistas, tidy farms, and tens of thousands of acres of wilderness. Because of its relatively high altitude (Mt. Davis, the state's highest point at 3,213 feet, is nearby), the region's climate is significantly colder and snowier in winter and cooler in summer than are the cities to the west and east.

The following rides start from Hidden Valley Resort, 12 miles west of Somerset, Pennsylvania. Hidden Valley is a vacation-home resort and ski area (both downhill and cross-country). Taking advantage of its beautiful setting (it's surrounded by 25,000 acres of state wilderness lands), the resort began renting mountain bikes in the mid-1980s. Hidden Valley made a financial commitment to mountain biking largely because of one of its employees, Jim Sota.

"I suggested we look into offering mountain bikes after I got my first bike six years ago," recalled Sota, who manages the bike shop in summer and the cross-country skiing facilities in the winter. "We started small, with only ten rental bikes, but it's proven popular. Now we've got a rental stable of 35 bikes, a bike shop, and we sponsor a race every fall."

All the trails from Hidden Valley lead to state forests. Where they cross private land Hidden Valley has permission for users to pass. Mountain bikers may park at the Ski Lodge or behind The Barn, the cross-country ski center on PA 31. Jim Sota asks that bikers check in at the shop (located at the Ski Lodge) to inquire about trail conditions, pick up a map, and let them know when you're returning.

RIDE 21 *RACE LOOP RIDE*

This is a moderately hilly 10-mile loop that will give experienced mountain bikers a good workout. The ride requires some technical skill due to short sections of rocky single-track. The first climb is long and steep, but the rest of the climbs are easier. The trail surface varies from mud to paved road, but most is packed dirt. At the higher elevations there are excellent views of the mountains to the west and of the Jones Mill Run Valley. The fall foliage in mid-October is spectacular. This area contains abundant wildlife (white-tailed deer, bear, rabbit, pheasant, turkey, squirrel, grouse) and a wide variety of plant species. The clear mountain streams and beautiful western Pennsylvania scenery attract visitors from all over the country.

The first part of the loop is paved road leading to a dirt-and-grass trail. Roots and rocks make for a bumpy ride on Lookout Trail. The pipeline adjacent to Fire Tower Road is smooth dirt with some muddy sections. Cherry Trail has some rocky and muddy portions. Timberhaul Road is a hard-packed and gravel double-track.

After the first climb you're rewarded with a delightful single-track through a mature white-pine forest. The rest of the loop is almost as enjoyable. Vistas of the mountains to the west are visible as you ride through a variety of settings, ranging from deciduous hardwood and coniferous forests to open meadows.

General location: Twelve miles west of Somerset, Pennsylvania.

Elevation change: The ride begins at 2,500′ of elevation and climbs to 2,800′ in the first mile. The highest point is 2,900′, at 3.5 miles. You descend to 2,300′, then climb for 2 miles to 2,800′ on Timber Haul Road. There's a quick descent to the ski area parking lot. The total elevation gain is 1,000′.

Season: Fall riding is the best. In summer, start the ride early in the day to avoid the mugginess. From November through March expect snow. In spring the trails are very muddy. Avoid riding during deer hunting season, which begins in late November.

RACE LOOP RIDE

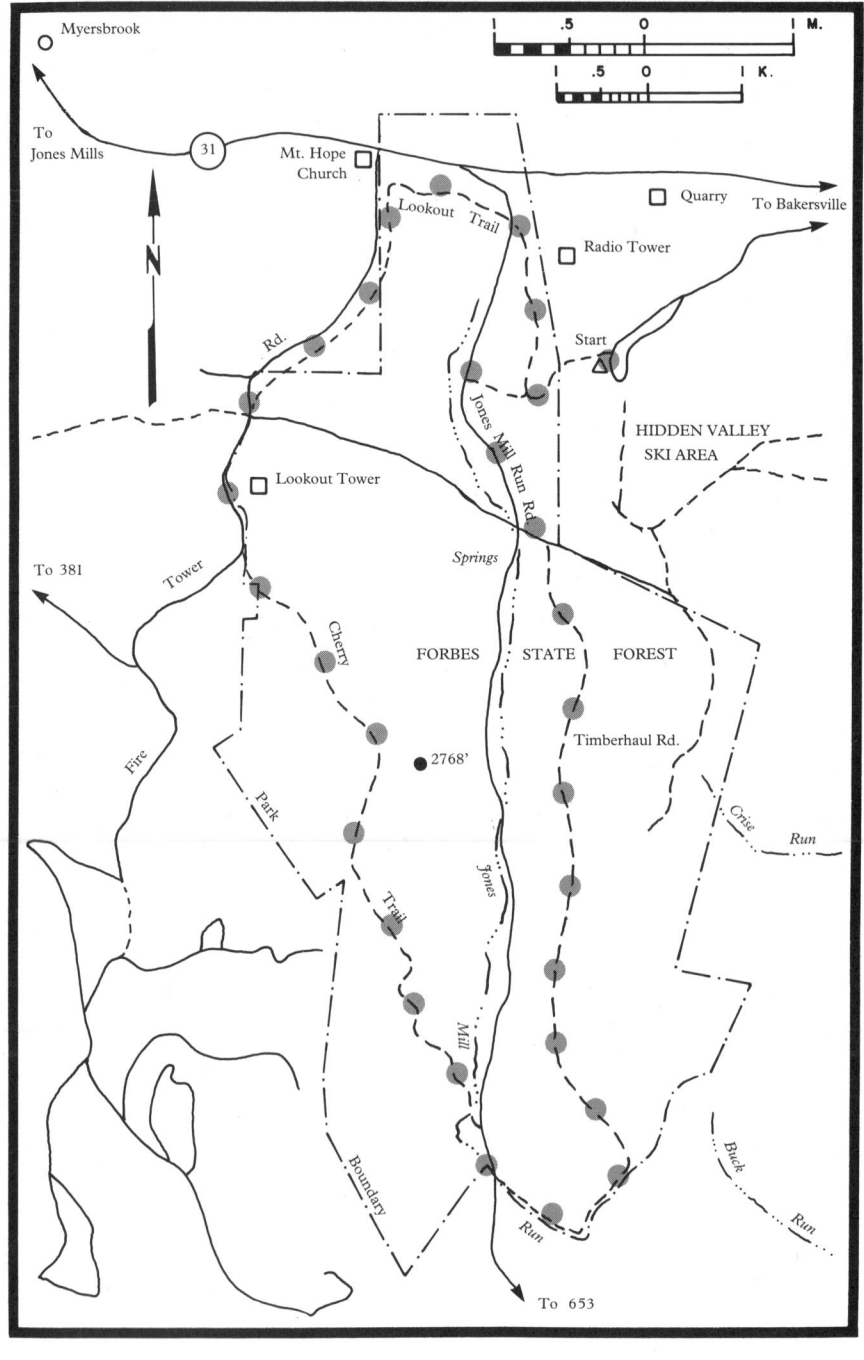

Services: All services are available at Hidden Valley Resort. Camp at Kooser State Park, 2 miles east of Hidden Valley on PA 31.

Hazards: Rocky areas approach very quickly on fast descents, so look ahead. Watch out for a sharp left turn on Cherry Trail that has a surface of large loose gravel.

Rescue index: Jones Mill Run Road carries light traffic that can be flagged down.

Land status: Private (Hidden Valley Resort) and state forest.

Maps: Bakersville quads of the USGS series. The Seven Springs Department of Forestry Snowmobile Trail Maps are also helpful, and are available from Hidden Valley Resort.

Finding the trail: Hidden Valley Resort is located off PA 31 between Somerset and Donegal, PA. From points north and west take the Pennsylvania Turnpike to Exit 9/Donegal. Continue 8 miles east on PA 31 to Hidden Valley. From Washington, DC, and points south and east, take the Pennsylvania Turnpike to Exit 10/Somerset. Continue 12 miles west on PA 31 to Hidden Valley. Follow the signs to the Lodge to start the ride.

Sources of additional information:

Mountain Bike Shop
Hidden Valley Resort
One Craighead Drive
Somerset, Pennsylvania 15501
(800) 458-0175, ext. 473

District Forester
Forbes State Forest
P.O. Box 519
Laughlintown, Pennsylvania 15655
(412) 238-9533

Notes on the trail: Start the ride in the parking lot of the ski area at Hidden Valley Resort. Exit the parking lot and make a left up Parke Drive. At Valley View Drive (just above the upper parking lot) you can either continue up Parke Drive (which is easier), or turn right onto Valley View Drive; Valley View Trail (which is very steep) is 40′ up the road on the left.

For the easier (and longer) climb continue up Parke Drive, make a left onto Gardner Road at the stop sign, and then take the next right, the Lookout Trail (there's a sign). Follow the trail 100 yards and make the next right; continue following Lookout Trail, which parallels Gardner Road. Either way the loop starts on the Lookout Trail, at the intersection of Valley View and Gardner Roads.

NORTH WOODS RAMBLE

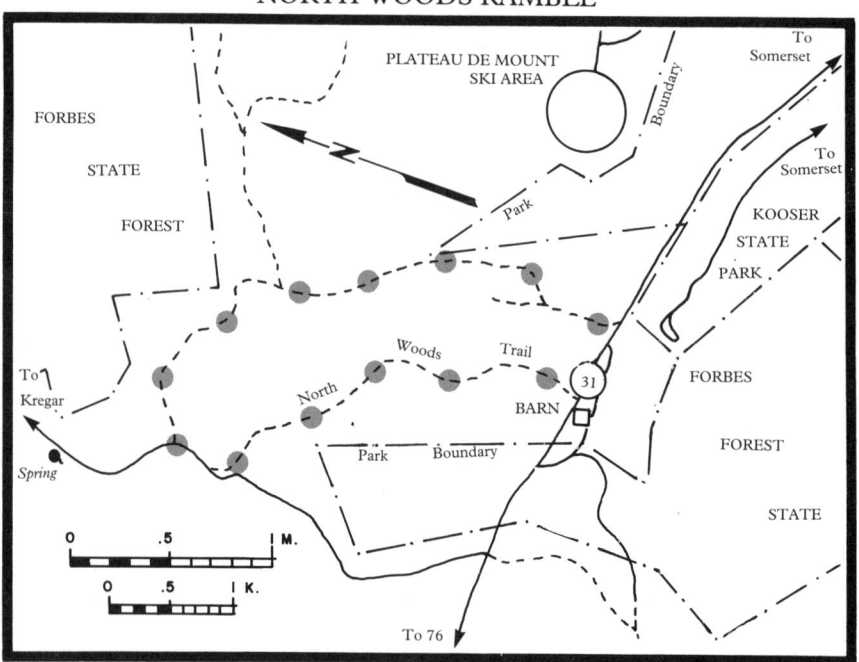

RIDE 22   *NORTH WOODS RAMBLE*

This 3-mile loop ride features some excellent views of the mountains of western Pennsylvania. Little technical skill is required, though there is one short section of loose rock. The first quarter mile is hard-packed; the next mile is a gradual climb on a grass trail. There are no steep hills. The top of the climb is a two-wheel-drive road, and the return trail is all grass. "Ramble" is a good name for this easy ride.

Somerset County is visible from the top of the trail, and there's a good view of Laurel Ridge looking north into the forest regeneration area. This region is typical of Pennsylvania forests and meadows. In addition to the views and excellent pedaling, you can visit a stone springhouse on the return.

General location: Forbes State Forest in the Laurel Highlands of western Pennsylvania. The ride begins at The Barn, the cross-country ski shop at Hidden Valley Resort.

Elevation change: There's a 300' climb in the first 1.5 miles.

Season: Late spring through fall are the best times to ride this loop. Spring

Photo by author

is usually very muddy. Expect snow from November through March. Avoid riding during deer hunting season, which typically begins on the first Monday after Thanksgiving.

Services: All services are available at Hidden Valley Resort. Camp at Kooser State Park, 2 miles east of Hidden Valley on PA 31.

Hazards: Watch for rocks while riding through the forest regeneration area on North Woods Trail. And look out for groundhog holes (which can devour front wheels, causing the dreaded face-plant) in the fields at the end of the ride.

Rescue index: Help is quickly reached at The Barn on PA 31.

Land status: Private land and state forest land.

Maps: Pick up the Hidden Valley Resort trail maps and Department of Forestry Snowmobile Trail Maps from Hidden Valley Resort.

Finding the trail: Hidden Valley Resort is located on PA 31 between Somerset and Donegal, Pennsylvania. From points north and west take the Pennsylvania Turnpike to Exit 9/Donegal. Continue 8 miles east on PA 31 to Hidden Valley. From Washington, DC, and points south and east, take the Pennsylvania Turnpike to Exit 10/Somerset. Continue 12 miles west on PA 31 to Hidden

Valley. Stop at The Barn (Hidden Valley's cross-country ski shop) on PA 31, 300 yards east of the Hidden Valley Resort entrance. Park behind the building.

Sources of additional information:

Mountain Bike Shop
Hidden Valley Resort
One Craighead Drive
Somerset, Pennsylvania 15501
(800) 458-0175, ext. 473

District Forester
Forbes State Forest
P.O. Box 519
Laughlintown, Pennsylvania 15655
(412) 238-9533

Notes on the trail: Start this easy trail at The Barn by pedaling out of the parking lot on the lower road and riding toward the stone house. Cross PA 31 (watch for traffic) just past the house, and keep left once you enter the driveway. Then follow the North Woods signs.

On the return you can either follow the dirt road back to PA 31, or follow the trail through the field on the left (an apple tree marks the beginning of the trail). This trail passes through a short section of woods followed by a view of orchards. And a note to allergy sufferers—in late summer the fields can become overgrown with goldenrod.

RIDE 23   *KUHNTOWN LOOP*

Riding the trails and roads on this 15-mile loop is a good introduction to the history of the Laurel Highlands. North Woods and Schaffer Trails were once railroad lines used to haul logs out from logging operations. The dirt roads provided access for early settlers who have long since moved on. The smooth sections of road near the Pennsylvania Turnpike are used by modern-day logging operations. Toward the end of the ride there's a stone spring house along the dirt road.

This ride, designed for experienced and well-conditioned cyclists, takes you to the heart of the Laurel Ridge area. The trails and roads are typical of many others found in the region. The top of the ridge provides several views of the surrounding mountains. Most of the ride is in woods, and with the rise and fall of elevation is representative of the region's topography. The first 2.5 miles are on grassy ski trails. After the warming hut at the bottom of

KUHNTOWN LOOP

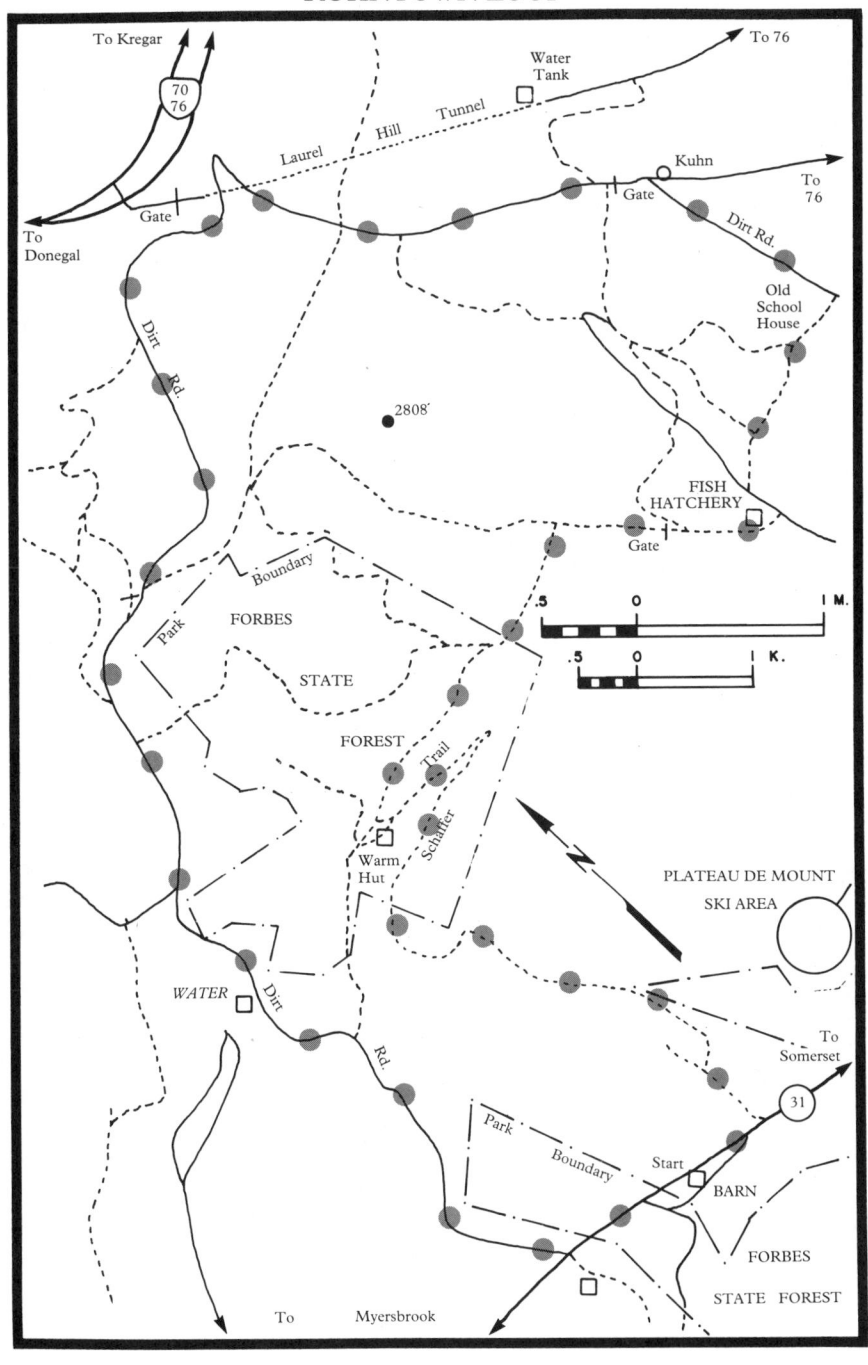

Schaffer Trail the surface is mostly dirt and gravel. Some sections are rutted and washed-out dirt road. There is a long, steep climb over loose rock after the fish hatchery. The climb out of the valley near the Pennsylvania Turnpike is mostly packed dirt. Once you reach the road at the top it's dirt road for the remainder of the ride.

General location: Forbes State Forest, 12 miles west of Somerset, Pennsylvania. The ride begins and ends at The Barn, the cross-country ski shop at Hidden Valley Resort.

Elevation change: The first 1.5 miles begin with a 300' climb followed by a 300' descent over the next 2 miles. A steep, half-mile climb after the fish hatchery is difficult due to the loose surface. Once at the top there is a slight elevation gain back to the very top of the ridge for the next 1.5 miles. A fast 250' descent to the Turnpike (with a sharp left turn) is followed by a 400' ascent (with 2 steep climbs) over the next 2 miles of the dirt trail. The road back is level with a fast descent near the end. The total elevation gain is about 800'.

Season: Late spring through fall are the best seasons to ride this loop. Spring can be very muddy from snowmelt. Expect snow between November and March. Avoid riding in deer hunting season, which begins in late November.

Services: All services are available at Hidden Valley Resort. Camp at Kooser State Park, 2 miles east of Hidden Valley on PA 31.

Hazards: Watch for rocky sections and four-wheel-drive traffic on some of the roads. There is a sharp left turn with loose gravel on the descent into the Turnpike area.

Rescue index: There are a number of residences near the fish hatchery and along the dirt road after the steep climb. After climbing the dirt trail past the Pennsylvania Turnpike, help is best reached at Hidden Valley Resort.

Land status: State forest, public roads, and private property.

Maps: Department of Forestry Snowmobile Trail Maps; Bakersville and Seven Springs USGS series quads.

Finding the trail: Hidden Valley Resort is located off PA 31 between Somerset and Donegal, Pennsylvania. From points north and west take the Pennsylvania Turnpike to Exit 9/Donegal. Continue 8 miles east on PA 31 to Hidden Valley. From Washington, DC, and points south and east, take the Pennsylvania Turnpike to Exit 10/Somerset. Continue 12 miles west on PA 31 to Hidden Valley. Stop at The Barn (Hidden Valley's cross-country ski shop) on PA 31, 300 yards east of the Hidden Valley Resort entrance. Park behind the building.

Sources of additional information:

Mountain Bike Shop
Hidden Valley Resort
One Craighead Drive

Photo by author

Somerset, Pennsylvania 15501
(800) 458-0175, ext. 473

District Forester
Forbes State Forest
P.O. Box 519
Laughlintown, Pennsylvania 15655
(412) 238-9533

Notes on the trail: See North Woods Ramble for details on the start of this ride.

Allegheny National Forest and Clarion

A glance at a road map reveals that a sizeable portion of central and western Pennsylvania is, well, empty—no roads, no towns, no superhighways. Cynics would say there's nothing there. Mountain bikers, on the other hand, know better. Empty space on a road map just might mean great off-road riding.

In this case they're right. Most of this empty territory is the Allegheny National Forest, 740,000 acres of wilderness in the northern Allegheny Mountains. The forest boasts 170 miles of hiking trails (including the 95-mile North County Trail, a National Scenic Trail), hundreds of camping sites, the Allegheny Reservoir Scenic Drive (part of the coast-to-coast Bike Centennial Route), and the 27-mile-long Allegheny Reservoir.

In addition, the Forest Service is busy expanding a system of off-road-vehicle trails, such as the Marienville, Willow Creek, and Rocky Gap O.R.V. Trails. These trails are maintained, well marked, and perfect for mountain biking. Furthermore, while the trails allow mountain bikes year-round, they're only open to motorized vehicles from Memorial Day through late September, leaving the trails free for mountain bikers the rest of the year.

So where do you start exploring this huge forest? Clarion, south of Allegheny National Forest on Interstate 80, is a perfect place. Clarion University of Pennsylvania doubles the population of the town to 14,000 when classes are in session. And where there are college students, you can usually find a good bike shop. In Clarion it's High Gear, located at 5th and Wood streets in downtown Clarion.

The shop serves as the focal point for Clarion's cycling community. On a typical sunny Friday afternoon the shop bustles with activity: A group of five riders returning from a ride in the national forest; owner Steve Shaffer and former employee Anthony DeBaldo assembling a unicycle and then test riding it around the repair stand; a group poring over topo maps before a ride on the state game lands around Clarion. The phone rings every two minutes. R.E.M. is on the CD player. A visiting writer declines a test ride on the unicycle; he's too busy taking notes. It's that kind of place.

High Gear also sponsors races (weekly time trials, and several road and mountain bike races) and teaches bike maintenance at the college. Twenty-six-year-old Steve Shaffer started the business while a sophomore at Clarion University and moved to his present quarters in 1990.

Everybody associated with the shop is into cycling, including Steve's college co-op student, Michelle, nominally a non-cyclist. Steve insists that she ride an exercise bike for 20 minutes before leaving the shop. "She's got to ride *something* if she's going to work here," says Steve. It's that kind of place.

RIDE 24 *MARIENVILLE ALL-TERRAIN-VEHICLE TRAIL*

This all-terrain-vehicle trail is just one of countless recreational trails throughout Allegheny National Forest, but it's especially popular with local mountain bikers. The many rustic wooden bridges over fast mountain streams are great places to stop, relax, and soak up the wilderness experience in this half-million acre forest. The ride is almost entirely through woods, so there are few signs of civilization. Check out the excellent views of the surrounding ridges at the gas line swath. Part of the trail winds along Spring Creek, a small trout stream. Wildlife, including white-tailed deer and wild turkeys, are often seen while riding this loop. Old oil and gas well relics are also visible along the trail.

Most of this 12-mile loop is along wide, smooth trails. There are a couple of short stretches along gas pipelines that are narrow, steep, rocky, and rutted. There are several steep climbs, including one toward the end of the ride that only strong climbers will ascend without dismounting. Most of the trail is hard-packed dirt and fast when dry. Occasionally there are short stretches of logging, fire road, and gas line right-of-ways that have rough, rutted sections. Watch for shallow diversion ditches (dug to prevent washouts) on the descents.

General location: In Allegheny National Forest, about 35 miles north of Clarion, Pennsylvania.

Elevation change: The ride starts at 1,900' of elevation. At the gas line the trail drops 100' over a half mile. At mile 2.5 a 320' descent begins and is followed by a 340' climb over 1 mile. After rolling over two 100' climbs and descents there is a gradual 300' drop over 1.5 miles. At the creek the trail turns around before a steep 360' climb over a half mile. The last climb is on the gas line and rises about 100' after a 135' drop. The total elevation gain on the ride is about 1,100'.

Season: The best months for riding this trail are from April through the fall. The trail is open to motorized off-road vehicles from Memorial Day through September 24, and for a brief time in the winter. Mountain bikes are permitted year-round, but be cautious when motorized vehicles are present. Fall is pleasant with the changing foliage and cooler temperatures. Avoid riding in deer hunting season, which starts in the late fall.

Services: All services are available in Clarion.

Hazards: Keep alert for motorized off-road vehicles. On descents look out

MARIENVILLE ALL-TERRAIN-
VEHICLE TRAIL

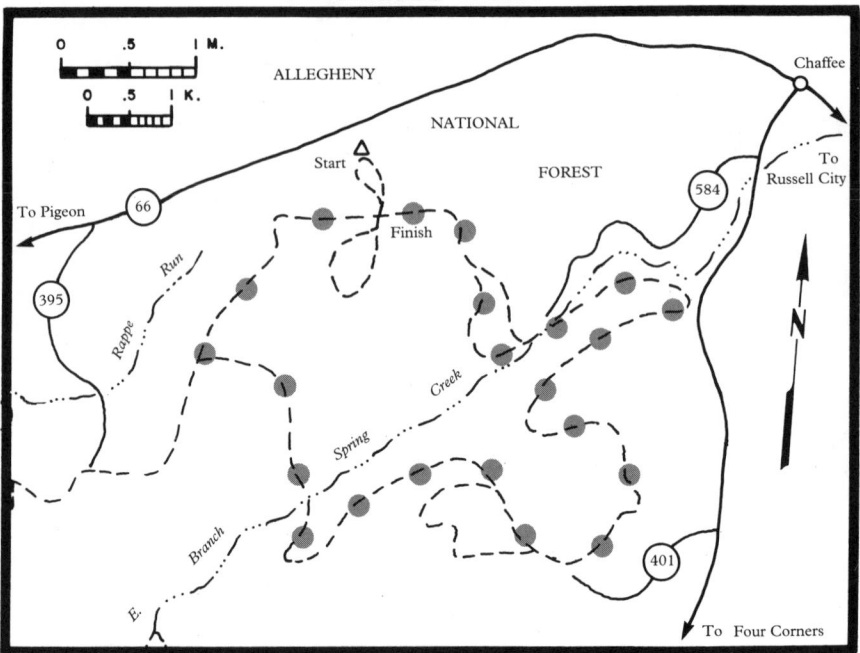

for diversion ditches dug across the trails to prevent erosion, which can drop daydreaming cyclists instantaneously.

Rescue index: The trail is well traveled in the summer months, and most of it is accessible from various maintenance and logging roads. Marienville Ranger Station is located 6 miles south on PA 66. The nearest phone is in Russell City, 3 miles north on PA 66.

Land status: National forest.

Maps: Trail maps are available at the trailhead and at the ranger station in Marienville. There are also 9 checkpoints with maps located along the trail. The USGS 7.5 minute topo is Lynch.

Finding the trail: The trail starts on PA 66 about 9 miles north of Marienville and 10 miles south of Kane, Pennsylvania. Park at the ORV Trailhead/Parking Area.

Sources of additional information:

District Ranger
Marienville Ranger District
Marienville, Pennsylvania 16239
(814) 927-6628

High Gear
34 S. 5th Street
Clarion, Pennsylvania 16214
(814) 226-4763

RIDE 25 *MILLCREEK TRAIL*

This 11.5-mile (one-way), out-and-back ride starts along the Clarion River and winds through State Game Lands #74 along Mill Creek. As you pedal these easy, pleasant state game land maintenance roads and trails the creek is usually in sight. Birds and wildlife are everywhere; keep an eye open for signs of beaver activity. The stream is usually stocked with trout, so packing a fly rod is a popular option. There are a number of springs along the trail. The greatest attraction of this ride is the beauty of the forest and the stream. Pack a lunch and make a leisurely day of it.

This ride requires almost no technical skill, except for stream crossings, which can be portages. The terrain varies from hard-packed dirt road to grassy meadows to single-track in the woods. There are many small stream crossings.

General location: Five miles northeast of Clarion, Pennsylvania.

Elevation change: The ride starts at 1,100' of elevation and gains 120' over the first half mile. The rest of the ride is a gradual uphill grade along the creek to an elevation of 1,400'.

Season: This ride is best from mid-summer through late fall. Sections of the trail are marshy in the spring and early summer. There are also a number of small streams that may be difficult to cross after heavy rains.

Services: All services are available in Clarion.

Hazards: Water crossings can be high after wet weather or in the spring and early summer.

Rescue index: Most of the trail is accessible by four-wheel-drive vehicles from various back roads that connect to it. These roads can be used to reach help.

Land status: State game land.

Maps: The USGS 7.5 minute quads are Strattanville and Corsica.

Finding the trail: From Clarion, drive east on US 322 to Strattanville. Turn left onto Millcreek Road. Look for the Penelec Recreation Area sign after about one-quarter mile. Stay on the dirt road for approximately 3 miles to the park. Park at the picnic area.

Sources of additional information:

High Gear
34 S. 5th Street

MILLCREEK TRAIL

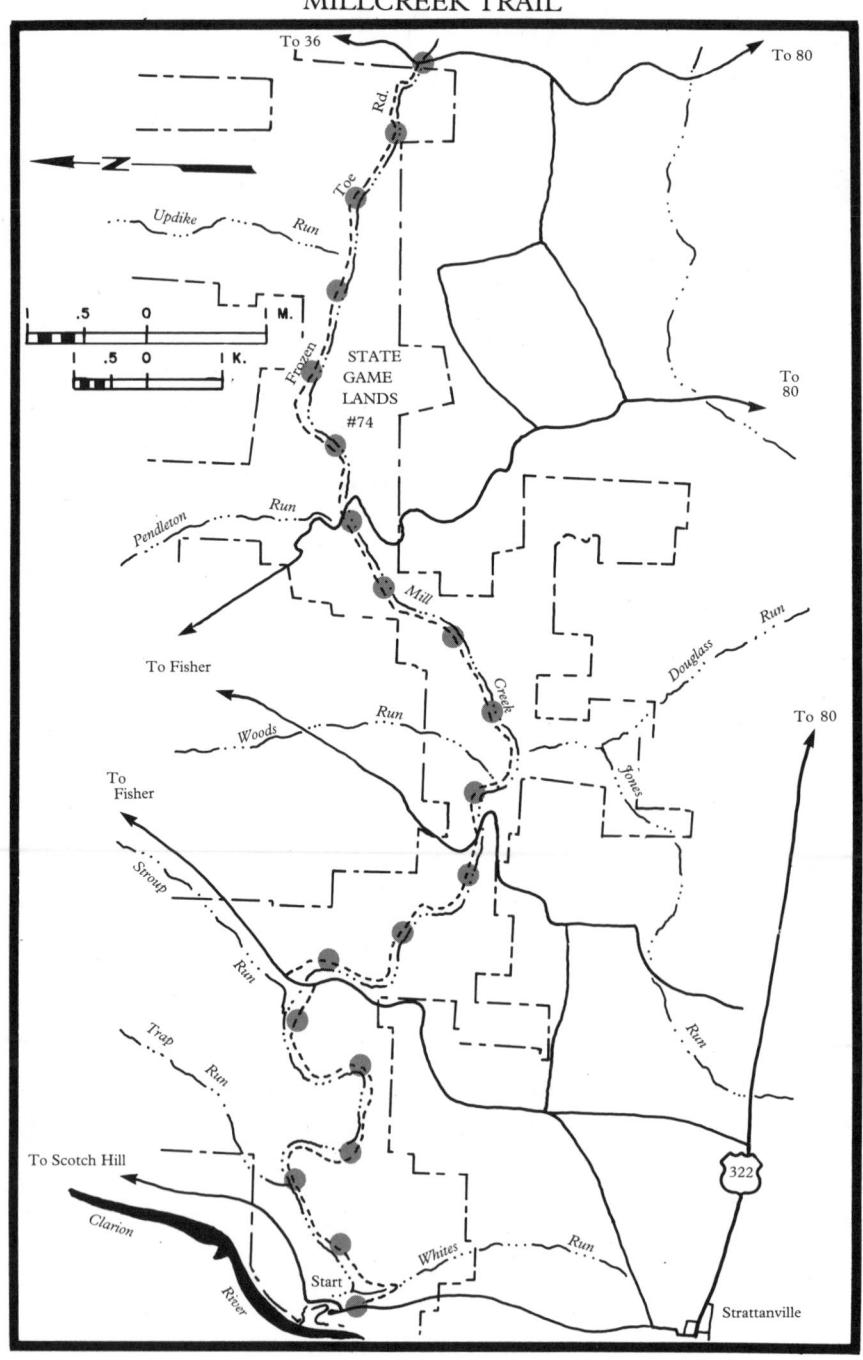

Clarion, Pennsylvania 16214
(814) 226-4763

Notes on the trail: This is a great leisure ride. On warm spring days the trail is lined with blooming trees and flowers. For riders wanting to make a loop out of the ride, obtain a local road map. Connect Frozen Toe Road (great name) back to Fisher Road and then back to the parking area.

RIDE 26 *BUZZARD SWAMP*

This is an easy 11-mile loop ride on cross-country ski trails. It demands only two easy climbs on paved and dirt roads leading to and from the plateau where the swamp is located. The ride starts and ends on paved and dirt roads, while the rest of the route is through meadows and forests on easy, grassy jeep trails used for cross-country skiing in the winter. However, the trails in Buzzard Swamp can be wet and soggy, especially in the spring or after a hard rain.

Buzzard Swamp is along a flyway for migrating Canada geese that stop here in early spring and late fall, so consider packing binoculars and a bird book. It's a unique area with 14 ponds, streams, bogs, meadows, and mixed hardwood and pine forests unique to Allegheny National Forest.

General location: Allegheny National Forest, about 25 miles north of Clarion, Pennsylvania.

Elevation change: Buzzard Swamp sits on a plateau. There are two 150' descents and climbs on the roads leading to and from the area.

Season: The loop is rideable spring through fall. While spring can be wet and muddy, summer and fall riding is great. Avoid riding in the deer hunting season, in the late fall. Expect snow between November and March.

Services: All services are available in Clarion. The Bucktail Motel in Marienville has an excellent restaurant.

Hazards: The trails can flood in the spring. Avoid riding in deer hunting season, in the late fall.

Rescue index: There are some residences along the dirt roads leading in and out of the area.

Land status: National forest.

Maps: Maps are available at the ranger station 1 mile north of Marienville. The USGS 7.5 minute topo is Marienville East.

Finding the trail: The ride starts in the center of Marienville, about 25 miles north of Clarion on PA 66. Park near the Bucktail Hotel.

BUZZARD SWAMP

Sources of additional information:

District Ranger
Marienville Ranger District
Marienville, Pennsylvania 16239
(814) 927-6628

High Gear
34 S. 5th Street
Clarion, Pennsylvania 16214
(814) 226-4763

Notes on the trail: From the center of town ride down Loleta Road, between the Bucktail Hotel and the Kelly Motel. Turn left on Forest Service Road 157. Follow the Buzzard Swamp Trail signs. After passing through the area, turn left at the gate onto Lomonaville Road and continue back to town.

RIMERSBURG RIDE-O-RAMA

RIDE 27 *RIMERSBURG RIDE-O-RAMA*

This 350-acre unreclaimed strip mine is the favorite playground of Clarion-area hammerheads. There are hundreds of hills and jumps on which you can hone your mountain biking skills, burn off excess calories, and generally goof off. One hill located in the southeast end (near the entrance road) is reminiscent of the first drop on a huge roller coaster. Non-experts and the sane can choose from a wide variety of less death-defying drops.

With hundreds of hills and jumps the area can be ridden tamely or aggressively, slow or fast. Good bike handlers (or those who aspire to improve) will get an excellent workout. The area is almost always hard-packed and fast to ride. The surface is mostly packed shale.

General location: Fifteen miles south of Clarion, Pennsylvania.

Elevation change: The elevation doesn't change more than 25' or 30' over the entire area.

Season: All year. The trails are well ridden by dirt bikes and four-wheelers, so the surface is always packed and in good condition.

Services: All services are available in Clarion, about 15 miles northeast of Rimersburg.

Hazards: This is a great place to fine-tune your bike handling skills, but you must know your limits. Be careful of loose shale in some spots and occasional interruptions by motorized dirt bikes.

Rescue index: There is a phone at the VFW across the road from the entrance.

Land status: Private. Call High Gear in Clarion to confirm that the area is open to the public.

Maps: USGS 7.5 minute quad is Rimersburg.

Finding the trail: Rimersburg is located on PA 68 about 15 miles south of Clarion and 20 miles northeast of Butler, Pennsylvania. Drive 1 mile south of Rimersburg; the entrance is on the right across from the VFW. Turn right and park along the entrance road.

Sources of additional information:

High Gear
34 S. 5th Street
Clarion, Pennsylvania 16214
(814) 226-4763

State College

State College, Pennsylvania, located near the center of the state, is aptly named: the 30,000-student campus of Pennsylvania State University dominates the town. To a mountain biker's eye, however, the town's major attractions are the mountains and neat-as-a-pin farmland that surround it. Riding a mountain bike right out of town is not only feasible, but the preferred way to reach the nearby hills.

So it's no surprise that State College is a mountain bike haven. With recent growth causing downtown congestion, mountain bikes are now the preferred way to get around. These days it seems like every Penn State student rides a mountain bike to class.

To support this kind of mountain bike activity, State College boasts several bike shops. And the biggest, The Bicycle Shop on West College Avenue, is impressive. Its large showroom is dominated by high quality, big ticket bikes, including both road and mountain tandems. The secret to the shop's large selection is sales volume.

"Bikes are the favorite form of transportation in State College," says sales manager Mike Hermann. "Every year we get a big rush of kids who spend between $300 and $500 for a bike. And it's a bargain for them, when you consider the cost of parking and car insurance." And every four years there's a complete turnover of students, guaranteeing continued sales.

The Bicycle Shop actively supports mountain biking by sponsoring several races throughout the year. On Sundays there's usually an informal ride led from the shop. The large staff is knowledgeable and willing to help visitors with maps and directions to trailheads. And if you're in the market for a tandem, call Mike Hermann.

RIDE 28 TUSSEY MOUNTAIN TO WHIPPLE DAM

This easy, 5-mile, out-and-back ride features classic Appalachian scenery. The woods, rocks, and mountain streams are reminiscent of New England. The verdant green foliage in spring and blazing colors in fall are spectacular. Most of the ride is through thick woods on well-maintained woods roads that pass several springs. The lookout tower provides spectacular views of the surrounding ridges and valleys. While this ride is non-technical, the climb to the fire tower and the climb on the return from Whipple Dam require good stamina.

TUSSEY MOUNTAIN TO WHIPPLE DAM

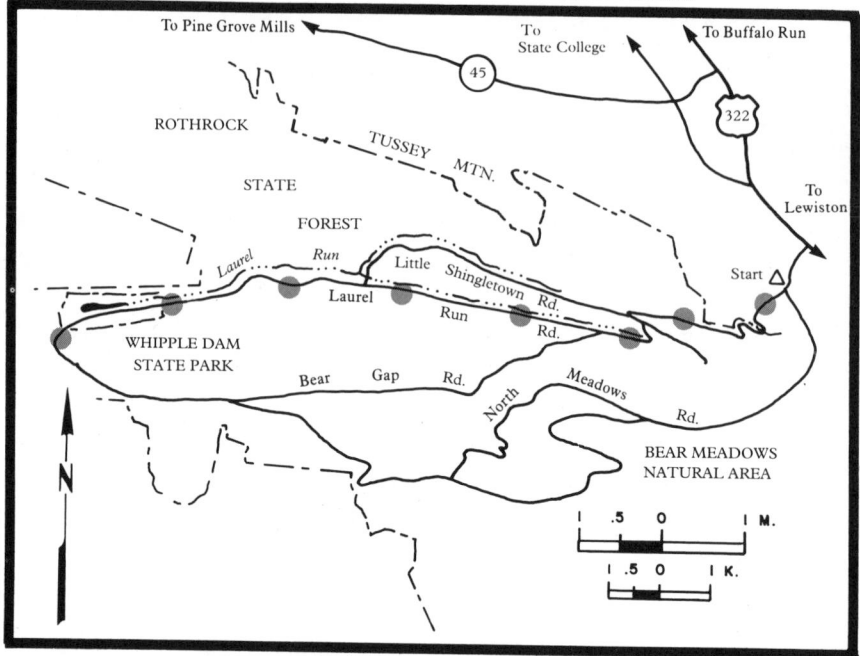

But the rewards are worth it. In summer you can swim at Whipple Dam. Look for a large field of blueberries surrounding the lookout tower—another reason for doing this ride in late summer. In addition to the views from the lookout tower, keep an eye open for the abundant wildlife in the area. You might even see a black bear.

General location: Rothrock State Forest, outside State College, Pennsylvania.

Elevation change: From the start at the ski area to the fire tower is a steep climb of approximately 800′ over 2 miles. On the return from Whipple Dam the elevation gain is about the same, but is spread over 5 miles.

Season: Spring and fall are the best times of year for mountain biking in central Pennsylvania. Summer is hot, humid, and buggy, and snow is possible between November and March. However, since the final destination of this ride is a public swimming area, this is a popular ride in the summer. Avoid riding in deer hunting season, after Thanksgiving.

Services: All services are available in State College. Whipple Dam has water and rest rooms available year-round. A snack bar is open between Memorial Day and Labor Day.

Hazards: Keep an eye peeled for snakes during warm weather, especially along the ridge. Watch for traffic on Laurel Run Road.

Photo by author

Rescue index: This is a well-traveled road, so you should have no problem flagging down a vehicle.

Land status: Pennsylvania state forest land and park.

Maps: The USGS 7.5 minute topo maps are State College and McAlevys Fort.

Finding the trail: From State College, take Business US 322 south to Tussey Mountain Ski Area. Park at the ski area parking lot.

Sources of additional information:

The Bicycle Shop
441 West College Avenue
State College, Pennsylvania 16801
(814) 238-9422

Notes on the trail: After parking, get on your bike and turn right at the first intersection. You will be turning onto a dirt road. From here climb up to the lookout tower. The turnoff to the lookout tower is not marked, but it's simple to find—it's the only left-hand turn within 100 yards of the top of the climb. Look for a gate.

After visiting the tower, retrace the route back down to the main road and continue downhill. From the ski area to the fire tower is all uphill, and from the fire tower to Whipple Dam is all downhill. Stay on the main road to reach Whipple Dam. To return, retrace the route back to the parking lot at Tussey Mountain.

RIDE 29 *STATE COLLEGE TO TUSSEY MOUNTAIN VIA LOOKOUT TOWER AND SHINGLETOWN GAP*

This is one of the prettiest sections in central Pennsylvania, featuring more than six stream crossings, huge ferns, rhododendron, and pine and mature forests that create a lush, deep-forest feel on the ride. Most of this 15-mile loop ride demands no technical skill. It starts out on paved road in State College, then climbs on dirt road at the Tussey Mountain Ski Area. A single-track descent at the end of the ride is rocky and has many stream crossings. Don't miss the fire tower on Tussey Mountain for great views of the surrounding mountains. Look for the gate on the left about 100 yards from the top of the mountain.

STATE COLLEGE TO TUSSEY MOUNTAIN

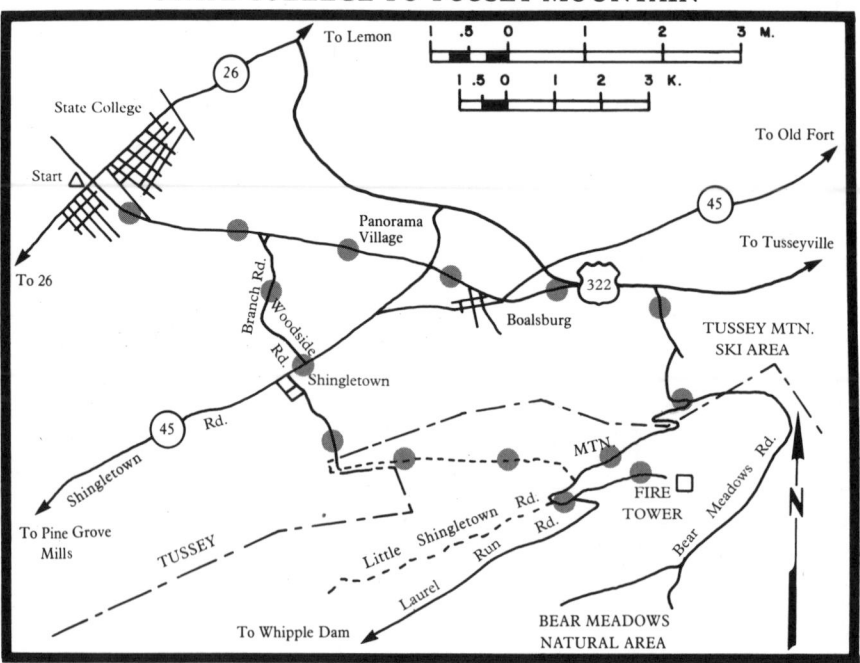

Photo by author

General location: State College, Pennsylvania.

Elevation change: There is about an 800' elevation gain on the climb up Tussey Mountain. The elevation is lost on the single-track descent to Shingletown.

Season: While rideable April through October, this loop is especially popular in the hot summer months. The thick vegetation guarantees a cool, shady ride on the descent to Shingletown. Avoid riding in deer hunting season, after Thanksgiving.

Services: All services are available in State College.

Hazards: Watch for snakes on the ridges in warm weather and for traffic on the roads.

Rescue index: Other than the descent to Shingletown, all the roads are well traveled. There are residences at the end of the single-track trail to Shingletown.

Land status: State forest land and county roads.

Maps: The USGS 7.5 minute topo maps are State College and McAlevys Fort.

Finding the trail: A convenient place to start this ride is The Bicycle Shop, near downtown State College. Or park anywhere along Business US 322 southbound out of town.

Sources of additional information:

The Bicycle Shop
441 West College Avenue
State College, Pennsylvania 16801
(814) 238-9422

Notes on the trail: From State College pedal out Business US 322 south to the turnoff for Tussey Mountain Ski Area (at Bear Mountain Road, on the right). Ride through the parking area, then turn right at the first intersection onto a dirt road. After leaving the fire tower retrace your route to the first left-hand option. (This is easy to miss—look for a small semi-circle parking area with a closed gate.) Behind the gate are two grassy jeep trails. Ride either one; they eventually meet again. This leads to the single-track (which is technical) and ends at a parking area near a small reservoir.

Follow the paved road down to the stop sign at PA 45. Turn right and go a short distance to Woodside Road, turn left, and then turn right at the "T" intersection onto Branch Road. This takes you back to US 322; turn left to get back into town.

RIDE 30 *PENN ROOSEVELT TO ALAN SEEGER*

This rigorous, 15-mile loop ride offers a special treat—a stop at a virgin forest at the Alan Seeger Natural Area. Hike down the trail (no bikes allowed) to view the huge pine trees. Rumor has it these might be the largest pine trees in North America. The area is thick with rhododendron and a large mountain stream flows through it. Also, the lookout tower is on one of the highest points around and provides great views of the surrounding ridges and valleys.

This ride features steep climbing and challenging terrain as it goes over ridges and through valleys covered with second-growth hardwood forests. There are many views of the surrounding mountains. Expect to shoulder your bike for about 300 yards on the climb out of the Penn Roosevelt picnic area. This is followed by twisting single-track that leads over terrain that changes on almost every turn, demanding total concentration. Next is a hard-packed dirt road that climbs very steeply to the lookout tower.

All the roads on the loop are either hard-packed dirt or paved. The single-track eventually turns into a jeep trail. The tough climbing starts at the intersection of Seeger Road and Stone Creek Road.

General location: Rothrock State Forest, between State College and Lewistown, Pennsylvania.

Elevation change: The ride has 2 major climbs of about 1,000' each. The

PENN ROOSEVELT TO ALAN SEEGER

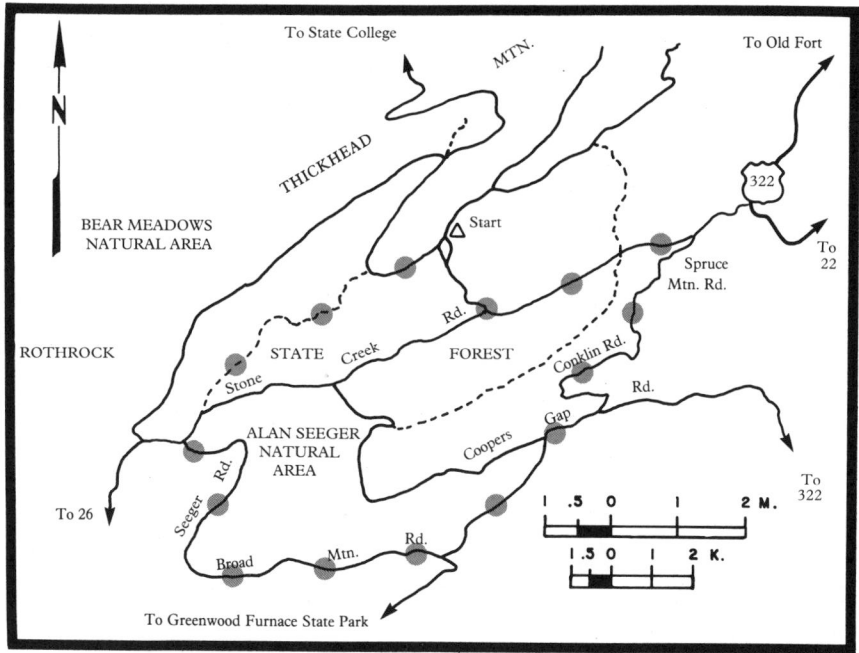

first is out of Penn Roosevelt Picnic Area. After the descent into Alan Seeger Natural Area, the second major climb leads 4.5 miles to the lookout tower. There are a couple of smaller climbs followed by a descent back to Penn Roosevelt Picnic Area.

Season: The roads on this loop are rideable from April through October. Spring can be muddy and snow is possible from November through March. Avoid riding in deer hunting season, after Thanksgiving.

Services: All services are available in State College. Water, bathroom facilities, and camping are available at the Penn Roosevelt picnic area.

Hazards: The descent on the single-track section out of the Penn Roosevelt picnic area is very fast and the terrain changes around every corner. Watch for snakes on the ridges in warm weather.

Rescue index: Except for the single-track and jeep trail sections, the whole ride is on public roads. However, this is a remote area that doesn't carry a lot of traffic, especially in late fall and early spring.

Land status: State forest.

Maps: The USGS 7.5 minute topo maps are State College and McAlevys Fort.

Finding the trail: From State College, drive out US 322 south toward Lewistown. Turn right near the bottom of the Seven Mountains descent (at the reservoir) and follow the paved road through Rothrock State Forest to the Penn Roosevelt State Forest picnic area. Park at the campground.

Sources of additional information:

The Bicycle Shop
441 West College Avenue
State College, Pennsylvania 16801
(814) 238-9422

Notes on the trail: The turnoff to the lookout is the only left-hand option available, so you can't miss it. And as the map indicates, there are several options for returning to the Penn Roosevelt picnic area from the lookout tower. They're all fun!

RIDE 31 *STATE COLLEGE TO WHIPPLE DAM AND BEAR MEADOWS*

Bear Meadows is a pristine area that's well worth the long ride. Observation platforms built over the marsh let visitors view birds and fish from ten feet in the air. This is even a nice place to visit on a rainy day, since it's so rich in flora and wildlife. The wet, swamp-like topography draws many birds. And they don't call it Bear Meadows for nothing—keep an eye peeled for both deer and bear. More fun things to do on this ride include climbing the lookout tower at Tussey Mountain and, in summer, swimming at Whipple Dam State Park.

Most of this 25-mile loop ride is on hard-packed dirt roads. The descent on Little Shingletown Road is on a rocky jeep trail. The trail around Bear Meadows Natural Area is rocky, and crossed by fallen logs and many streams. Be warned: This ride requires technical skills and good stamina, since it has two long climbs of around 800' to 1,000' of elevation gain each.

General location: Rothrock State Forest, near State College, Pennsylvania.

Elevation change: There's a steep 800' climb to the lookout tower at Tussey Mountain. The loop then descends and climbs about 800' to Bear Meadows Natural Area.

Season: Rideable between April and November, although mid-summer can be hot and humid. Spring can be muddy, and expect snow from November through March. Avoid riding in deer hunting season, after Thanksgiving.

Services: All services are available in State College. Whipple Dam has water and rest rooms; between Memorial Day and Labor Day a snack bar is open.

Hazards: Watch for snakes on the ridges in warm weather. Be alert for traffic on the dirt roads.

Rescue index: Whipple Dam and Bear Meadows are both popular areas.

STATE COLLEGE TO WHIPPLE DAM AND BEAR MEADOWS

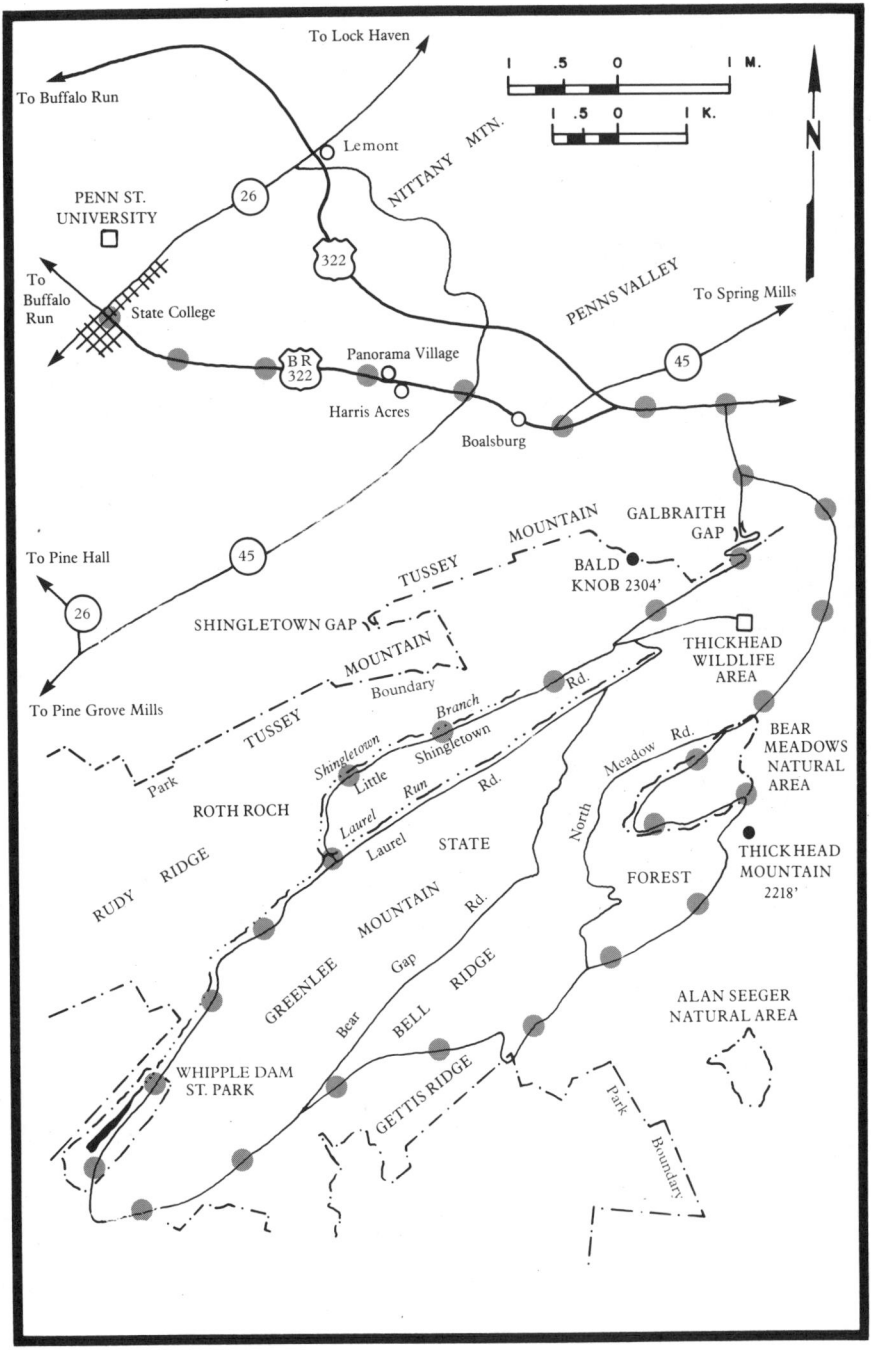

Little Shingletown Road, however, is remote, with no residences or farms along it.

Land status: Pennsylvania state forest and parks.

Maps: The USGS 7.5 minute topo maps are State College and McAlevys Fort.

Finding the trail: From State College, pedal out Business US 322 south to the turnoff for Tussey Mountain Ski Area (at Bear Mountain Road, on the right). After the lookout tower watch for the turn onto Little Shingletown Road (which isn't marked) at the very top of the climb. The turn is at the same elevation as the tower.

Sources of additional information:

> The Bicycle Shop
> 441 West College Avenue
> State College, Pennsylvania 16801
> (814) 238-9422

Notes on the trail: Bear Meadows Natural Area is a day-use-only area that is in pristine condition, since no fishing or boating is allowed. The large, flat bog, punctuated by a slow-moving stream, changes appearance with the seasons, making it a popular destination throughout the year.

RIDE 32 *STATE COLLEGE TO ALAN SEEGER*

This 45-mile, out-and-back ride, popular with racers training for competition, features three major ascents of 800' to 1,000' of elevation gain each. Overall, this is a ride for experienced, hard-core mountain bikers. Most of this ride is along forest roads that provide frequent views of the surrounding ridges and valleys. Try to allow enough time to explore Bear Meadows and Alan Seeger Natural Areas.

While there are several steep ascents and descents on the dirt roads, watch out for the extremely technical trail that drops from the lookout tower to Alan Seeger Natural Area. It's only for the very experienced. Most riders should backtrack down the dirt road, which is one of the steepest, fastest drops in the region.

Other neat features on this ride include the lookout tower above the Alan Seeger Natural Area, which offers excellent views. And there's a short hiking trail (no bikes allowed) in Alan Seeger that shouldn't be missed. Bear Meadows Natural Area is a bog that features a wide variety of wildlife.

General location: The ride starts in State College, runs through Bear Meadows Natural Area to Alan Seeger Natural Area, and then returns to State College.

STATE COLLEGE TO ALAN SEEGER

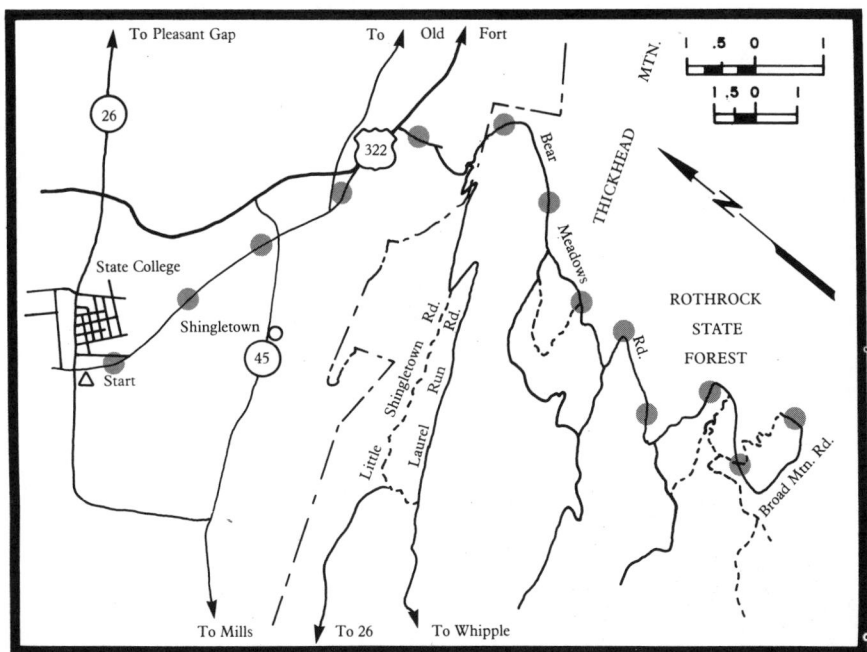

Elevation change: There are 3 major climbs: Tussey Mountain to Bear Meadows Natural Area, Alan Seeger Natural Area to the lookout tower and, on the return, Alan Seeger to Bear Meadows. The ride then drops for the return to State College. Total elevation gain is about 3,000′.

Season: Rideable between April and November. Mid-summer can be hot and humid. Expect snow after November and through March. Spring can be muddy. Avoid riding in deer hunting season, after Thanksgiving.

Services: All services are available in State College.

Hazards: The descent from the lookout tower into Alan Seeger Natural Area is very difficult and should only be attempted by expert riders.

Rescue index: Most of the ride is along traffic-bearing roads. However, traffic gets lighter as the ride moves away from US 322.

Land status: State forests, state and county roads.

Maps: The USGS 7.5 minute topo maps are State College and McAlevys Fort.

Finding the trail: From State College, pedal out Business US 322 south to the turnoff for Tussey Mountain Ski Area (at Bear Mountain Road, on the right). At Tussey Mountain Ski Area turn right onto Meadows Road.

Sources of additional information:

The Bicycle Shop
441 West College Avenue
State College, Pennsylvania 16801
(814) 238-9422

Notes on the trail: Mike Hermann, the sales manager at The Bicycle Shop in State College, has this warning about the optional descent from the lookout tower to Alan Seeger Natural Area: "We originally named this trail 'Herm's Ride from Hell' when we first attempted it, and people do get hurt riding this. To be ridden well, it must be ridden fast. This section of trail is for extreme mountain bikers—only the hard-core need apply!"

Bald Eagle State Forest

Bald Eagle State Forest, located near the geographical center of Pennsylvania, lies midway between State College to the west and the Susquehanna River to the east. Named after a famous Indian chief, the forest comprises 191,858 acres in the ridge and valley region of the state. The dominant features are sandstone ridges that rise as much as 2,300 feet above sea level. The many streams in the area originate in the forested ridges and drain southeasterly toward the Susquehanna River.

With over 340 miles of roads, as many miles of foot trails, and 300 miles of designated snowmobile trails, Bald Eagle State Forest draws mountain bikers from throughout Pennsylvania and the Northeast. Since 1987 the Bald Eagle Mountain Bike Jamboree has been held at R. B. Winter State Park (one of four state parks located in the forest) and offers a wide selection of rides, full technical support, maps, and camping. The Jamboree is held every October and attracts hundreds of mountain bikers for three days of riding during the peak of the fall foliage season.

When pedaling north-central Pennsylvania, stop by The Bicycle Peddler in Lewisburg to pick up maps and get final directions to trailheads. Owner Mike Kryzytski is a rabid mountain biker who will make sure you get the most from your visit to the area. And don't forget to ask Mike for the dates of this year's Bald Eagle Mountain Bike Jamboree.

RIDE 33 COWBELL HOLLOW / TOP MOUNTAIN TRAIL

This 15-mile loop ride is a typical north-central Pennsylvania combination of forest roads and trails. It features Top Mountain Trail, one of the best mountain bike rides in Bald Eagle State Forest. This abandoned jeep trail, which varies from smooth to very rocky, is fast and challenging, with lots of turns, short climbs, and descents. It also has excellent views of the surrounding mountains. Sugar Valley Narrows Road is a hard-packed dirt road, while all the other forest roads on this ride are hard-packed dirt covered with loose stones. Cowbell Hollow Trail is one of the most rideable single-track trails in this area—but watch out for deadfalls.

With steep climbs and rocky, technical single-track, this trail is for experienced riders. Less experienced mountain bikers will find large parts of the loop rideable, but should have good stamina and be ready to push their bikes over the rocky sections of trail. White Deer Creek, which is crossed twice, is

COWBELL HOLLOW/TOP MOUNTAIN TRAIL

one of the larger creeks in the area. It's a rocky, fast-flowing trout stream that has some excellent camping spots along it. Mook's Spring on Running Gap Road, 100 yards south of the Top Mountain Trail intersection, is a dependable source of water.

General location: The ride starts in Bald Eagle State Forest, 10 miles northwest of Lewisburg, Pennsylvania (60 miles north of Harrisburg).

Elevation change: The ride begins at 1,000' of elevation and climbs to over 1,750' on Cowbell Hollow Trail. After descending to about 1,100' at White Deer Creek, the trail climbs to 1,800' on Top Mountain Trail. Descend to 1,300' on White Deer Creek Road and follow the creek back to 1,000' at the start. Total elevation gain is around 1,500'.

Season: The best time to ride this loop is between April and October. Spring can be very muddy. The best views are in the fall after the leaves are off the trees. (But don't ride in deer hunting season, usually after Thanksgiving.) The winter months are risky. Expect snow after November, and the forest roads are often ice-covered, even after long spells of warm weather.

Services: All services are available in Lewisburg, Pennsylvania. Camp at R. B. Winter State Park, about 12 miles southwest of this loop.

Hazards: Sections of Top Mountain Trail are extremely rocky. In winter and early spring expect parts of the trails to be covered with ice.

Photo by author

Rescue index: There's light traffic along White Deer Creek Road. Interstate 80 parallels most of this ride.

Land status: Pennsylvania state forest.

Maps: Pick up a Bald Eagle State Forest public use map at The Bicycle Peddler in Lewisburg. USGS 7.5 minute quads are Carroll and Williamsport S.E.

Finding the trail: Take Exit 29 from I-80 (10 miles west of PA 15). From the exit ramp, go down the hill a few hundred yards to the dirt road and park near the intersection with Sugar Valley Narrows Road.

Sources of additional information:

Department of Environmental Resources
Bureau of Forestry
P.O. Box 147
Laurelton, Pennsylvania 17835-0147

The Bicycle Peddler
PA 45 West
Lewisburg, Pennsylvania 17837
(717) 524-4554

Notes on the trail: This ride starts from an interstate exit that inexplicably leads directly onto a desolate state forest road. From your car, ride west on Sugar Valley Narrows Road, then bear left onto Garden Hollow Road, which is followed by an almost immediate left onto Cooper Mill Road. There's a steep climb to the top; on the downhill, turn left onto Cowbell Hollow Trail at the first 180-degree hairpin turn (look for a sign). This up-and-down jeep trail turns into a brushy single-track. It descends to White Deer Creek. Cross the creek at the small bridge and turn right onto White Deer Creek Road.

Make a sharp left almost immediately onto Running Gap Road and climb to the top. Turn right on Top Mountain Trail. Following this single-track is self-evident; but if in doubt, follow the blue blazes and bear left. Turn right at the first forest road, Cooper Mill Road. Follow it downhill (you may have a short climb first, depending on which branch of Top Mountain Trail you finished on) to White Deer Creek Road. Turn right and ride to the end. Turn right again and ride back to your car.

RIDE 34   *THE BEAR GAP RIDE*

This 12-mile figure-8 ride is a challenging route designed for experienced mountain bikers. However, intermediate riders with good stamina and the willingness to walk some sections will be able to complete the double loop.

Most of the trail is through second-growth hardwood forests, with many vistas of the surrounding ridges and valleys. Stop at Sand Mountain Tower and climb to the top for breathtaking views, which are especially spectacular on a clear day at dusk or during a full moon. You can also swim at the state park.

These forest roads are mostly hard-packed dirt covered with loose stones. Spring Mountain Trail is relatively flat and rideable by novice mountain bikers. Parts of Bear Gap are expert only, but are short enough to walk. The Old Tram Trail is moderately rocky.

General location: R. B. Winter State Park, 15 miles west of Lewisburg, Pennsylvania.

Elevation change: Start at 1,600' of elevation and climb the Cracker Bridge Trail to 1,700'. Climb to 1,767' at the intersection of Cooper Mill and Sand Mountain Roads. Drop down Bear Gap Trail to around 1,000' and climb back up again to 1,767' at Sand Mountain Road. On the return to the park you will reach 2,047' at the fire tower. Total elevation gain is about 1,400'.

Season: Generally rideable between April and November. Spring can be very muddy. Autumn, after the leaves are off the trees, offers the best views. The trails and roads can be icy in winter, even after prolonged warm spells. Expect snow from November through March.

THE BEAR GAP RIDE

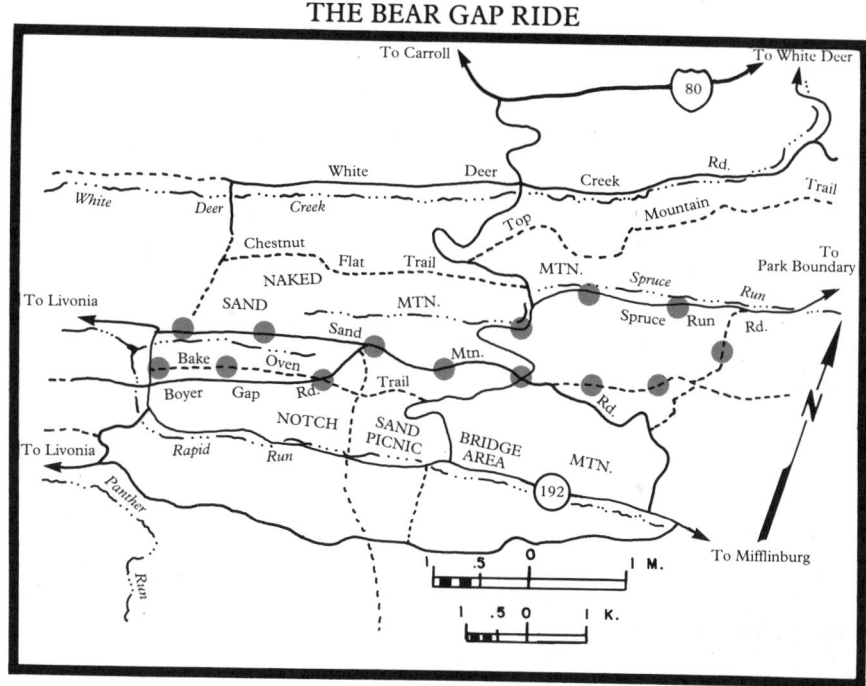

Services: All services are available in Lewisburg, Pennsylvania, 18 miles east of R. B. Winter State Park.

Hazards: Bear Gap Trail is very rocky and in wet weather can be filled with flowing water. Avoid riding in deer hunting season, after Thanksgiving.

Rescue index: R. B. Winter State Park is usually staffed. Traffic can be flagged down on PA 192.

Land status: Pennsylvania state forest.

Maps: The USGS 7.5 minute topos are Carroll, Williamsport S.E., and Hartleton. Also, pick up a copy of the Bald Eagle State Forest public use map at The Bicycle Peddler in Lewisburg.

Finding the trail: R. B. Winter State Park is 18 miles west of Lewisburg, Pennsylvania, on PA 192. Follow the signs to the camping area. Park in the lot between the lake and the camping area.

Sources of additional information:

Department of Environmental Resources
Bureau of Forestry
P.O. Box 147
Laurelton, Pennsylvania 17835-0147

The Bicycle Peddler
PA 45 West
Lewisburg, Pennsylvania 17837
(717) 524-4554

Notes on the trail: From the parking lot, ride north on the paved park road a half mile uphill to the first intersection with a dirt forest road; turn right onto Sand Mountain Road. Go to the first intersection (Boyer Gap Road is to the right) and take Cracker Bridge Trail to the left. At the bottom of the hill, turn right and follow the Old Tram Trail east to Cooper Mill Road and turn right. Turn left at the top, after the long climb. Very soon you'll reach a fork; bear left (which is almost straight) and continue to Bear Gap Trail (no trail sign).

Here's how to verify you're on Bear Gap: The trail goes slightly downhill at first, with a grassy meadow on the left, followed by a steep downhill through trees and across a small stream. Follow the trail downhill to Spruce Run Road. Turn left. At the next intersection, go left onto Cooper Mill Road.

Repeat the climb on Cooper Mill Road. At the top turn right onto Sand Mountain Road. After the short climb to the top you'll see the fire tower. Continue downhill on Sand Mountain Road. At Boyer Gap Road turn left, then turn right onto Bake Oven Trail and back to the park.

RIDE 35 *CHERRY RUN / PENN'S CREEK RAILROAD BED*

While this is a long ride with several rocky single-tracks and three long climbs on forest roads, beginning mountain bikers with good stamina will enjoy it. Most of the route is along hard-packed forest roads covered with loose sand and gravel. The single-track trails on the ride are rocky and technical. The section of Old Mingle Road from the grave (see below) to the railroad bed is along a narrow, steep bank that requires good bike handling skills. The Mid-State Trail is steep and rocky.

This 20-mile ride has lots to offer besides a great workout. Along Penn's Creek there is great swimming in the summer, an abandoned railroad tunnel to ride through, and the century-old grave of a drowning victim erected by his heart-broken lover. The Joyce Kilmer Natural Area, on the left along Bear Run at the beginning of the ride, is a 77-acre tract of virgin white pine and hemlock. Hike down the trail at the sign on Bear Run (bikes aren't allowed) to explore the forest.

There are many vistas of the surrounding forest-covered ridges. The abandoned rail bed along Penn's Creek is one of the most beautiful spots in the state. The creek is huge and flows through a big valley covered with a mature

CHERRY RUN/
PENN'S CREEK RAILROAD BED

forest free of underbrush. With no road along the creek, the area has a real wilderness feeling to it.

General location: Bald Eagle State Forest, 25 miles west of Mifflinburg, Pennsylvania.

Elevation change: The ride starts at about 1,100' of elevation and slowly climbs to 1,900' on Bear Run Road. Rupp Hollow is a ridge with an elevation of about 1,700' along its length; you then drop to 1,200' at Old Mingle Road. The road drops to just below 1,000' of elevation at Penn's Creek. At the former trestle, start a slow climb to 1,200' at Cherry Run Road. Climb to 1,717' at Rupp Hollow Road. Along Paddy Mountain Road the elevation climbs to 2,100', then drops to below 900' at PA 45. Total elevation gain is around 1,900'.

Season: Rideable from April through November. Spring can be muddy; the best views are in late fall after the leaves are off the trees. Avoid riding in deer hunting season, after Thanksgiving. Expect snow from November through March.

Services: All services are available in Lewisburg, 25 miles east of the ride.

Hazards: The mud on Old Mingle Road in wet weather is the worst in north-

Photo by author

central Pennsylvania. The single-track is rocky and technical. The downhill on Paddy Mountain Road is fast and technical.

Rescue index: This ride is in the heart of Bald Eagle State Forest and mountain bikers are, for the most part, on their own. The village of Weikert, on Penn's Creek past Cherry Run, has year-round residents. Traffic can be flagged down on PA 45.

Land status: State forest.

Maps: Bald Eagle State Forest public use map, available at The Bicycle Peddler in Lewisburg.

Finding the trail: Take PA 45 west from Mifflinburg through Hartleton and past Laurelton Center. After entering the state forest, look for a left turn onto Bear Run Road. The parking lot is 100 yards down the road on the left.

Sources of additional information:

Department of Environmental Resources
Bureau of Forestry
P.O. Box 147
Laurelton, Pennsylvania 17835-0147

The Bicycle Peddler
PA 45 West
Lewisburg, Pennsylvania 17837
(717) 524-4554

Notes on the trail: After parking, pedal uphill on Bear Run Road to the end. Turn left on Woodward Gap Road and then turn right on Rupp Hollow Road. Turn left onto the Mid-State Trail, a rocky, downhill single-track. Turn right onto Old Mingle Road and follow it to the dead end at Penn's Creek. To find the unnamed trail to the left, look about 100 yards above the creek bank. Follow the creek downstream along the rocky remnants of the logging trail. Look for the tombstone of a drowning victim. Turn toward the creek at the tombstone and continue downstream a short distance to a cabin; turn left at the cinder path and ride through an abandoned railroad tunnel.

Continue along this old railroad grade to the former site of a trestle. Leave the grade and go left (uphill), which leads to Cherry Run Road, followed by a long climb to Rupp Hollow Road. Turn right and continue straight. (The road's name changes to Paddy Mountain Road.) At the end of the downhill turn left and continue to PA 45; turn left again and return to the parking lot.

Jim Thorpe

In the western Pocono Mountains of Pennsylvania, the Lehigh River cuts a spectacular 1,000-foot-deep gorge through table-top mountains and thousands of acres of state park and game lands. Taking advantage of 30 miles of abandoned railroad grade along the river, Pennsylvania created Lehigh Gorge State Park, 6,000 acres of spectacular park land that stretches south from an Army Corps of Engineers dam near Wilkes Barre to a town with the unlikely name of Jim Thorpe, Pennsylvania. This combination of scenic river gorge, state game lands, and a restored Victorian-era village results in one of the best mountain biking destinations in the East.

The rich history of the area is also an attraction, especially to mountain bikers. This is coal country, and many of the old rail lines used to haul coal from mines to river ports are now converted trails that make for easy pedaling. In the mid-nineteenth century industry was booming and, as the transportation hub of the region, so were the towns of Mauch Chunk and East Mauch Chunk (today's Jim Thorpe). Canal, railroad, and river traffic converged in the towns. Millionaires built mansions, hotels, an opera house, and churches in fine Victorian style on the hillsides overlooking the Lehigh River. When the boom ended later in the century the towns and the mountainous region around them became a popular summer resort known as "The Switzerland of America."

The Great Depression of the 1930s clinched the area's decline and the towns fell into disrepair. Unemployment took its toll and young people fled the region. In the early 1950s the local newspaper started an economic development fund and urged citizens to contribute a nickel per week. In 1954 the communities were rewarded for their spunk when the widow of Jim Thorpe, the hero of the 1912 Stockholm Olympic Games (who died a pauper in a Philadelphia hospital in 1953), agreed to let the two towns merge under the great athlete's name and build a monument and mausoleum for him.

The 1980s marked the beginning of an era of prosperity and restoration for this handsome town on the Lehigh. Tourism is now big business. Shops, restaurants, bed-and-breakfasts, and lots of cars now line the streets of Jim Thorpe. You'll also see plenty of mountain bikes.

And no wonder. With Lehigh Gorge State Park at its doorstep and miles of hiking trails winding through the town to the overlooks nearby, Jim Thorpe was made for fat-tired bikes. The trails, converted from old railroad right-of-ways, are on two-percent grades, making for effortless riding. Close by are thousands of acres of state game lands, which extends the variety of mountain biking from the town.

Since 1986 Jim Thorpe has hosted the Mountain Bike Weekend, held every June in nearby Mauch Chunk Lake Park. Bill Drumbore and Galen Van Dine, local riders who help organize the event, discovered mountain biking when it was virtually unheard of in the East. (Bill built his first mountain bike in a garage using old 10-speed and BMX parts. It's stored in the basement of the Hotel Switzerland in Jim Thorpe and displayed in the bar during the Mountain Bike Weekend.) Every year Bill and Galen help organize and plan mountain bike rides for the hundreds of mountain bikers who converge on the town for a weekend of camaraderie and great cycling. They also assisted in the trail descriptions that follow.

Here's how to get there. Jim Thorpe is located between Allentown and Scranton, off the Northeast Extension of the Pennsylvania Turnpike (about 90 minutes from Philadelphia). From New York City take Interstate 80 west to PA 209 south, about a three-hour drive.

RIDE 36 *THE WEEKEND WARRIOR*

The mountains in the western Poconos were sheared by glaciers, making the tops smooth and rolling—and perfect for mountain biking. This entire 14-mile ride, which can be ridden as a loop or a figure-8, follows double-track roads on top of Broad Mountain. The road passes through mixed-hardwood forests (mostly oak with some maple and gray birch) interspersed with open fields. The mountain borders the Lehigh River Gorge, providing different views of the river and mountains, and glimpses of hawks soaring at eye level.

The optional ride to the first overlook is down a rocky power line cut; the view up the river gorge (almost 1,000 feet deep) makes it worth the return climb. The second overlook is even better. The village of Jim Thorpe, with Flagstaff Park towering over it (see Galen's Surprise), straddles both sides of the river flowing deep inside the gorge.

General location: Five miles north of Jim Thorpe, Pennsylvania, off PA 93.

Elevation change: The optional, out-and-back drop down the power line to the first overlook is about 350′. The elevation at the start is about 1,700′ and gradually drops to about 1,300′ at the second overlook. There is about 600′ of climbing spread over the entire ride.

Season: Summer and fall are the best seasons to ride this loop. The mountaintop is relatively cool in the summer and the fall colors are spectacular (early and mid-October). Spring can be very muddy and snow is possible from November through March. These are state game lands, so avoid riding during fall hunting season.

THE WEEKEND WARRIOR

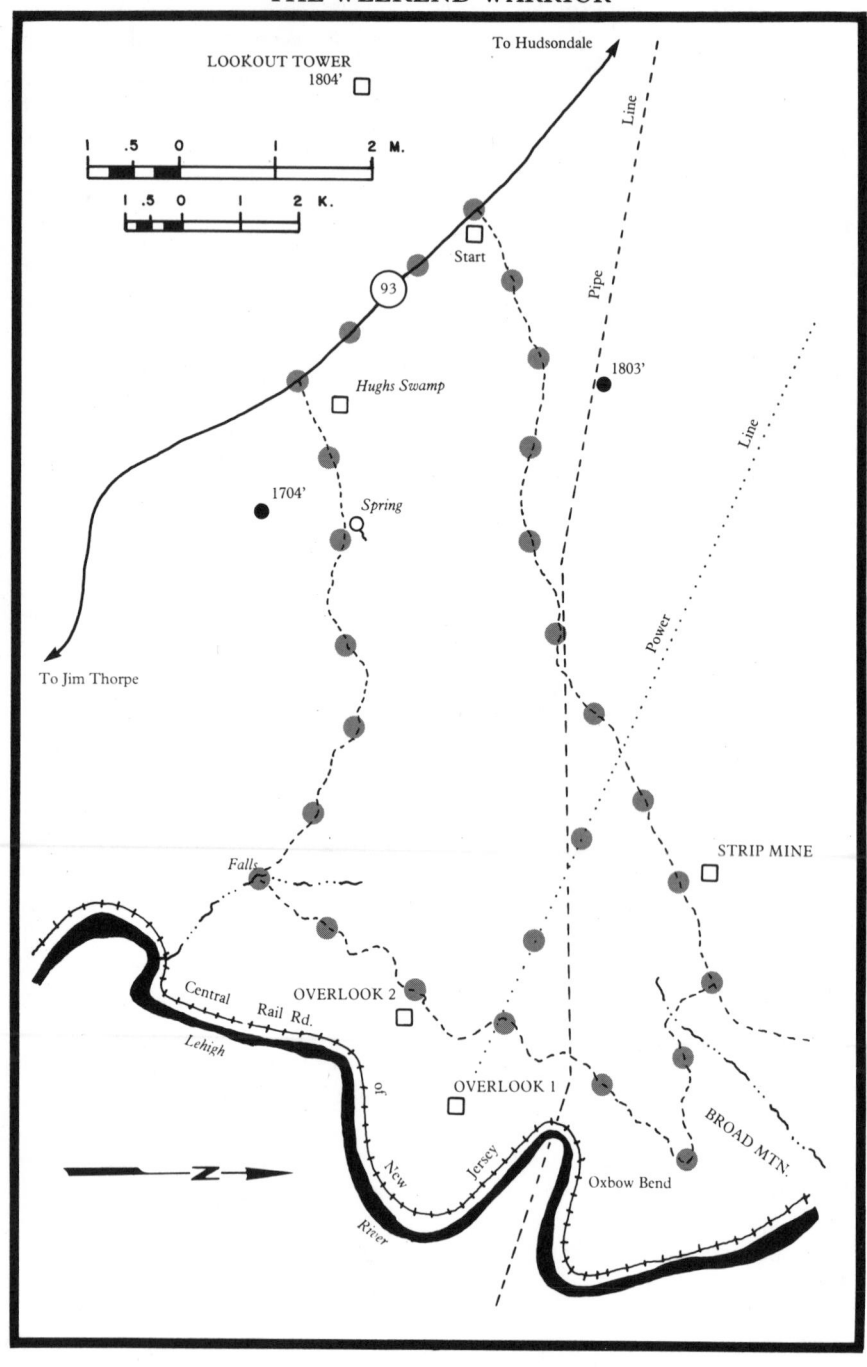

Services: All services are available in Jim Thorpe. Mountain bikes can be rented at Blue Mountain Sports.

Hazards: The descent to the first (optional) overlook is steep and rocky. Watch for heavy truck and car traffic on PA 93 for the last mile of the ride.

Rescue index: PA 93 is the only traffic-bearing road on the loop. There are no residences on the ride. The farthest point from PA 93 is about 5 miles.

Land status: State game lands.

Maps: Copies of the Mountain Bike Weekend Maps are available at Blue Mountain Sports in Jim Thorpe. The USGS topo maps are Christmans and Weatherly quadrangles.

Finding the trail: From Jim Thorpe, Pennsylvania, go north on PA 209 for 2 miles to the first traffic light (PA 93) and turn right. Go approximately 3 miles and park in the second lot on the right near the gate.

Sources of additional information:

Carbon County Tourist Promotion Agency
P.O. Box 90
Railroad Station
Jim Thorpe, Pennsylvania 18229
(717) 325-3673

Blue Mountain Sports
34 Susquehanna Street
Jim Thorpe, Pennsylvania 18229
(717) 325-4421

Notes on the trail: The recommended way to ride this loop is a figure-8. From the second pulloff on PA 93, ride out the fire road beyond the gate. After 2.5 miles, turn right and follow the power lines. At the intersection a mile later, go straight for the descent to the first overlook. Return to this intersection from the overlook and turn right. (It would be a left if you were coming down the power lines.) Follow this loop for 2.5 miles back to the first intersection. Turn left and retrace the ride along the power lines; at the intersection where you went straight to the overlook, now turn right.

After a half mile there is a "T" intersection; turn left to reach the second overlook. Double back to the "T" and go straight. Follow the road for 3 miles (through 2 stream crossings and a steep climb) to the next intersection; continue straight. At the gate in the parking lot on PA 93, turn right and ride 1 mile along the road back to your car.

RIDE 37 *GALEN'S SURPRISE*

This 14-mile loop ride is a great example of the tremendous diversity of off-road riding that Jim Thorpe offers. For example, the view from Flagstaff Park of the Lehigh River Gorge and the town of Jim Thorpe spans a whopping 65 miles. The park, containing a restaurant, a nightclub, and a view to die for, was known as "The Ballroom of the Clouds" during the Swing Era of the 1930s and 1940s and was home base for the Dorsey Brothers Band. Sound too civilized for a mountain bike ride? Relax—the next section of the ride features bone-jarring single-track, followed by fast double-track along a ridge and a steep descent to a huge lake.

The ride starts with an easy cruise on the Switchback Trail, but then climbs for 1.5 miles to the top of Mauch Chunk Ridge and Flagstaff Park. Next is two miles of rough single-track on a narrow, rocky trail. You will follow the ridge on an old dirt road, and make a right for a steep descent along a power line cut to the Shoreline Trail. Most of the ride on the ridge is through second-growth hardwood forest. After the descent, follow the wooded shoreline of Mauch Chunk Lake. This trail twists through evergreen forests and has views of the lake and Mauch Chunk Ridge. Look for the bird sanctuary and observer's shack built on the marshy lake shore. There's an excellent view of the entire lake and the wetlands teem with birds. The shack is also a good shelter in a storm. Keep an eye peeled for wildlife (including black bear) while riding.

General location: The ride begins in Mauch Chunk Lake Park, located 3 miles west of Jim Thorpe, Pennsylvania, on PA 209 (the Lentz Trail Highway).

Elevation change: This ride does all of its climbing on the paved road to Flagstaff Park—about 450' of elevation gain. After that it's all ridge riding, followed by a steep descent to the lake.

Season: Summer is excellent—consider a swim at the lake following the ride. In fall the spectacular foliage is mirrored on the lake. Spring can get very muddy, especially along the lake. Expect snow between November and March. Avoid riding in hunting season (late fall).

Services: All services are available in Jim Thorpe. Mountain bikes can be rented at Blue Mountain Sports.

Hazards: Watch for cars on the paved road up to Mauch Chunk Ridge. The drop off the ridge at the power lines is very steep.

Rescue index: No point on the trail is more than a couple of miles from paved roads. Also, Mauch Chunk Lake Park is staffed from April through October.

Land status: The trail along Mauch Chunk Ridge is on private property. Obtain permission to ride at Flagstaff Park (just past the turnoff for the

GALEN'S SURPRISE

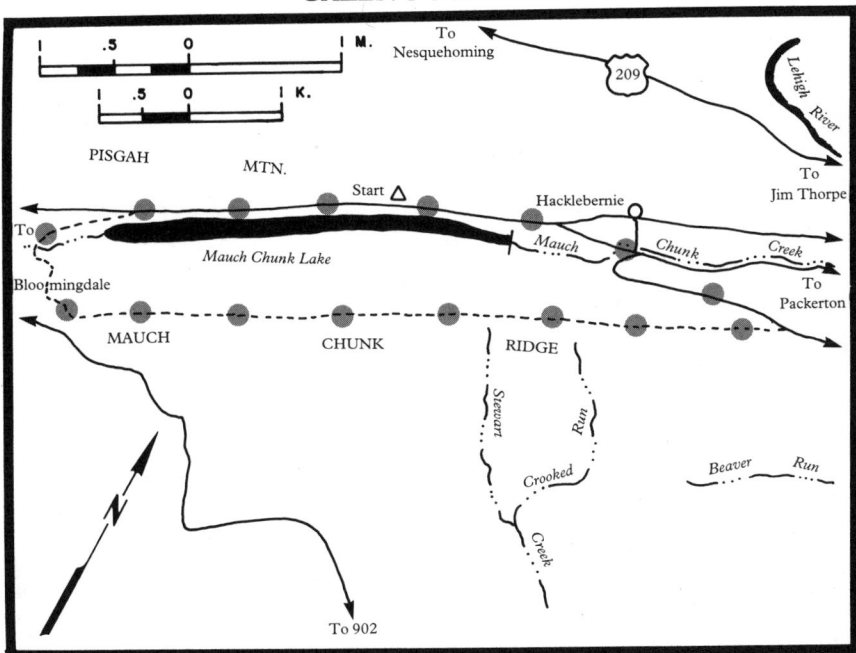

single-track trail). Mauch Chunk Lake Park is owned by the Carbon County (Pennsylvania) Parks and Recreation Commission.

Maps: Maps showing this ride are available at Blue Mountain Sports in Jim Thorpe. The USGS topo is the Nesquehoning quadrangle.

Finding the trail: Mauch Chunk Lake Park is located 3 miles from Jim Thorpe, Pennsylvania, on PA 209 (the Lentz Trail Highway). The Switchback Trail is located at the park entrance. Park at the office or at any of the other parking lots.

Sources of additional information:

Mauch Chunk Lake Park
P.O. Box 7
Jim Thorpe, Pennsylvania 18229
(717) 325-3669

Blue Mountain Sports
34 Susquehanna Street
Jim Thorpe, Pennsylvania 18229
(717) 325-4421

Notes on the trail: The ride starts on the Switchback Trail, which crosses PA 209 at the entrance of Mauch Chunk Lake Park. Follow it past the dam, where it bears left. At the intersection with the paved road turn right and climb 1.5 miles to the top of the ridge; the trailhead is on the right. Continue a short distance on the road to Flagstaff Park, catch the view, and get permission to ride the ridge trail.

Double back to the single-track (now on the left). After about 2 miles the trail turns into a grassy road for another 3 miles. At the "T" intersection turn right and descend at the power lines. Look for the single-track to the left that goes into the woods (about two-thirds of the way down). In the woods, follow the path over 2 wooden bridges and emerge in a field. Turn right and keep the woods to your right as you bear around to the lake. Once you arrive at the lake the Shoreline Trail is easy to find.

RIDE 38 *LEHIGH GORGE STATE PARK*

The Lehigh River cuts a spectacular gorge through the Poconos, and this pleasant ride through Lehigh Gorge State Park provides great views from the bottom up. The fast-moving river, steep walls of rock, waterfalls, and thick vegetation characterize the trail along its 30 miles. The Lehigh River is almost always in sight, frequently coursing over rocks and rapids. On this easy ride the emphasis is on the scenery, not bike handling. The grade along this wide, cinder-covered trail is virtually unnoticeable riding north (upriver), and riding downriver is even easier. On long rides take head winds into consideration: It's usually best to ride out with the wind in your face and return with a tail wind. And while this is usually ridden as an out-and-back ride, it's easy to set up a shuttle for a one-way ride—say, Jim Thorpe to Rockport.

Highlights: At the first river crossing north of Jim Thorpe, explore an abandoned railroad tunnel adjacent to the bridge. At various points along the trail, look for ruins of the old canal that parallels the river. Look up and you'll see many waterfalls emptying into the river through siltstone and sandstone rock formations.

General location: Jim Thorpe, Pennsylvania.

Elevation change: Negligible.

Season: Summer and fall are the best seasons. The fall foliage viewed from the bottom of the gorge is dramatic. Spring can be wet and muddy. Expect snow from November through March. Hunting is permitted in the park, so avoid riding in the late fall.

Services: All services are available in Jim Thorpe. Mountain bikes can be rented at Blue Mountain Sports.

LEHIGH GORGE STATE PARK

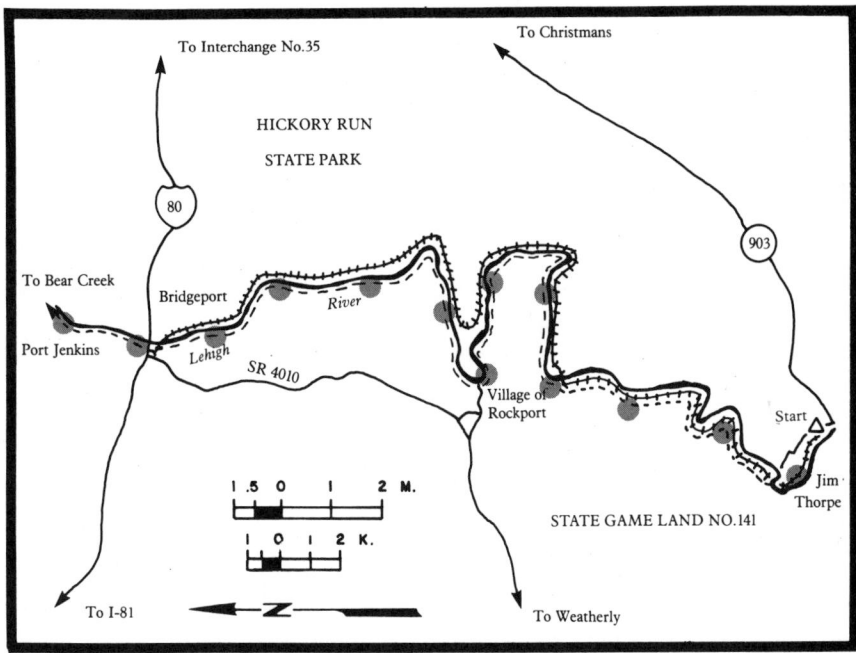

Hazards: The trail is along, and occasionally crosses, railroad tracks still in use.

Rescue index: The trail is closed to motor vehicles and is in a deep gorge surrounded by state game lands, so help is only available at park entrances.

Land status: State park.

Maps: Pick up maps at Blue Mountain Sports and the tourist bureau in Jim Thorpe.

Finding the trail: From Jim Thorpe, either drive or pedal your bike across the Lehigh River on PA 903 and turn left onto Coalport Road. The entrance to the Coalport Access Area is on the left.

Sources of additional information:

Department of Environmental Resources
Lehigh Gorge State Park
RD 2 Box 56
Weatherly, Pennsylvania 18255
(717) 427-8161

Blue Mountain Sports
34 Susquehanna Street
Jim Thorpe, Pennsylvania 18229
(717) 325-4421

RIDE 39 *THE SWITCHBACK TRAIL*

Here's an easy 10-mile loop that includes forest trails, great views of the Lehigh River Gorge, a ramble through old Jim Thorpe, and a spin along a babbling mountain stream. And if that sounds too good to be true, consider this: there aren't any steep climbs, either.

The trail is in two sections—the Back Track and the Down Track, references to the days when the trail was a gravity railroad. Loaded coal cars traveled the Down Track to waiting barges and returned to the coal mines empty on the Back Track. Today the Back Track follows a wooded ridge (watch for deadfall) into Jim Thorpe; the Down Track returns to Mauch Chunk Lake Park along the stream. A wide cinder path winds through some woods in the heights above the town. The grade never exceeds two percent.

Watch out for: a steep, rocky descent into town on the Back Track; a side trail to "The Point," a rock outcropping with an unobstructed view north of the Lehigh River Gorge where hawks soar at eye level; a young black bear spotted around dusk on the Down Track.

General location: Jim Thorpe, Pennsylvania.

Elevation change: The ride starts at Mauch Chunk Lake Park and descends about 600' in elevation to Jim Thorpe. Recovering the lost altitude on the 2 percent grade back up to the park is very easy.

Season: Summer and fall are the best seasons for riding. Spring can be very muddy, especially on the Back Track. Stay out of the woods during deer hunting season (late fall). Expect snow between November and March.

Services: All services are available in Jim Thorpe. Mountain bikes can be rented at Blue Mountain Sports.

Hazards: There is a steep, rocky descent from the Back Track into Jim Thorpe that novice riders may want to walk.

Rescue index: The Back Track section is along a mountain ridge away from paved roads. The rest of the trail is either in town or parallels PA 209.

Land status: County park lands.

Maps: Blue Mountain Sports and the tourist bureau in Jim Thorpe carry maps.

Finding the trail: From Mauch Chunk Lake Park, ride out the main entrance, turn left onto PA 209 and ride a half mile to where the Back Track intersects

THE SWITCHBACK TRAIL

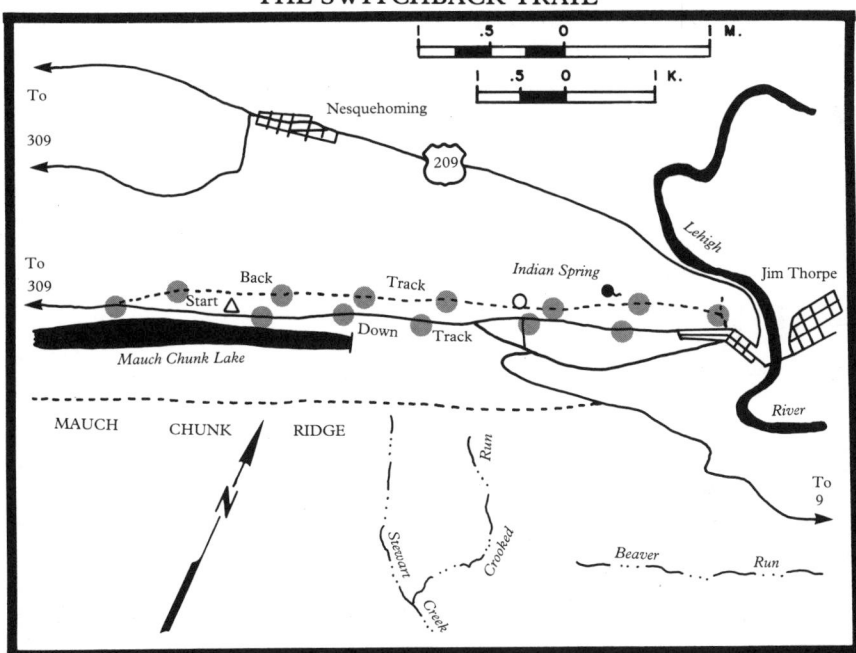

on the right. (Here's a shortcut, if you don't mind pushing your bike 100 yards up a very steep bank: Turn right from the park entrance and look for a dirt road on the left. Follow it straight up the side of the mountain to the Back Track section and turn right.)

Sources of additional information:

Carbon County Tourist Promotion Agency
P.O. Box 90
Railroad Station
Jim Thorpe, Pennsylvania 18229
(717) 325-3673

Blue Mountain Sports
34 Susquehanna Street
Jim Thorpe, Pennsylvania 18229
(717) 325-4421

Notes on the trail: The Switchback Trail is built on the right-of-way of one of America's first railroads, the gravity railroad between old Mauch Chunk and the coal mines in Summit Hill. Cars full of coal rolled to waiting barges in Jim Thorpe; mules pulled the empty cars up a steep incline where they rolled back to the mines. (Steam power later replaced the mules.) The gravity railroad began operating in 1828 and ran until 1933. After the Civil War and the decline of the canal system that the railroad fed, it was converted into a passenger ride, foreshadowing the development of the roller coaster.

One last note: While the ride can be started in Jim Thorpe, be sure to ride out of town on the Down Track section, to avoid a steep climb on the Back Track.

RIDE 40 *SUMMER'S LOOP*

This 15-mile loop on Pennsylvania state game land is characterized by deep forests, making this a nice ride on hot days. An added attraction is the great view of the Lehigh River Gorge, especially in fall when the foliage is turning. The mountain laurel is in full bloom in mid-June. Keep on the lookout for wildlife, including deer, black bear, and birds.

While this ride is entirely on forest roads, there are sections of steep descents and climbs on rutted surfaces that make it challenging, especially if ridden fast. After starting on pavement the trail changes to dirt, with some stretches of coarse gravel. On the return leg there's a creek crossing followed by a packed-dirt uphill. Midway through the ride the trail passes over the Rockport Tunnel, a live railroad tunnel that runs through the mountain. The view of the Lehigh River Gorge is one of the best and one that few visitors to the area ever see. A series of steep, short climbs ends the ride.

General location: Summer's Loop is 10 miles from Jim Thorpe, Pennsylvania, in the western Pocono Mountains.

Elevation change: The elevation changes are minor, with the lowest point of the ride at 1,100′ of elevation and the highest only 1,680′. This difference accumulates over many short climbs.

Season: Summer and fall are the best seasons. The mountain is usually covered by snow in winter and deep mud from melting snow in early spring. Avoid riding during hunting season (late fall).

Services: All services are available in Jim Thorpe. Mountain bikes can be rented at Blue Mountain Sports.

Hazards: The biggest danger on this ride, with its easy grades and wide roads, is running out of water. Watch out for snakes in warm weather and avoid riding in deer hunting season (late fall). Be careful on the long descents.

Rescue index: There's the small private community of Christmansville near the start of the ride. If you've begun the descent toward Drake's Creek and need help, keep going in that direction to your car.

SUMMER'S LOOP

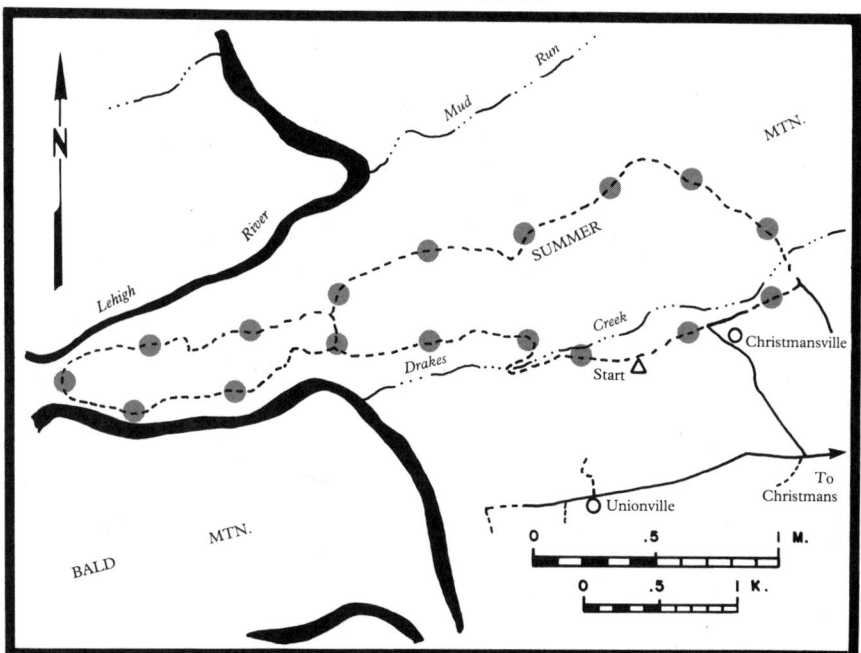

Land status: State game lands.

Maps: The topo map for this ride is the Christmans USGS quadrangle.

Finding the trail: To reach Summer's Loop, drive north from Jim Thorpe on PA 903 for 10.5 miles. At the sign for Penn Forest Garage (directly across from Smith's Hardware Store), turn left onto Unionville Road. Follow this road (don't turn off on side roads) for 2.5 miles to a power line and turn right onto Schoolhouse Road. Drive to the "Y" intersection and take the dirt road to the left. About a half mile down the road look for a small open area by the power line; park there. To start the ride, head back out the dirt road to the "Y" intersection and go straight. Follow the road to another "Y" intersection. Look for a house on the corner and a gate across the road to the left. Take the left past the gate and ride uphill. Go straight until the road turns to dirt at a "Y" intersection. Turn right to begin the loop.

Sources of additional information:

Blue Mountain Sports
34 Susquehanna Street
Jim Thorpe, Pennsylvania 18229
(717) 325-4421

Notes on the trail: Pennsylvania state game lands provide a lifetime of mountain biking opportunities, but offer nothing in the way of road signs, trail signs, blazes, or anything to help riders find their way around. Carry a topo map and compass, and give yourself enough time to explore. And don't forget your spirit of adventure.

NEW YORK

Shawangunk Mountains / Catskill State Park

In a two-hour drive north of the cold concrete canyons of New York City, intrepid mountain bikers are transported to the scenic Hudson Valley. Overlooking the valley to the west is Catskill Park, featuring 650,000 acres of mountains and forests—and some of the best mountain biking and alpine scenery in the East. South of the park, the Shawangunk (SHON-gum) Mountains have become a favorite destination for off-road riders.

The Hudson Valley's rich history is also a boon to mountain bikers. The region was settled in the early seventeenth century, and the many carefully carved carriage trails crisscrossing the nearby Shawangunks reflect nearly three centuries of use. For off-road cyclists, this translates into many miles of moderate-grade climbing through spectacular mountains. Dramatic rock outcroppings and vistas of mountain ridges and lakes mark almost every turn along many of these trails.

If riding carriage trails sounds a little too tame, the Shawangunks also feature excellent single-track trails. For hammerheads seeking anaerobic bliss, all-day rides leading to distant peaks are easy to plan.

With New York City only a few hours away the Shawangunks get a lot of use by hikers and increasingly over the last five or so years by mountain bikers as well. When I visited on a mid-week morning the trails in Minnewaska State Park were filling up with hikers, and at least a dozen mountain bikes were being unloaded in the parking lot. The word is out: the Shawangunks are a hot place to bike.

With the growing popularity of the Shawangunks as a mountain bike destination, it hasn't taken long for an entrepreneurial spirit to see a need and fill it. Bob Henninger is an expert-class mountain bike racer who operates two bike shops in the Catskills—his original shop in Kingston, and a second shop in New Paltz (where Bob rents mountain bikes and organizes tours).

He calls the Shawangunk Mountains "the East Coast Boulder, Colorado," and anticipates the continued growth of mountain biking's popularity throughout the nineties. With a decade of riding experience in the area, Bob is a regional expert on where to ride off-road. Whenever you're looking for a mountain bike adventure in the Shawangunks, Catskill Park, or the Hudson Valley, stop in at one of his shops to talk about mountain bikes, good trails to ride, and to get directions to the trailhead. The rides that follow are some of Bob's favorites.

MINNEWASKA STATE PARK

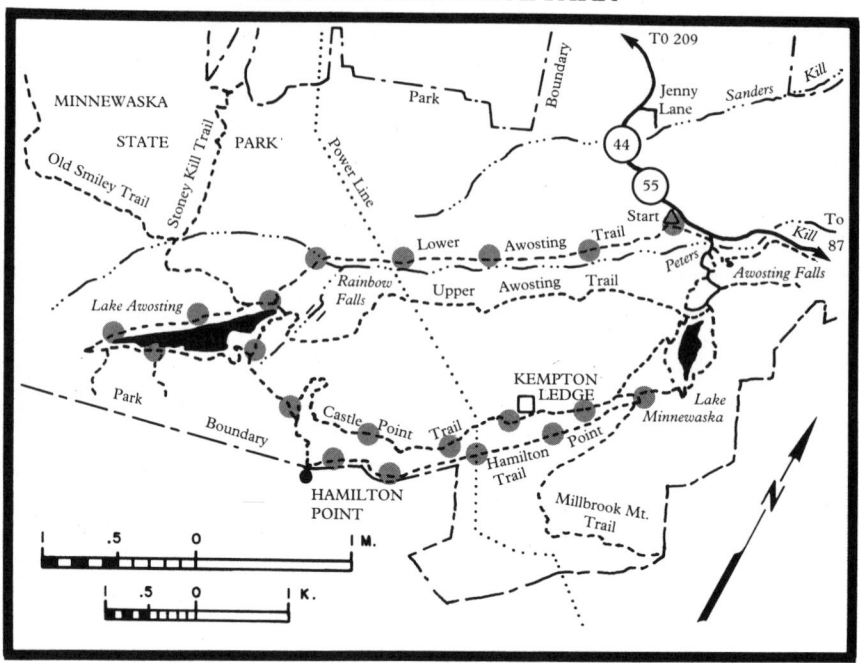

RIDE 41 *MINNEWASKA STATE PARK*

For spectacular mountain scenery, this 17-mile loop ride may qualify as one of the best on the East Coast. The carriage roads carved out of the mountains gently switchback up the mountain face, revealing higher and grander views of the surrounding mountains and lakes at each turn. From Castle Point the nearly 360-degree view is breathtaking, as high ridges recede in the distance in all directions. The scenery never lets up.

And for more good news, you don't need to be a LeMond or Tomac to enjoy this ride. Although there are some long climbs, most of the riding is on six-foot-wide converted carriage roads. The gentle grades require endurance, not technical riding ability. The trails are well maintained and heavily used.

General location: Minnewaska State Park lies 25 miles southwest of Kingston, New York, off NY 44/55 in the Shawangunk Mountains.

Elevation change: The loop begins at around 1,400′ of elevation and gently climbs to about 2,100′ at Castle Point. Total elevation gain is around 1,000′.

Season: These well-groomed trails make for fine riding year-round. Fall, with

Photo by author

its spectacular foliage, is a favorite season with most visitors, with spring and summer right behind. Expect snow between November and March.

Services: All services, including bike shops and rentals, are available in New Paltz and Kingston.

Hazards: The park is popular with hikers, so maintain a reasonable speed when descending on the carriage trails. Watch for wheel-eating crevasses when riding on the large rock formations that lead to the overlooks.

Rescue index: The park is heavily used by both hikers and mountain bikers, even on weekdays.

Land status: State park.

Maps: The USGS 7.5 minute topos are Gardiner and Napanoch. A trail map is available at the park entrance.

Finding the trail: From New York State Thruway (Interstate 87) Exit 18, turn left onto NY 299 west. Go through the village of New Paltz and cross the iron bridge. Continue on NY 299 until it ends 6 miles later. Turn right onto NY 44/55. The park entrance comes in about 4 miles, on the left.

Sources of additional information:

Minnewaska State Park
New Paltz, New York 12561
(914) 255-0752

Catskill Mountain Bicycle Shop
RD 6 Box 386
Kingston, New York 12401
(914) 336-2737

Catskill Mountain Bicycle Shop
5 ½ N. Front Street
New Paltz, New York 12561
(914) 255-3859

RIDE 42   *WALLKILL VALLEY RAIL TRAIL*

This beautiful, 12-mile hiking/biking trail passes through two quaint seventeenth-century villages, skirts farms, goes through woods, and crosses over rivers and streams. The elevated rail bed provides a view of the surrounding area including woodland ponds, the Wallkill River, and the Shawangunk Mountains in the distance. Wildlife frequently sighted along the trail includes wood turtles, woodcocks, songbirds, broadwing hawks, great horned owls, fox, white-tailed deer, and raccoons.

The well-maintained cinder trail is essentially flat. It can be ridden as an out-and-back, or as a loop by returning to the start via one of 21 paved roads that cross the trail. The trail passes through the New Paltz Historical District, which features seventeenth-century stone houses and the old railroad station that served the trains on this former Conrail route. There's also a Mexican restaurant, a bistro, a bakery, and several pizza parlors to round out a leisurely ride.

General location: The ride begins in the town of New Paltz, 15 miles south of Kingston and 1.5 miles from the New York State Thruway (I-87).

Elevation change: Negligible.

Season: The best riding is from late spring to mid-fall.

Services: All services, including two bike shops and rentals, are available in New Paltz. Gardiner has several bed-and-breakfast inns.

Hazards: Parts of the southern section of the trail are frequently covered with water after heavy rain. The bridge over the Wallkill River has been slated for repair; if the work isn't completed before your visit take special care.

WALLKILL VALLEY RAIL TRAIL

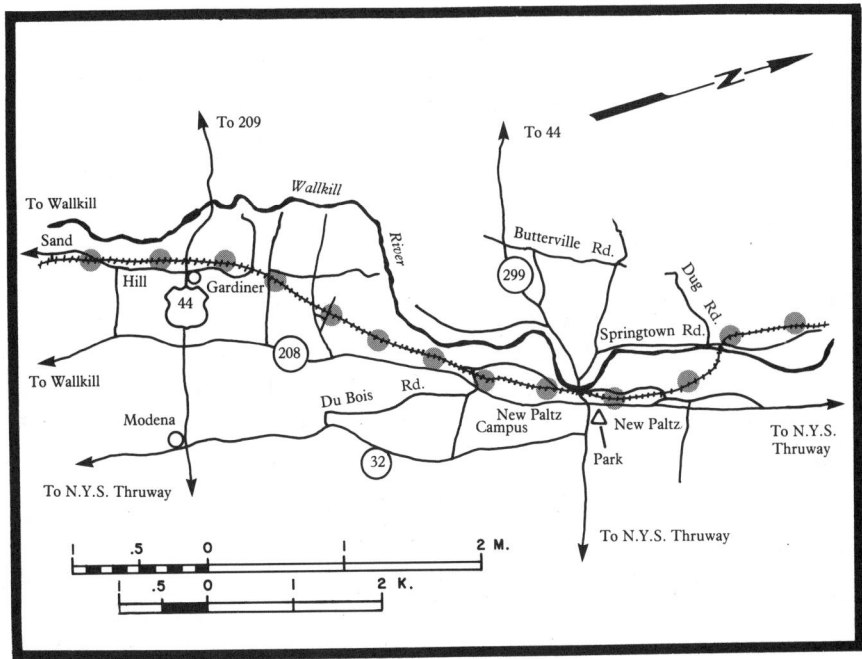

Rescue index: Help can be flagged down on the paved roads which cross the trail or from nearby residences.

Land status: The linear park is jointly owned by the village of New Paltz and the Land Trust of Wallkill Valley.

Maps: The USGS quadrangles are Gardiner and Rosendale. Brochures of the trail include a map and are available at the Town Hall on North Chestnut Street in New Paltz—phone (914) 255-0100.

Finding the trail: From I-87 take Exit 18 (NY 299) west for 1.5 miles to New Paltz, where the Wallkill Valley Rail Trail crosses the road. Park on a side street in the village or in the lot near the Historic District.

Sources of additional information:

Wallkill Valley Rail Trail Association
P.O. Box 1048
New Paltz, New York 12561

New Paltz Chamber of Commerce
257 ½ Main Street
New Paltz, New York 12561
(914) 255-0243

Catskill Mountain Bicycle Shop
5 ½ N. Front Street
New Paltz, New York 12561
(914) 255-3859

RIDE 43   *VERNOOY KILL FALLS TRAIL*

On this scenic ride in the mountains of Catskill Park watch for wildlife such as bear, deer, porcupine, turkey, and a wide variety of bird life. Other attractions include a beautiful waterfall and swimming hole surrounded by pines and shrubs about 2 miles into the ride. The trail passes through dense forests of pines, maples, and oaks, and along streams, waterfalls, and swamps. And don't forget to pack a fly rod. Vernooy Kill is an excellent trout stream.

This 10-mile loop, however, is for the technically adept mountain biker. It features rough, washed-out fire roads and technical single-track trails. There are steep climbs and long, technical descents that will challenge expert riders. Additional challenges include slippery wet rocks, black muck, and swamps. This is a ride for strong cyclists.

General location: Upper Cherrytown Road near Kerhonkson, New York, in the southern Catskill Mountains.

Elevation change: The ride starts with a long climb on technical single-track that gains about 1,000′ over 1.5 miles. This is followed by some gradual climbing and then rolling hills on a fire road. About 6 miles into the loop the trail begins to descend the mountain. The total elevation gain is around 1,200′.

Season: Local riders say that summer is the best time of year for this ride, for it's warm enough to swim and the trails are usually dry. In fall the foliage is considered "better than Vermont." Expect snow from November through March.

Services: All services are available in Kingston, New York.

Hazards: Watch for wet, slippery rocks. Watch out for other trail users on steep descents.

Rescue index: The trails are all within 5 miles of roads with residences and traffic.

Land status: State park.

Maps: The USGS 7.5 minute quadrangles are Peekamoose Mountain, Roundout Reservoir, and Kerhonkson.

Finding the trail: Take Exit 19 (Kingston) from the New York State Thruway (I-87) to NY 209 south, toward Ellenville. Go about 16 miles, through Accord. Turn right at Kerhonkson onto Pataukunk Road. At the intersection with Cherrytown Road continue straight onto Sampsonville Road. Bear left onto

VERNOOY KILL FALLS TRAIL

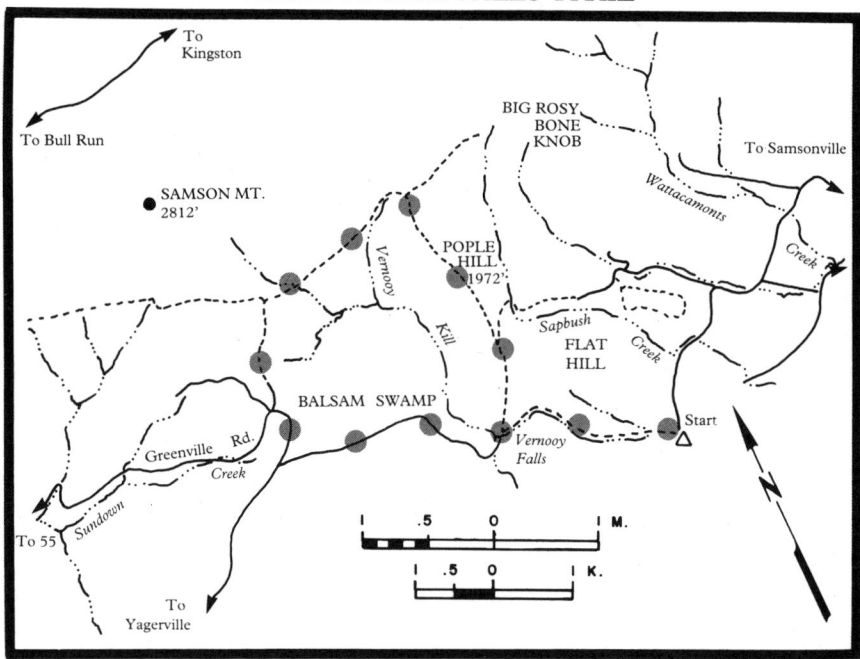

Lower Cherrytown Road. The name changes to Upper Cherrytown Road in Cherrytown. Continue to the parking area on the left at the state trail marker. Park here.

Sources of additional information:

Catskill Mountain Bicycle Shop
RD 6 Box 386
Kingston, New York 12401
(914) 336-2737

Catskill Mountain Bicycle Shop
5 ½ N. Front Street
New Paltz, New York 12561
(914) 255-3859

Notes on the trail: When first reaching the falls at the beginning of the ride take the trail to the right. When returning to this point on the loop you will return from the left, crossing over a wooden hiking bridge.

Syracuse

Syracuse, near the geographical center of New York, sits on the edge of the great northeastern sweep of the Appalachian Mountains. Its proximity to Lake Ontario, Adirondack Park, the Finger Lakes, and numerous hills and swamps affords a wide variety of riding to mountain bike enthusiasts.

A good example is Old Erie Canal Park, which starts in Syracuse and includes 35 miles of partially restored canal. The towpath gives mountain bikers not only glimpses of the region's history and early commerce, but a look at the considerable natural diversity of the area. The canal, begun in 1817, took advantage of a comparatively level route between the Hudson River and Lake Erie through the only break in the Appalachian chain. Finished in 1825, the canal was the work of self-made engineers, and was the greatest engineering feat of its time.

Another popular off-road destination near Syracuse is Highland Forest, a county-owned and -operated park on a tall hill overlooking lush farmland. Popular as a cross-country skiing area in the winter, the park welcomes mountain bikers to its trails in the warmer months. While foot trails are closed to cyclists, over 20 miles of ski trails and all roads and fire lanes are open to mountain bikes.

Syracuse is close to Adirondack Park, which at six million acres is the largest park east of the Rockies. While the park is an immense area containing 2,000 miles of hiking trails, mountain biking is relatively limited. For one thing, the old systems of logging roads that make up most of the trails rarely link up, making loop rides scarce. And in the spectacular—and highly popular—High Peaks region near Lake Placid, off-road cycling is discouraged because of the large numbers of hikers who visit the area and resistance from the powerful Adirondack Mountain Club.

But all is not lost in the Adirondacks. Moose River Recreation Area, on the western edge of the park, is one destination open to mountain bikers. What it lacks in stunning vistas and loop rides, it makes up for with the many miles of trails to explore in a rugged wilderness setting.

Another good mountain biking area in Adirondack Park is Streeter Lake. The trails lead to a beautiful, moss-covered meadow near two lakes. An overnight shelter overlooking the lake has been described as one of the most beautiful spots in the Adirondacks.

Steve Johnson is a Syracuse-based cyclist who lent his knowledge and expertise of the area in putting together several of these rides. Steve works out of his home teaching bicycle maintenance and repairing bikes. He's also active with the Onandoga Cycling Club, which promotes both road and mountain biking. If you're in Syracuse and have any questions about cycling in the area, give him a call at Meltzer's Bicycle Store, (315) 446-6816.

RIDE 44 *ERIE CANAL STATE PARK BICYCLE PATH*

This historic trail along the Erie Canal slowly curves eastward from Syracuse through farmland, wetlands, woods, and meadows which are home to white-tailed deer, woodchucks, and painted turtles. On this ride don't forget to bring binoculars and a bird book, for many types of woodpeckers, hawks, osprey, and a large number of great blue heron (with a wingspan over 5 feet) feed along the canal. Red maple, elm, and black willow trees predominate along the trail. The fall foliage peaks in early to mid-October.

The 38.5-mile (one-way) trail follows the old towpath used when mules pulled barges on the Erie Canal. Most of the towpath is flat, hard-packed dirt and stone that is 5- to 8-feet wide and maintained for bicycling and hiking. No technical riding skills are required. Road bikes with touring tires should have no problems on the first 15 miles. The towpath stops and roads parallel to the canal must be ridden after Durhamville for about 2 miles (NY 46), and from Lock Road to the New York State Barge Canal (NY 46).

In the first 2 miles the trail traverses huge stone aqueducts built to carry the canal over rivers and streams. Cedar Bay Picnic Area (.8 miles from the start) has picnic and playground facilities, bathrooms and water, as well as a Canal Center with historic information and displays (open on summer weekends). The large footbridge at Cedar Bay is a replica of the bridges that carried foot traffic and horses across the canal in the nineteenth century. Further along the trail are Green Lakes State Park, Poolsbrook Picnic Area (with the ruins of an 1800s brick factory), dry docks (used to maintain and repair canal boats) under restoration, the Canastota Canal Museum and, at the end of the trail, the Erie Canal Village, where you can catch a ride on a canal boat pulled by a mule!

General location: The trail begins at Butternut Drive in Dewitt, about 1 mile from the Dewitt exit of Interstate 481, and continues along the old Erie Canal to the Erie Canal Village near Rome, New York.

Elevation change: Negligible.

Season: The trail is rideable from spring to mid-fall. Bugs are a nuisance in June and in the evenings from July through September. Wear goggles or glasses, especially near dusk. Bugs in the daytime are usually no problem after June.

Services: Water, food, and beverages are available during the summer months

ERIE CANAL STATE PARK BICYCLE PATH

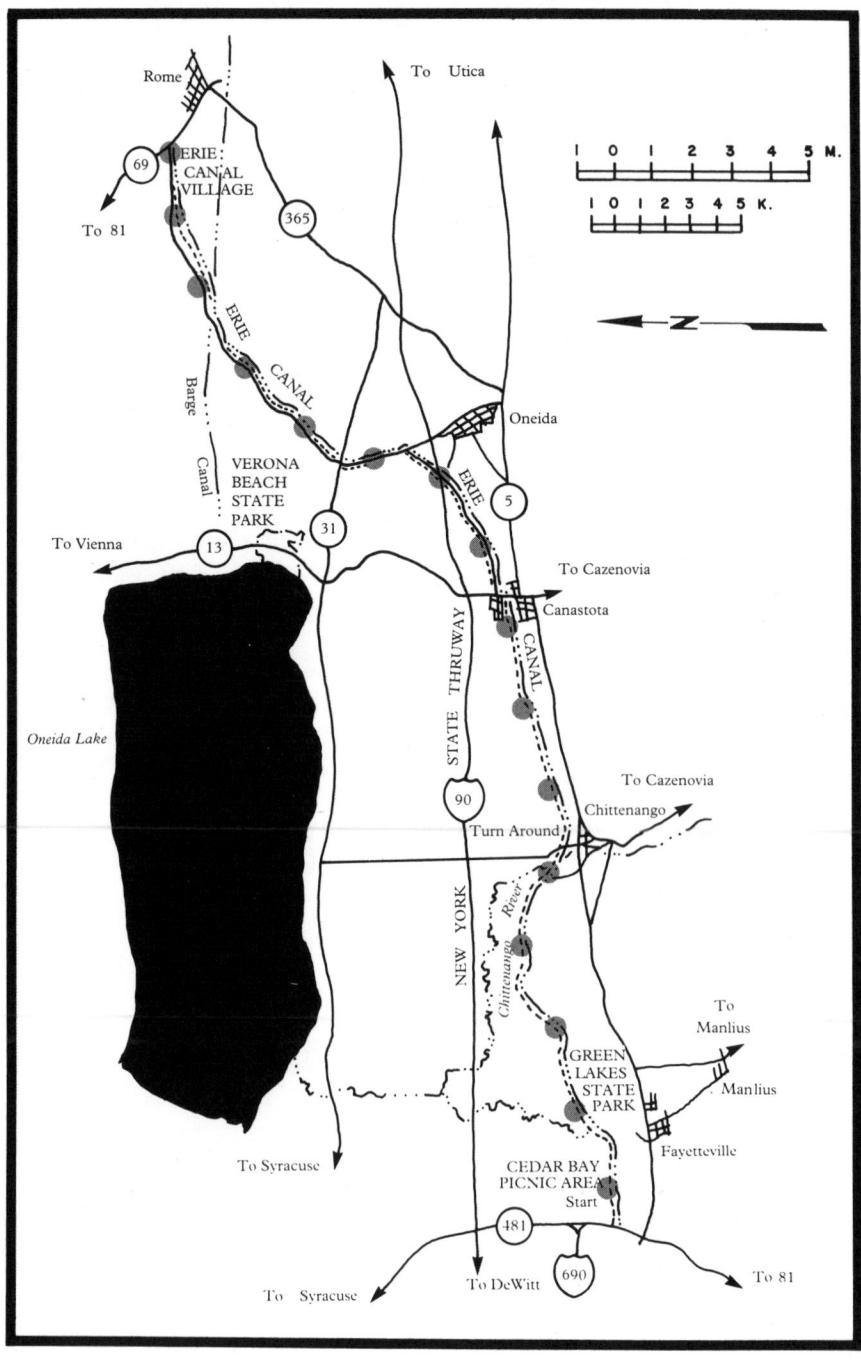

at Green Lakes State Park and the towns of Dewitt, Chittenango, Canastota, and Durhamville. Water is also available at Cedar Bay picnic area and Pools Brook Picnic Area. Overnight camping and swimming are available at Green Lakes State Park and nearby Verona Beach State Park. Bicycle service is available at Nipponose Adventure Outfitters in Dewitt.

Hazards: Watch for high-speed motor traffic when crossing the many roads that intersect with the trail.

Rescue index: The canal is popular and well-traveled; also, traffic can be waved down at intersections.

Land status: State park.

Maps: Maps of the Erie Canal Bicycling Path are sometimes available on the post at the bridge in Cedar Bay Park. Maps of Green Lakes State Park are available at the park office. The USGS quad maps are Syracuse East, Manlius, Canastota, Oneida, Sylvan Beach, and Verona.

Finding the trail: The trail begins at Butternut Drive in Dewitt, New York. From NY 5 (Erie Boulevard) in Dewitt, take Kinne Road east. Continue past a cemetery on the left and over I-481. Turn left immediately after the bridge onto Butternut Drive. The parking area is at the bottom of the hill on the right. The ride can also start at the parking area at Cedar Bay Park (.8 miles from Dewitt). Take Kinne Road east from NY 5 in Dewitt and continue to the end. Turn left at the "T" intersection and follow the road around a sharp, uphill curve to the right. Cedar Bay Picnic Area is on the left at the top of the hill.

Sources of additional information:

New York State Parks
Recreation and Historic Preservation
Empire State Plaza, Agency Building 1
Albany, New York 12238
(518) 474-1456

Onondaga Cycling Club
P.O. Box 6307
Teall Station
Syracuse, New York 13217

Meltzer's Bicycle Store
2714 Erie Blvd. East
Syracuse, New York 13224
(315) 446-6816

RIDE 45 *HIGHLAND FOREST*

About 30 miles south of Syracuse is a wonderful destination for mountain bikers: Highland Forest, a 2,759-acre county park and reforestation area atop a small, wooded mountain. This 10-mile loop ride, a good introduction to the park, passes through mixed-hardwood forest and conifers (at the southern end of the park) on wide, grassy cross-country ski trails. The hardwood forests are predominantly maple, ash, and beech, while conifers are mostly Norway spruce, and red and white pines. In the summer and fall the trails are shaded by the trees, providing cool cycling in hot weather.

While on the loop, stop and see an operating sawmill that makes picnic tables and other park equipment. On Road 16, about 8 miles into the ride, is Highland Tree—largest in the park. But the best part of Highland Park is the quiet, and the sense of isolation imparted by the forest on top of the small mountain.

The well-maintained fire roads and ski trails on this loop make for fairly easy riding. While some of the climbs are long, few are steep; bike handling skill requirements are minimal. Since the clay soil holds water long after rain, expect to get at least a little wet. And keep an eye peeled for deadfalls on Road 30, midway through the ride.

General location: Highland Forest is 30 miles south of Syracuse, New York.

Elevation change: The ride begins at the park office at about 1,700' of elevation and climbs to around 1,800' on the paved road at the sawmill. In the woods the trail drops about 200', passes a shelter on the left, and is followed by a short, steep climb. Over the next couple of miles the elevation slowly drops to about 1,500' at the end of Road 32. Along Road 30 the elevation is slowly regained. On Road 20 the elevation drops, then regains about 200'. The rest of the ride is fairly level, with a few long descents and easy climbs back up. The total elevation gain is about 1,000'.

Season: The trails are open to mountain bikes from May 1 through November 1. This area gets a lot of snow and Highland Forest is a popular cross-country skiing spot. Because of the high clay content of the soil, the trails tend to stay soggy long after it rains.

Services: All services are available in Syracuse. Water and rest rooms are located near the park office.

Hazards: Carry a forest map, available at the park office. Not all the trails and roads in the forest are marked, and a wrong turn could lead you out of the park.

Rescue index: The main park road, which carries traffic, runs north and south through the park.

HIGHLAND FOREST

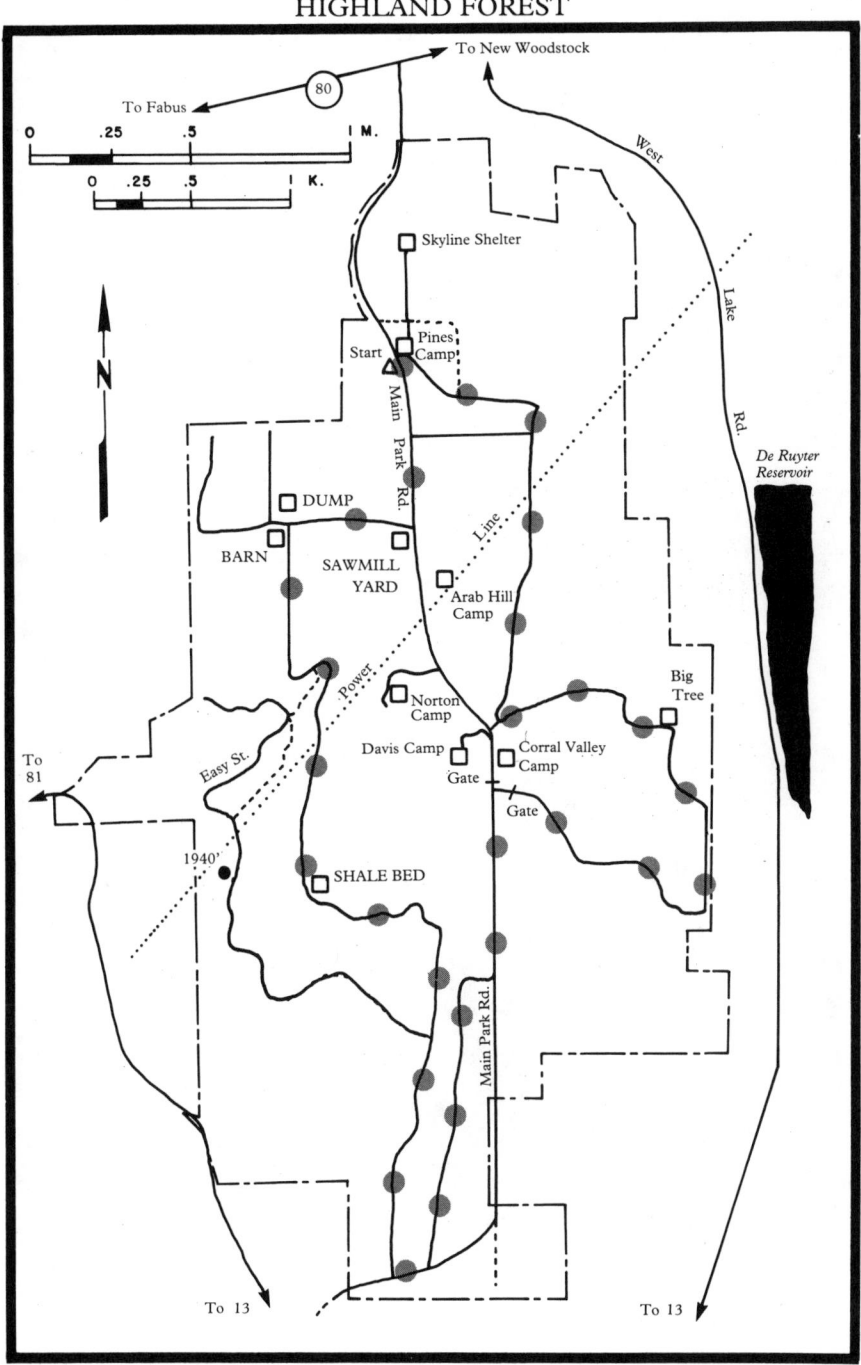

Wide, cross-country ski trails in Highland Forest offer mountain bikers non-technical —and well-shaded—routes. *Photo by author*

Land status: Onondaga County park.

Maps: A trail map is available at park headquarters. The USGS 7.5 minute topo is De Ruyter.

Finding the trail: From Syracuse drive south 18 miles on I-81 to the Tully exit. Drive east on NY 80 for 12 miles. The park is on the right. Park in the lot near the main office.

Sources of additional information:

Highland Forest
Box 31
Fabius, New York 13063
(315) 683-5550

Onondaga Cycling Club
P.O. Box 6307
Teall Station
Syracuse, New York 13217

Meltzer's Bicycle Store
2714 Erie Blvd. East
Syracuse, New York 13224
(315) 446-6816

RIDE 46 MOOSE RIVER RECREATION AREA

The greatest attraction to Moose River is the intense wilderness feel that comes from riding inside a 50,000-acre recreation area deep inside Adirondack Park. And the second greatest attraction? It's the network of trails that leads to the many ponds and streams deep in the forest. Adding to the sense of deep-woods isolation are tens of thousands of acres of other public lands surrounding Moose River. Many foot trails lead into the ridges and mountains in the West Canada Lakes Wilderness Area (no mountain bikes permitted).

Camping and mountain biking go together very well here. Moose River is scattered with campsites (all primitive, most with privies); many are perched on scenic spots over streams. There is also a swimming beach at the Limekiln Lake campground, near the west entrance to the area.

The Moose River Plains, which are the heart of the region, are surrounded by mixed-hardwood and pine forests interspersed with many lakes and ponds. While dramatic views aren't the rule, the area where the main road crosses the Moose River has a wide open look with low ridges visible in the distance. A ride to one of the ponds results in a dramatic change in scenery when a

MOOSE RIVER RECREATION AREA

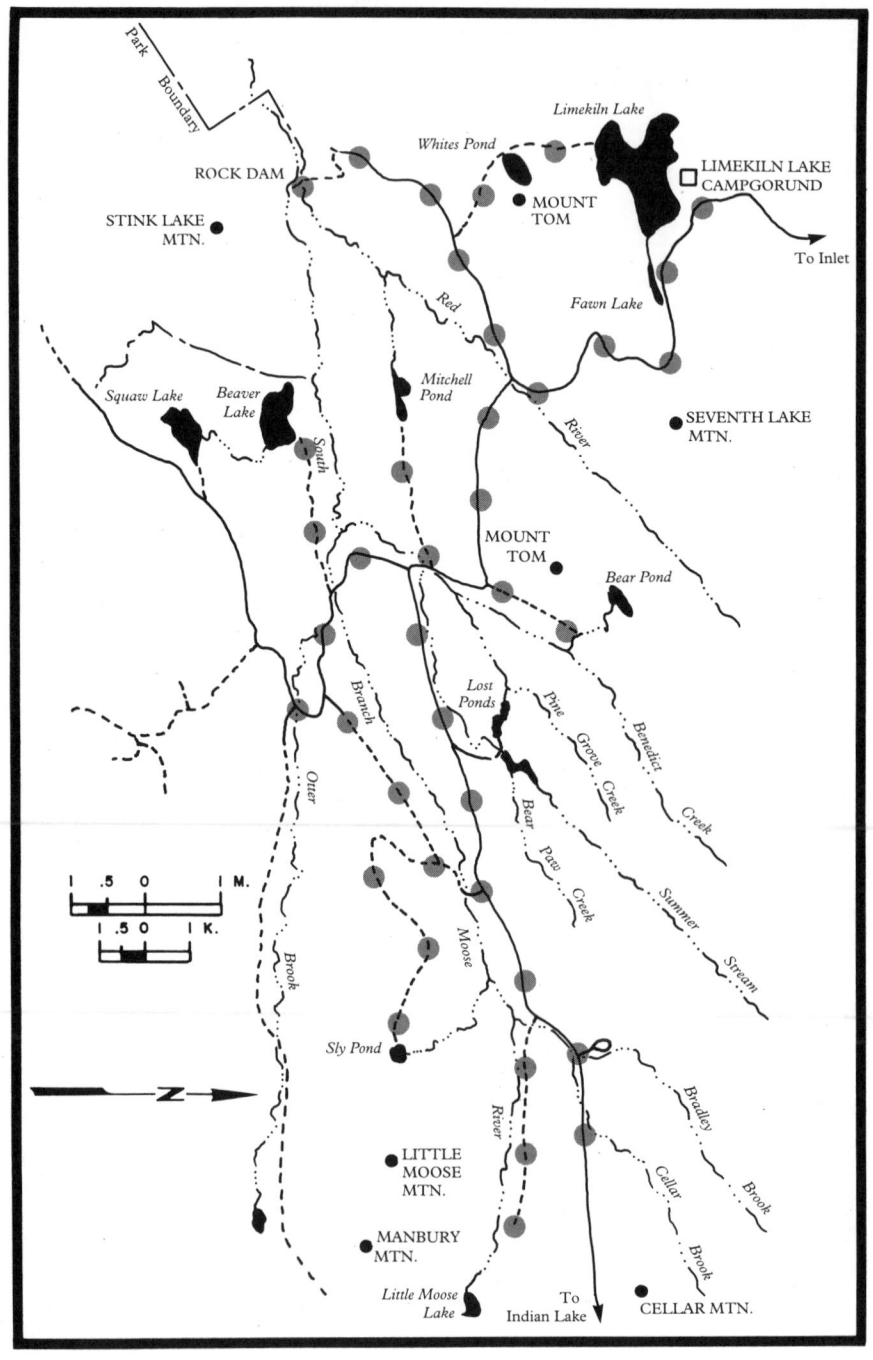

Photo by author

large pond comes into view. These trails follow a maze of abandoned logging roads through the recreation area. More than 27 miles of easy-to-ride access trails lead to ponds and streams scattered throughout the rolling terrain, providing a wide variety of out-and-back rides. These trails connect to a 41.3-mile main road system. The double-track trails (closed to motor vehicles) are usually grassy and flat, are often wet, and are frequently narrow, overgrown, and crossed by deadfalls. The main road system is hard-packed dirt, passable in two-wheel-drive vehicles, and well maintained.

General location: About 5 miles from Inlet, Hamilton County, New York, in western Adirondack Park.

Elevation change: The elevation of the area is around 2,000'. Frequently, the only descent on a trail occurs on the approach to a pond or stream. On most of the trails the maximum elevation gain or loss is only a few hundred feet. The area is surrounded by higher ridges and mountains that are in wilderness areas (off-limits to mountain bikes).

Season: Moose River Recreation Area is open from Memorial Day through the end of deer hunting season in the late fall. Avoid the area in blackfly season, which starts around Memorial Day and lasts through the Fourth of July.

Services: The closest town is Inlet, which has groceries and lodging. There is a spring on the main road 1.3 miles from where it crosses the Moose River.

Hazards: Avoid riding in deer hunting season, in the late fall. When camping, keep food and garbage secure against black bears.

Rescue index: The primary roads carry light traffic. There is a ranger residence at the Limekiln Lake entrance.

Land status: State park.

Maps: A trail map is available at the park office at the Limekiln Lake entrance. The USGS 7.5 minute topo maps are Old Forge and West Canada Lakes.

Finding the trail: From Inlet, New York, on NY 28, turn onto Limekiln Road and drive about 3 miles to the entrance of the recreation area. There is another entrance at the east end on Cedar River Road, which intersects NY 28/30 near Indian Lake. This entrance may be closed during or after inclement weather. Register at either gate. From either the Limekiln Lake or Cedar River entrance, drive about 5 miles into the area and park at a campsite.

Sources of additional information:

Forest Ranger
Limekiln Lake
Inlet, New York
(315) 357-4403

Meltzer's Bicycle Store
2714 Erie Blvd. East
Syracuse, New York 13224
(315) 446-6816

Notes on the trail: The Moose River Recreation Area is open for public use from Memorial Day through the end of deer hunting season. To get the most out of this scenic area, plan a leisurely camping trip and explore by mountain bike the many trails in the area.

RIDE 47 *STAR LAKE/STREETER LAKE TRAIL*

Two beautiful lakes, a tenth of a mile apart, are the destination of this Adirondack Park ride. The lakes are quite different. Streeter Lake is darkly colored, which is typical of Adirondack lakes. But Crystal Lake, one-fifth the size of its neighbor, is clear with a white sandy bottom. A large, moss-covered field near the lakes was once used to grow potatoes for potato chips—an incongruous yet beautiful sight. The Streeter Lake Lean-to is a great place to camp and is widely considered one of the most scenic spots in the Adirondacks.

This 13-mile loop ride passes through rolling terrain with low hills, ex-

STAR LAKE/STREETER LAKE TRAIL

posed outcrops of crystalline rocks, bogs, swamps, and streams. The forests consist of second-growth hardwoods that include sugar maple, black cherry, and beech. The area supports a large deer population, black bear, moose, Eastern coyote, fisher, beaver, porcupine, raccoon, and rabbits. The trail is a mixture of single-track and fire roads which roll through deep forests.

While there isn't much climbing on this ride, marshy and wet conditions require some strength and good bike handling ability. The trail and road conditions vary from marshy to sandy, with some hardpack on dirt roads and grassy areas in meadows. Except for minor stream crossings this is a non-technical ride in a beautiful setting.

General location: The ride is in western Adirondack Park and starts in Star Lake, located on NY 3 between Watertown and Tupper Lake, New York.

Elevation change: Star Lake, at the start of the loop, is at an elevation of about 1,450'. Streeter Lake has an elevation of 1,487'.

Season: The trail is usually rideable from late spring through early fall. Avoid the area from Memorial Day through the Fourth of July, when blackflies take over the Adirondacks. The mountains can get cold at night in the summer, so be prepared if an overnight trip is planned. Avoid riding in deer hunting season, which usually starts in October.

Services: There is a grocery store and gas station in Star Lake and a motel in Fine, New York (6 miles west on NY 3). A restaurant, the Cranberry Lake Inn, is 10 miles east on NY 3.

Hazards: The biggest hazard is the remoteness of the area. Carry a map and compass.

Rescue index: Traffic can be waved down on Youngs Road and Lake Road.

Land status: State park.

Maps: The Adirondack Mountain Club Northern Region Map is an excellent trail map of the area. The USGS 7.5 minute topo maps are Oswegatchie and Oswegatchie S.E.

Finding the trail: From NY 3 in Star Lake turn south onto Griffin Road to Lake Road. Turn right and park at the trailhead on the left.

Sources of additional information:

Adirondack Mountain Club
174 Glen Street
Glens Falls, New York 12801
(518) 793-7737

Meltzer's Bicycle Store
2714 Erie Blvd. East
Syracuse, New York 13224
(315) 446-6816

Notes on the trail: The trail starts as a single-track that is maintained for summer use and cross-country skiing in the winter. Follow the yellow markers as the trail winds south and crosses a couple of streams by footbridge.

The lakes can be used as a base for exploring more trails that lead out of the area. To complete the loop return on the trail from Star Lake, then bear right on the Youngs Road section of the trail. After 5 miles the trail ends at Youngs Road. Turn left and then take the second left, which leads to Lake Road and the start of the loop.

Ithaca

The town of Ithaca, located at the southern tip of 40-mile-long Cayuga Lake in the Finger Lakes region of central New York, is best known as home to Cornell University and Ithaca College. And true to form for a college town, Ithaca has a large cycling community. During warm weather, road riders and racers are a common sight as they train in the long glacial valleys that surround the town.

Many of these dedicated Ithaca cyclists switch to mountain bikes in the fall, when the racing season is over and the black fly population in the woods is KO'd by frost. They're on to a good thing. Ithaca is surrounded by state forests featuring spectacular gorges, numerous waterfalls, and many miles of trails and dirt roads. Moreover, the fall foliage in the Finger Lakes is legendary. The combination of nearby state forests, fall weather, and great trails makes for excellent mountain biking.

But a word of caution. These state forests are honeycombed with technical single-track trails and dirt roads, and appeal to strong riders with good bike handling skills. Less-experienced riders may wish to avoid the single-track and stick to the dirt roads.

Another caveat. Virtually no trail signs are posted to help visitors find their way around these state forests. Plan accordingly by bringing a topo map and compass, and allowing plenty of time. Since the forests are small and laced with unsigned roads and single-track trails that defy step-by-step directions, the trail descriptions that follow depict the area as a whole, without specific routes.

Ithaca-area riders Ed Zieba and Henry Schomacker recommended Hammond Hill, Yellow Barn, and Shindagin Hollow State Forests as the best mountain biking areas close to town. They ought to know. Ed races both road and mountain bikes and lives at the edge of Hammond Hill State Forest. (With a backyard like that, no wonder he wins races.) Henry, who died in 1990, was a devoted cyclist and the reigning champion technical single-track descender among the Ithaca elite. His spirit rages on in the woods and hollows around Ithaca.

RIDE 48   *HAMMOND HILL STATE FOREST*

Spectacular descents on the main seasonal roads and serpentine single-track trails make Hammond Hill the most popular mountain bike destination around Ithaca. An example: "Hammond Roubaix" is a stretch of single-track that's notorious with local hammerheads and named after the infamous Paris-Roubaix bicycling classic. For experts only, the trail weaves its way through a rough, stony, muddy creek bed that is best ridden from north to south. Other trails wind through thick pine stands planted in uniform rows. Some descents are several miles long (notably the trail down to Six Mile Creek and Six Hundred Road). Loop rides of 5, 10, 15 or more miles are possible here.

Hammond Hill, although rated difficult by local mountain bikers, is still within the capabilities of strong recreational bikers. The forest contains many short climbs (usually less than 1 mile) that are often steep for short stretches. From the top of Hammond Hill, the elevation gain and loss moderates. Good bike handling skills are necessary to negotiate narrow trails with sharp drop-offs on the shoulders. The constantly changing terrain—leaf-covered hard-pack, boggy sections with deep ruts, dry creek beds with pizza-sized shale chips and baseball-sized rocks—makes riding in this area a real challenge.

Hammond Hill Road is an unpaved seasonal road, hardpack at the start but with changing conditions on the climb that vary with the seasons. The trails off the main seasonal roads generally are narrow double-track used by snowmobiles or single-track hiking trails used by all-terrain vehicles. All the trails tend to be wet except after dry spells. Most of the roads and trails in this area cut through verdant forest, a mixture of deciduous and coniferous species. A variety of pine, much of it planted in the 1930s by the Civilian Conservation Corps, stands interspersed with birch, beech, cherry, oak, maple, and many other hardwood species.

Fall is the prettiest time of year in the forest, but spring can also be delightful, if a bit wet. Peak time for fall riding is mid- to late October, when the foliage is spectacular. The area is bisected with gorges and creeks containing small waterfalls and swimming holes. Some open spots along ridge tops offer great views of the surrounding hills, which are dotted with farms and fields. Hammond Hill is also home to a wide variety of wildlife. Look for white-tailed deer, hawks, red-winged blackbirds, chickadees, grosbeaks, cardinals, woodpeckers, sparrows, and finches. Occasionally, great blue herons and barn and horned owls are spotted. Also common are gray and red squirrels, and the ubiquitous chipmunk.

General location: The forest is located between the towns of Caroline and Dryden, 8 miles east of Ithaca, New York.

HAMMOND HILL STATE FOREST

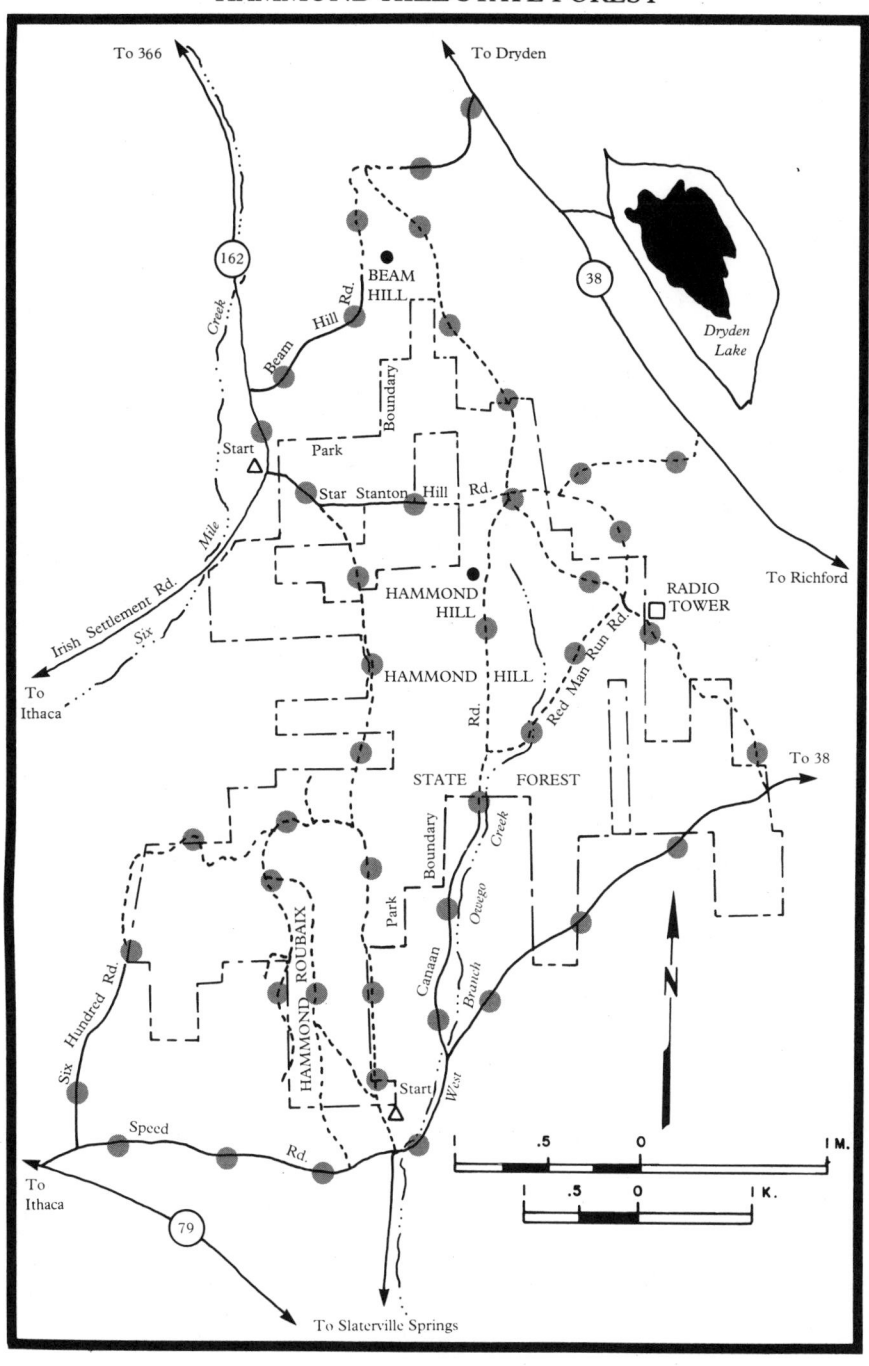

Elevation change: The north end of Hammond Hill Road begins with an elevation of 1,500' and climbs to Hammond Hill, elevation 2,014', the highest point in the forest. The starting point at the south end of the forest is at an elevation of 1,300'. The average gain in vertical feet from the valley to the ridges is between 500' and 800'. Many trails are roller coasters with negligible elevation gain.

Season: The best riding is in the fall, when conditions are driest and most of the bugs are gone. Deerfly and blackfly season lasts from July into September; insect repellent is a must. Spring is the wettest season. Winter is great for "Idita-biking" because the snow-covered trails are packed down by snowmobiles. Avoid riding in deer hunting season, which starts in mid-November.

Services: All services are available in Ithaca. A grocery store is located on the corner of Midline Road and NY 79. A natural spring is located in front of the courthouse next to the store.

Hazards: Watch for four-wheel-drive and logging vehicles on the seasonal roads. The area is popular with moto-cross motorcycles. The forest is littered with deadfall, hanging branches, and fallen limbs. Don't forget bug repellent during blackfly season, from July into September.

Rescue index: Most trails are within walking distance of paved roads where passing motorists can be flagged down. There are also a few isolated residences in the forest.

Land status: State forest.

Maps: The USGS 7.5 minute topo is Ithaca East.

Finding the trail: There are 2 places to start rides in Hammond Hill State Forest. The northern beginning point is reached by driving east from Ithaca on NY 79 to Slaterville Springs; turn left onto Midline Road, which changes name to Irish Settlement Road. Hammond Hill Road is on the right, 4.4 miles from NY 79. Pull off and park near the intersection.

To reach the southern starting point continue through Slaterville Springs on NY 79 for .5 miles to Harford Road and turn left. Go straight for 2 miles to the intersection of Hammond Hill Road and Flatiron Road, and turn left onto Hammond Hill Road. Park at the foot of the hill.

Sources of additional information:

The Bike Rack Bicycle Shop
Collegetown
Ithaca, New York 14850
(607) 272-1010

Ed Zieba
522 Harford Road
Brooktondale, New York 14817
(607) 539-7672

Notes on the trail: As with other state forest lands around Ithaca, trails and roads are not marked in Hammond Hills State Forest. The best approach to riding the area is to bring the Ithaca East topo map, a compass, and a spirit of adventure. Since even local mountain bikers who know the area occasionally get disoriented (lost, they say, is too strong a word), you can avoid frustration by allowing plenty of time and carrying extra food, water, and tools.

RIDE 49 *YELLOW BARN STATE FOREST*

Local hammerheads all agree: Come to Yellow Barn for the screaming descents. But that's not all. Views of the surrounding hills from clearings are spectacular on the many loop rides ranging from 5 to 10 miles in length that you can do here. (For longer rides it's easy to link up with nearby Hammond Hill State Forest via a short ride on paved road.) Yellow Barn's mix of forest includes deciduous and coniferous trees typical to the Finger Lakes area. Many small creeks flow through the forest into small gorges and then to the major creeks that feed the Finger Lakes. These gorges often have waterfalls and small circular swimming holes.

Short, steep climbs are the trademark of mountain biking in Yellow Barn State Forest. The area is often wet and muddy, increasing the power output needed on climbs. The short, rapid descents off the top of the ridge require good bike handling skills. Yellow Barn Road is an unpaved seasonal road that's rocky in sections. Many of the trails in the forest are rutted from logging activity. Furthermore, Yellow Barn is infamous for its lake-sized puddles and oozy mud. Like all other forests in the Ithaca area, the terrain changes constantly. Trails along the pipeline and power line are single-tracks used by moto-cross motorcycles and are usually hardpack.

General location: About 8 miles east of Ithaca, New York.

Elevation change: The southern end of Yellow Barn Road is at an elevation of 1,460'. The highest point in the forest is 1,888'. The northern end (at NY 13) is 1,140'. The average elevation gain is between 400' and 700' on any particular climb.

Season: The best riding starts in the early fall and continues through mid-November. Spring tends to be wet, and summer riding can be plagued by heat, humidity, and bugs. The fall foliage is excellent. Lake-effect snow flurries from the north occur frequently, so carry extra clothes when riding in the fall.

Services: All services are available in Ithaca, 8 miles from the forest. A small grocery store is located at Midline Road and NY 79; the courthouse next to it has a spring.

YELLOW BARN STATE FOREST

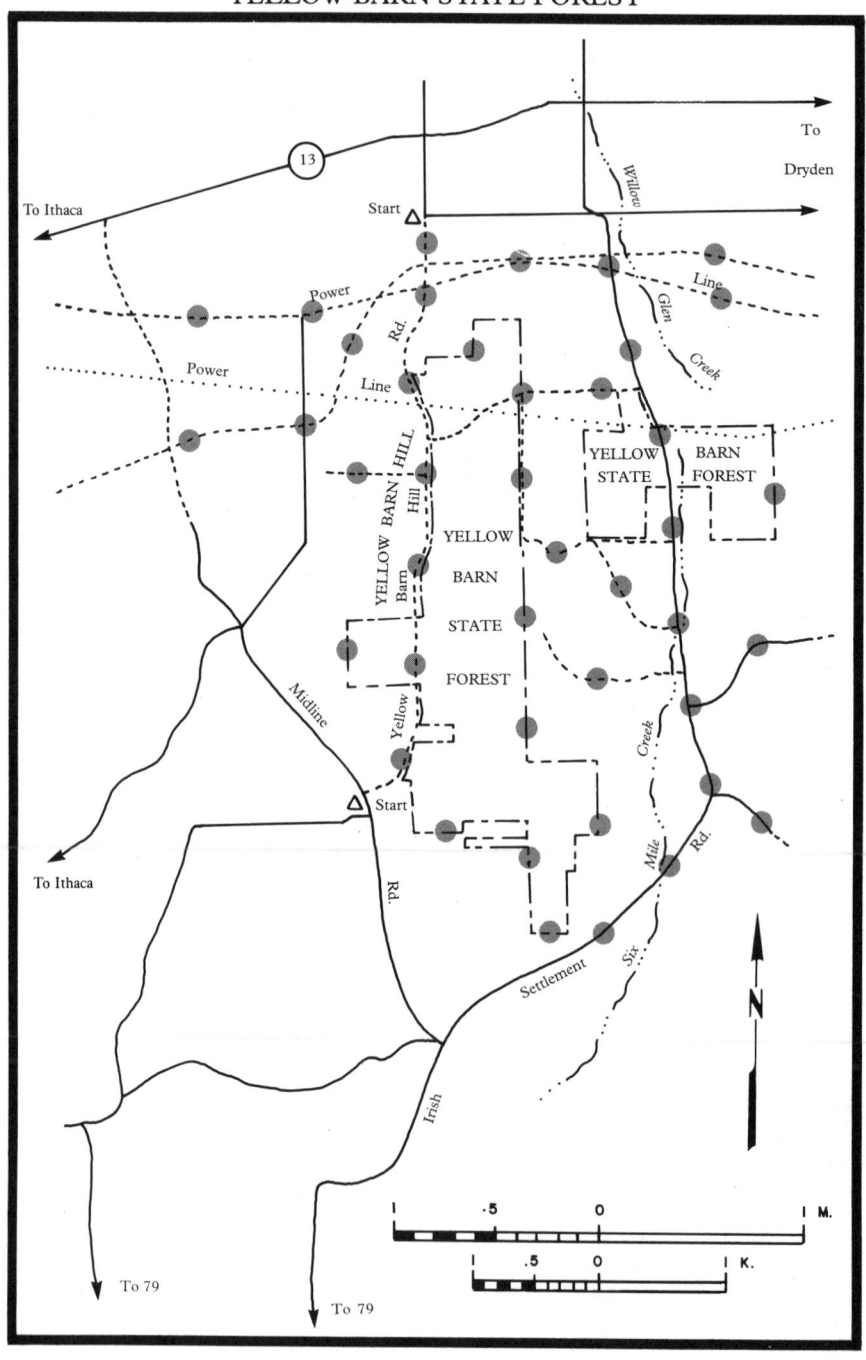

Hazards: Avoid the towers when riding on the power lines. Also, ruts made by logging trucks are dangerous on the descents. Bring bug repellent during blackfly season, from July into September.

Rescue index: The area is within walking distance of paved roads where cars can be waved down. There are many private residences along the paved roads at the southern end of the forest.

Land status: State forest.

Maps: The USGS 7.5 minute topo is Ithaca East.

Finding the trail: There are 2 starting points for rides in Yellow Barn. To reach the southern starting point take NY 79 east from Ithaca to Slaterville Springs and turn left onto Midline Road. Go straight 2 miles to the intersection with Irish Settlement Road (at a dip in the valley). Turn left, following Midline Road for another 2 miles to Yellow Barn Road, at the sign for the Dusenberry Sportsmen's Club. Turn right and park anywhere along the shoulder at the foot of the hill.

To reach the northern starting point take NY 13 east from Ithaca toward Dryden. Turn right on Yellow Barn Road, drive to the unpaved section, and park at the plow turnaround.

Sources of additional information:

The Bike Rack Bicycle Shop
Collegetown
Ithaca, New York 14850
(607) 272-1010

Ed Zieba
522 Harford Road
Brooktondale, New York 14817
(607) 539-7672

Notes on the trail: This area shares a trait with other New York state forests—no trail signs are posted. Explore the area by riding loops that radiate from the central unpaved road. The forest is also crisscrossed by cleared power lines and pipelines that are rideable. Carry a topo map and allow plenty of time for the ride.

RIDE 50 *SHINDAGIN HOLLOW STATE FOREST*

Ithaca mountain bikers consider Shindagin Hollow a double-whammy: the riding is both technical *and* steep. This beautiful forest is known for its twisting descents punctuated by roots lying across the trails. The single-track trails

SHINDAGIN HOLLOW STATE FOREST

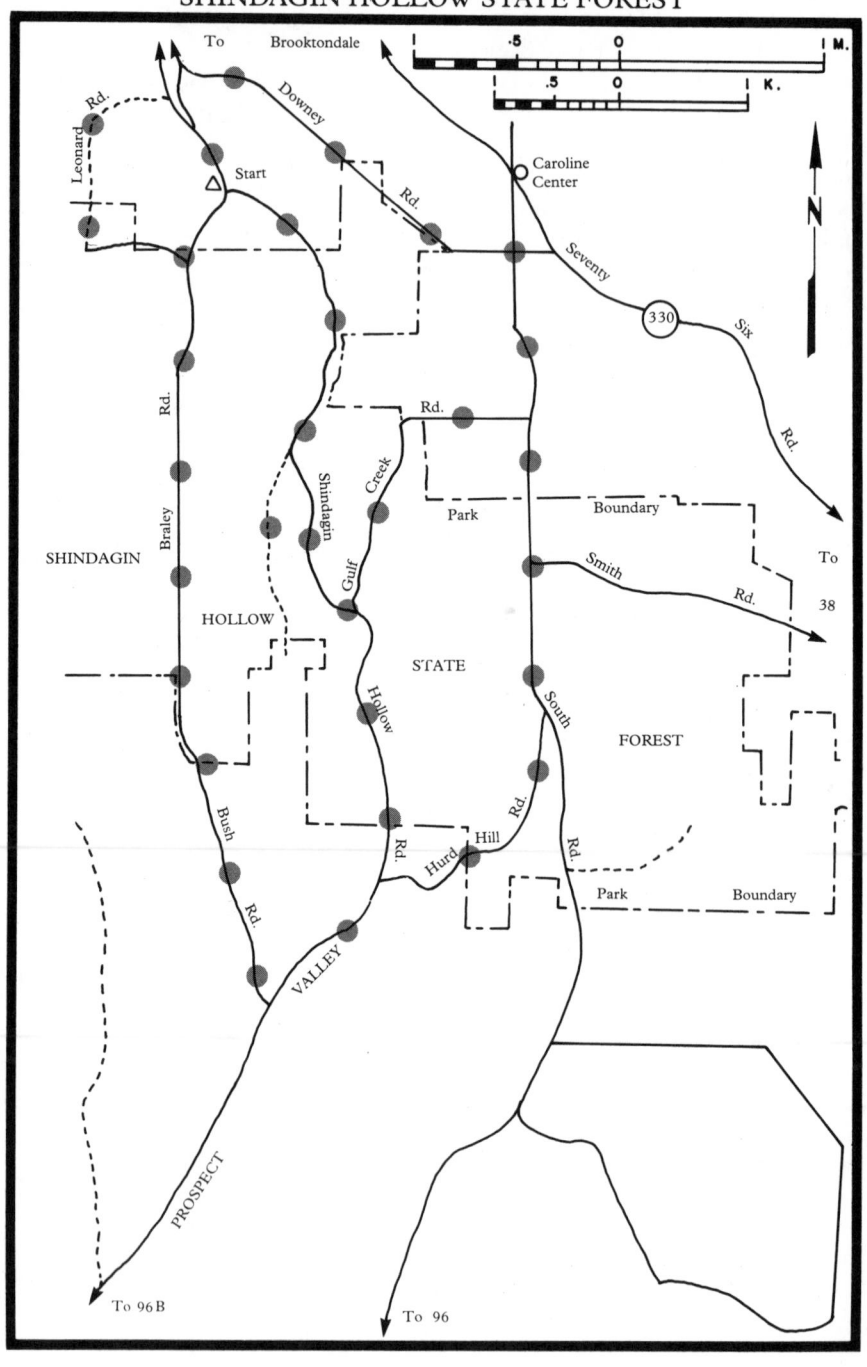

are fast and narrow, and they pass close to trees. Ruts created by moto-cross motorcycle activity add to the difficulty of the trails. In general the climbs are gradual and short, but there are lung-searing exceptions.

The forest is covered with mixed deciduous and coniferous trees, and small gorges and glens bisect the hillsides. Many creeks and waterfalls add to the beauty, while Prospect Valley offers bucolic views of small dairy farms nestled in a gorge. Shindagin Hollow Road and Braley Hill Road are unpaved, hard-packed dirt roads suitable for two-wheel-drive vehicles. But most of the riding in Shindagin is on narrow single-track, which can be wet and covered with standing water. The trails are fast when dry. All roads above the valleys tend to be unpaved.

Since the forest is a maze of single-track trails connected by seasonal roads, it accommodates all riding styles. Loop rides of 5, 10, and 15 miles or longer are possible. Huge pine stands in the forest are great places to take a break and feature a pristine, cathedral-like ambience.

General location: About 10 miles southeast of Ithaca, near the town of Caroline in Tompkins County, New York.

Elevation change: Shindagin Hollow Road and Braley Hill Road start at an elevation around 1,400'. Bald Hill, the tallest peak in the area, is around 1,850'. The average elevation at the tops of the trails is about 1,600'. Shindagin Hollow bottoms out near 1,100'.

Season: The best time to ride this area is from mid- to late October through mid-November. The fall foliage is spectacular in the Shindagin Hollow Valley. Spring can be wet. Heat, humidity, and bugs are strong arguments against summer riding. After the first frost conditions improve dramatically. Avoid riding in deer hunting season, in late November.

Services: All services are available in Ithaca, a 20-minute drive. There is a small grocery store in Brooktondale on Central Chapel/Brooktondale Road. There are no sources of potable water in the forest.

Hazards: Deep ruts made by moto-cross motorcycles can grab front wheels, resulting in a face-plant. Watch for four-wheel-drive trucks and logging vehicles. Some hills have washouts cut into trails to drain runoff, which can pitch unwary riders over the handlebars. Blackfly season runs from July into September, so bring repellent.

Rescue index: Most trails are within walking distance of paved roads, where cars can be waved down. The main roads in the forest carry light traffic.

Land status: State forest.

Maps: The USGS 7.5 minute topo is Ithaca East.

Finding the trail: From Ithaca, drive east on NY 79 for 4 miles to the Brooktondale exit. Turn right and go straight for about 5 miles, where Brooktondale Road becomes Central Chapel Road. Continue straight and bear right onto Braley Hill Road at the fork (Shindagin Hollow Road is to the left). Park at the foot of the hill.

Sources of additional information:

The Bike Rack Bicycle Shop
Collegetown
Ithaca, New York 14850
(607) 272-1010

Ed Zieba
522 Harford Road
Brooktondale, New York 14817
(607) 539-7672

Notes on the trail: Shindagin Hollow State Forest shares many characteristics of the other forests in the Ithaca area—great single-track, beautiful views, tough climbs, and no trail signs.

The key to riding the single-track is to find the trails that branch off the main roads. A topo map, a compass, and a philosophical attitude about getting lost are indispensable. Just allow plenty of time.

Corning

Corning, a small town famous for its glassworks, is located in southeastern Steuben County, just above the Pennsylvania border in central New York state. Geographically, this part of the state rests on a section of the Appalachian Plateau that is sharply eroded by river valleys. The result is that the landscape is dominated by large hills that rise as much as 1,200 feet above the narrow valley floors.

Here's a brief outline of the topography: The principal river valleys in the region are formed by four rivers—the Tioga, the Canisteo, and the Cohocton, all of which join to create the fourth river—the Chemung, near Corning. The Chemung then flows eastward through the center of Corning to meet the Susquehanna River, which continues through Pennsylvania and Maryland to spill into Chesapeake Bay. The best mountain bike trails in the Corning area are on the hills over these river valleys.

In addition to being famous for its glass industry, Corning serves as the Southern Gateway of the popular Finger Lakes vacation area; tourism is second only to industry in the region's economy. The town has some 15 hotels and motels, and several campgrounds to accommodate visitors, making it a good base of operations for exploring the region.

The mountain biking around Corning is mostly on wide dirt roads that lead up to the tall hills between the river valleys. Vistas of forests and orderly farmlands stretch into the distance from the summits. In fall the foliage of the wide variety of trees is brilliant.

Jeff Loik is the founder of the Crystal City Mountain Bike Club in Corning. He has been an avid mountain biker for over four years, and has pioneered many rides in the Corning area. The following rides are some of his favorites.

RIDE 51 *HIGMAN HILL / BLENCOWE ROAD TRAIL*

The Southern Tier of New York state, with its Finger Lakes region and large state forests, is a naturalist's paradise. This 9-mile out-and-back ride is a good example. Thanks to the reforestation efforts of the Civil Conservation Corps in the 1930s, this area contains a myriad of tree species. From the overlook at the top of the first climb is a view north down the NY 414 valley toward Beaver Dams, New York. The railroad through this valley in the 1800s and early 1900s was the primary route into northern New York state. Looking left and right are views of General Sullivan's Trail, which was carved during

HIGMAN HILL/BLENCOWE ROAD TRAIL

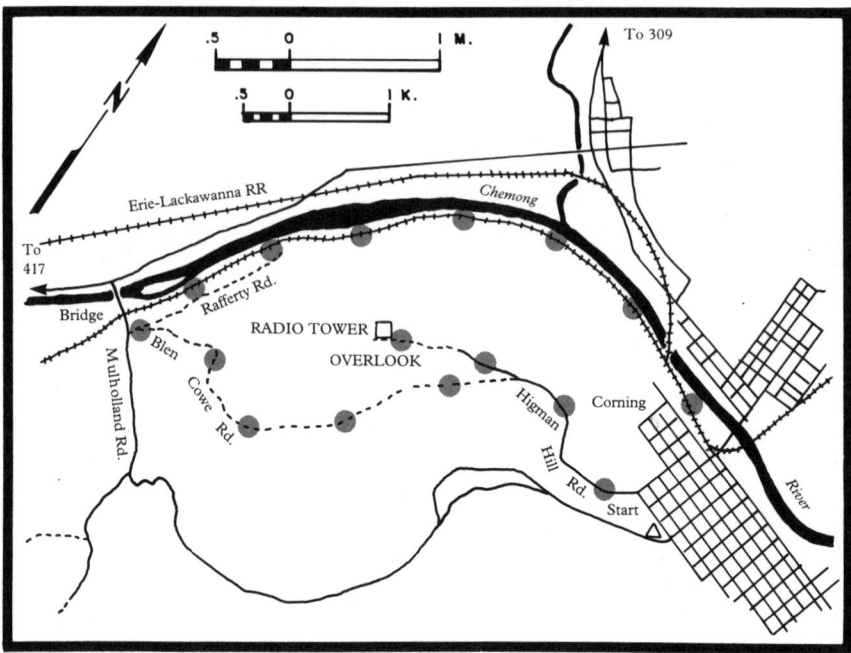

the Indian wars of the 1700s and 1800s. (General Sullivan was given charge of clearing hostile Indians from the area.) Stop at the radio tower for the best view of the Chemung River Valley to the east and the Post Creek Valley to the north. Also, at the top of the climb, look for an informal "playground" for off-road vehicles and mountain bikes on the right.

This is an easy ride, requiring no technical skills. Most of it is on four-wheel-drive roads and dirt roads maintained by New York State Electric and Gas. Good aerobic fitness is required for the climb. All the roads on this ride are wide, hard-packed dirt. Following the linkup with the Erie-Lackawanna railroad track (at the bottom of Blencowe Road), large stones used to maintain the tracks make for a bumpy ride. Keep an eye open for wildlife on this ride, particularly the many types of hare and white-tailed deer.

More historical notes: The early settlers made great use of the fertile Chemung Valley for the growing of grains, corn, and tobacco. The periodic flooding of the Chemung River provided rich, workable soil and an ample supply of water for irrigation. The level top of Higman Hill was mostly logged clear of trees and was planted with grain for livestock and human consumption. For the most part the hill has now been abandoned due to its inaccessibility. The last reference to any settlement is seen in the remains of the burned-out farmhouse at the start of the Blencowe Road descent.

General location: Higman Hill, outside Corning, New York.

Elevation change: The first mile of the ride climbs about 650', followed by about 4 miles of level riding. The last mile or so is a steep descent. The elevation is about 1,100' at the start and rises to 1,736' for a total elevation gain of 636'.

Season: This ride is good year-round, except for early spring (which is usually muddy) and late fall (during hunting season). Mid-summer may be hot and humid, so remember to carry plenty of water. In late September and early October the famous western New York fall foliage sets the rolling hills ablaze with a multitude of colors.

Services: All services are available in Corning.

Hazards: Keep alert for four-wheel-drive traffic when riding. Watch out for off-camber turns on the Blencowe Road descent, which are further complicated by 3 half-covered culverts. At high speeds these can throw your bike off-line.

Rescue index: There is a house with a phone on the left at the bottom of Blencowe Road.

Land status: Seasonal-use roads maintained by New York State Electric and Gas Company.

Maps: The USGS 7.5 minute topo is Corning.

Finding the trail: The dirt road starts at the corner of Sixth Street and Washington Street in Corning. Park on either side of the road.

Sources of additional information:

Corning Bike Works
96 E. Market Street
Corning, New York 14830
(607) 962-7831

RIDE 52 *SUGAR HILL TRAIL*

Great views of forests, hills, valleys, lakes, and fertile farmland are the highlight of this long but scenic ride. Reforestation efforts provided the Sugar Hill area with a variety of trees, including the apple trees harvested for raw fruit and cider making. (The sugar from the apples is what gives the area its name.) The 360-degree view from the top of Sugar Hill includes Lamoka Lake and Wanet Lake, which are joined by a canal. No technical bike handling ability is required on this 20-mile loop, since it follows seasonal-use and abandoned dirt roads. However, a wide variety of road surfaces and large elevation gains make this ride challenging. The first 2.5 miles are fairly steep and rough. Look for a large stand of pine trees on the left during the return leg of the loop.

SUGAR HILL TRAIL

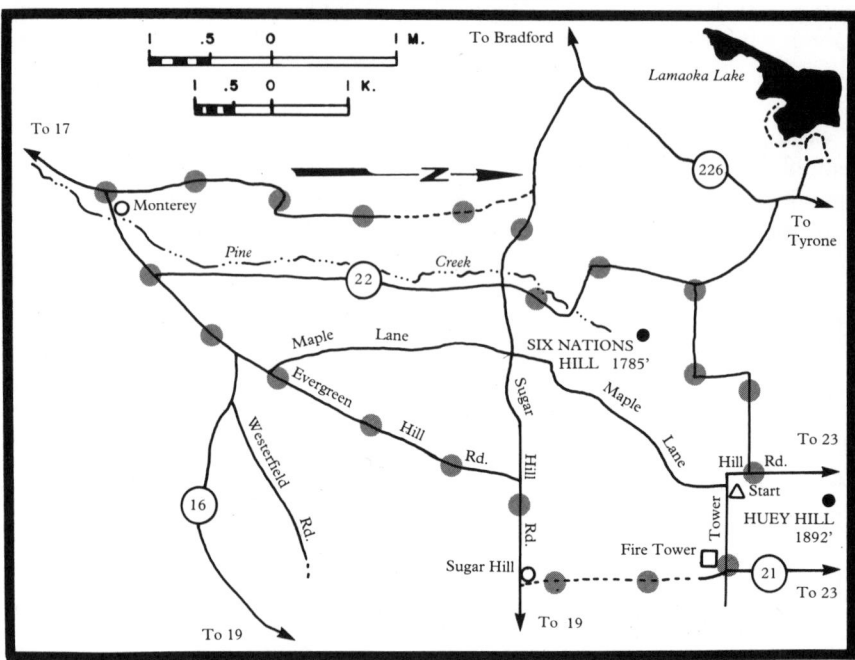

They were hand-planted to study methods of halting soil erosion in the area.

The first mile or so is on a hard-packed dirt road followed by 2.5 miles of steep climbing on an unmaintained dirt road that can be rough and rutted, especially after wet weather. This is followed by 3 miles of fairly straight and level single-track. The return trip is partially on a paved road, and includes a climb on the unpaved Evergreen Hill Road.

General location: Twelve miles north of Corning, New York.

Elevation change: The ride begins at the summit of Sugar Hill, elevation 2,080', and descends to around 1,212' halfway through the ride. The elevation is slowly recovered at the finish for a total gain of 878'.

Season: The best time to ride this loop is from mid-summer through late fall. Spring can be muddy and fall has spectacular foliage. For the hearty rider, mid-winter offers hard fast trails and views of the frosted and snow-covered hillsides.

Services: All services are available in Corning. Overnight camping is permitted in the fire tower area, and there are 4 lean-tos available.

Hazards: Watch for traffic on County Road 16.

Rescue index: The fire tower is usually manned in the summer. Also, traffic can be waved down on CR 16. The closest town is Monterey.

Land status: New York State Recreation Area.

Maps: Maps of Schuyler County are available at the Schuyler County Highway Department in Watkins Glen.

Finding the trail: Sugar Hill is located west of Watkins Glen and north of Corning. From Corning take NY 414 north; turn left onto CR 19 at North Beaver Dams. From Watkins Glen take CR 16 past the speedway to CR 21, which leads to Sugar Hill Road. Park near the tower.

Sources of additional information:

Corning Bike Works
96 E. Market Street
Corning, New York 14839
(607) 962-7831

RIDE 53 *POST CREEK TRAIL*

This is a flat, easy trail that is perfect for a quick ride in the morning or on a late summer afternoon. The railroad switching yard, the Ferenbaugh Campground, and the turnaround point at the end of the trail are interesting sights. And for anglers there is excellent fishing in Post Creek.

The approach to this 5-mile (one-way), out-and-back trail passes through Penn Central Railroad switching yard, which is used to transport large supplies of salt from underground mines near Seneca Lake. Paralleling the trail is Post Creek, a popular stocked brown trout stream (that produced a record 4-pound, 21.5-inch trout caught by Jeff Loik in 1989). The trail is lined by a wide variety of trees and passes through farmland. The ride is along a dirt road used by utility trucks. The road is frequently muddy and there are a few creek runoff crossings.

General location: Corning, New York.

Elevation change: Negligible.

Season: Summer is the best time of year to ride this trail. Other seasons tend to be wet and muddy.

Services: All services are available in Corning. Camp at the Ferenbaugh Campground, which is along the route.

Hazards: Watch for a few runoff crossings (used to prevent erosion) on the trail. Keep alert for trains.

Rescue index: Help is available at Ferenbaugh Campground or in Corning.

Land status: Private—New York State Gas and Electric Company and Penn Central Railroad.

Maps: The USGS 7.5 minute topo is Corning; the Steuben County Highway map also shows this route.

POST CREEK TRAIL

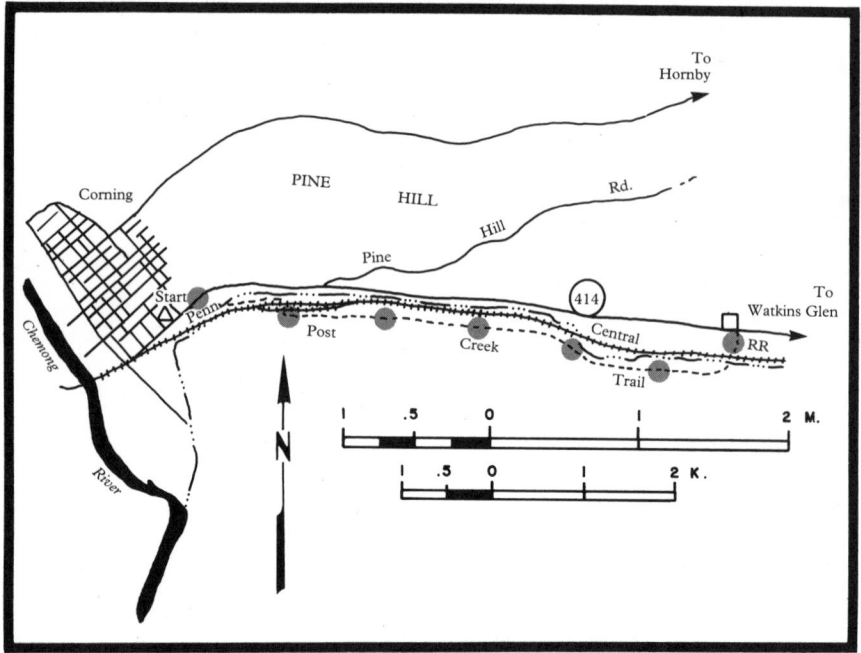

Finding the trail: The ride starts near the north side of Corning. Park in the Hotel Central parking lot, near Spruce Street (past the railroad bridge on Baker Street).

Sources of additional information:

Corning Bike Works
96 E. Market Street
Corning, New York 14839
(607) 962-7831

Notes on the trail: Ride out Baker Street in Corning, through the railroad overpass to the Hotel Central Bar and Grill (which, by the way, serves very good food). Turn right into the lot and continue past the baseball field behind the bar. Follow the road to the left that passes over a wood plank bridge. Parallel the railroad tracks for about .5 miles to the first railroad track crossing; turn left. Go about 30 yards to a small turnoff on the right (past a small railroad pump building). Ride up a short hill to the main trail on the left.

Follow the Post Creek Trail about 3 miles, where it reconnects with the railroad tracks. Follow the tracks to the campground. Here, either turn around or link up with NY 414 south for a loop ride on a paved road that leads back to Corning.

Western New York State

The huge Allegany National Forest in northwestern Pennsylvania continues north into New York as the 65,000-acre Allegany State Park, the largest in the New York state park system. Even more enticing to mountain bikers are the 80 miles of hiking trails, 25 miles of cross-country ski trails, and more than 50 miles of snowmobile trails found in the park.

The topography of Allegany State Park is marked by steep, wooded hillsides, huge rock outcroppings, fast mountain streams, deep valleys dotted with grassy meadows, and wooded wetlands. The park is forested with Allegheny Plateau hardwoods that yield legendary fall foliage. Wildlife is abundant. Look for white-tailed deer, black bear, fox, raccoon, porcupine, hawks, owls, woodpeckers, wild turkey, and numerous breeding and migratory songbirds.

North of the Allegheny River, the topography evokes Vermont. The mountain biking up here is different than in the forest—two of the rides that follow wind their way through small towns and state-owned forest lands along a combination of dirt and paved roads.

In Olean, New York, Hojo's House of Wheels serves as mountain bike headquarters for the area. Owner Tim Houseknecht sponsors both road and mountain bike races and carries maps of nearby Allegany State Park and other prime mountain biking locations. And should misfortune strike and require a fast bike repair, trust Hojo's to do a timely and correct job. After all, with 65,000 acres of state park to explore, who wants to waste time?

RIDE 54 ART ROSCOE SKI CENTER RIDE

The foothills of the Allegany Mountains remind a lot of visitors of Vermont, with low ridges blanketed with forests of maple, pine, and oak. Stone Tower, at the top of the first climb on this scenic, 19-mile loop, provides excellent views of these surrounding mountains, forests, and Red House Lake. For the best scenery try to catch the fall foliage in early October.

The 10-foot-wide ski trails winding through the forests are delightful to pedal. Be sure to stop and enjoy the views from the Stone Tower and the overlook on Christian Hollow Ski Trail. On the climb, keep your eyes peeled for a beaver dam. In summer you can end the ride with a swim at Red House Lake.

No technical skills are required to ride these roads and ski trails—just be in fairly good physical shape. The route is fairly long with only a few steep (but

ART ROSCOE SKI CENTER RIDE

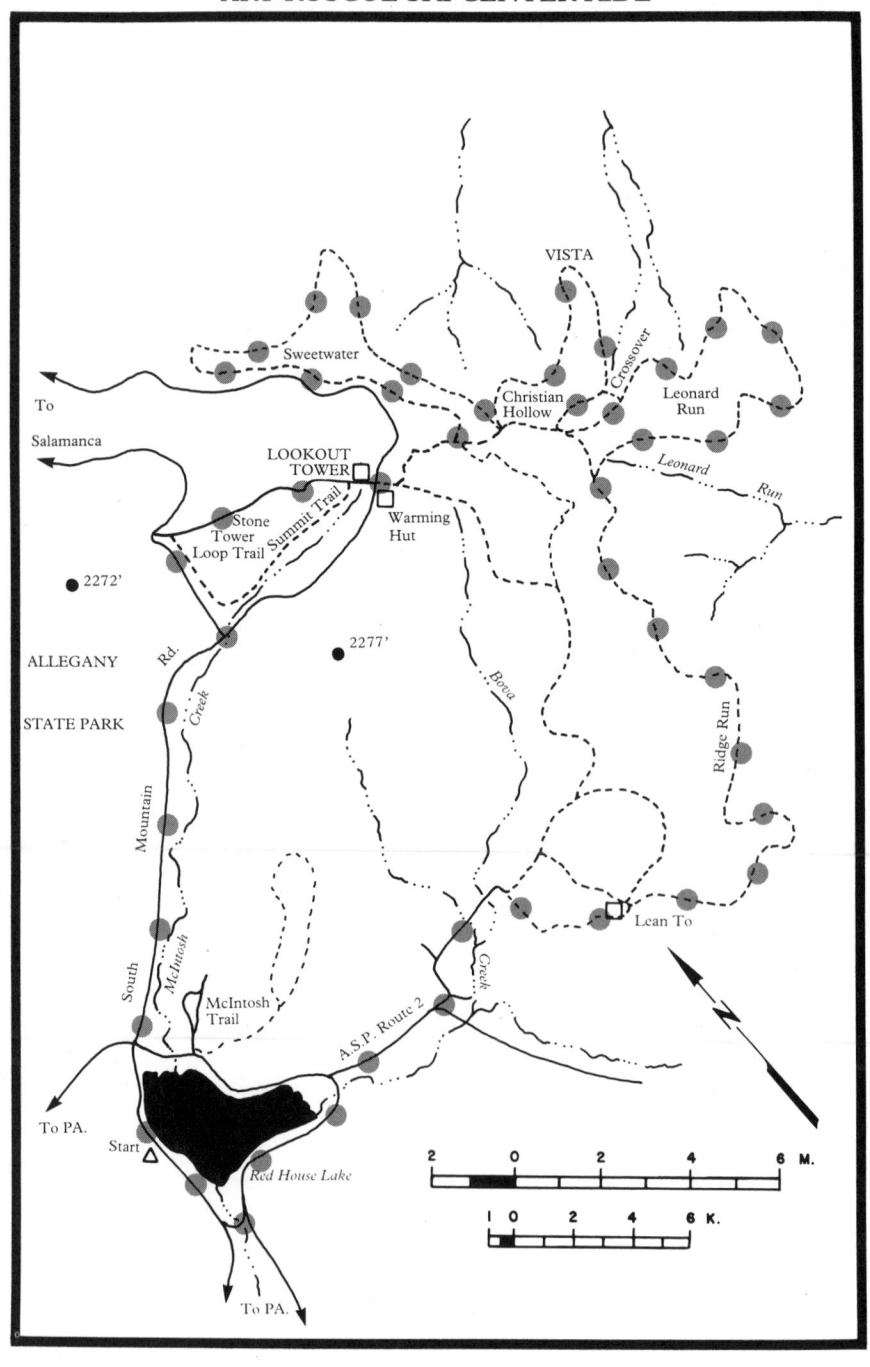

short) climbs on the ski trails. The ride starts out with a steady 3-mile climb on paved road followed by a mile on a packed-stone surface. The majority of the riding is on grassy, well-packed cross-country ski trails.

General location: Allegany State Park, Salamanca, New York, in the Red House Lake Area.

Elevation change: The ride starts at Red House Lake at an elevation of 1,456', then climbs to the Stone Tower at 2,202'. At the entrance to the cross-country ski trails the elevation is 2,300'. On the 3 trails (Sweetwater, Christian Hollow, and Leonard Run) the elevation gain is about 400'. Ridge Run descends gradually to the old Bova Ski Run, where the trail drops dramatically. The total elevation change is around 1,150'.

Season: The best season to ride this area is fall, for the trails are dry and the foliage is spectacular. In summer a long hot ride can be rewarded with a swim in Red House Lake. Spring riding tends to be soggy, due to snow thaw. Expect snow between November and March.

Services: All services available in Olean.

Hazards: Watch out for steep descents on the ski trails. Avoid riding during deer hunting season in the late fall.

Rescue index: There are cabins at the entrance to the ski trails where help may be found in an emergency. Otherwise, go to the administration building at Red House Lake.

Land status: New York state park.

Maps: The USGS 7.5 minute topo is Red House. Trail and topo maps are available at the administration building near Red House Lake.

Finding the trail: Take NY 17 (the Southern Tier Expressway) 5 miles west of Salamanca, New York, to the Red House exit. Follow the signs to the park entrance. (There is a $3 admission fee between Memorial Day and Labor Day.) Drive 1.6 miles to the intersection and bear right. Red House Lake is on the left. Park in one of the lots halfway around the lake.

Sources of additional information:

Allegany State Park
Administration Building
Salamanca, New York 14779
(716) 354-2545

Allegany State Park
Art Roscoe Ski Touring Area
Administration Building
Salamanca, New York 14779
(716) 354-2535

Hojo's House of Wheels
213 North Union Street

Olean, New York 14760
(716) 373-BIKE

Hojo's House of Wheels
9059 Main Street
Clarence, New York 14031
(716) 632-2631

Notes on the trail: To reach the trail from the parking lot, ride back past the state park administration building (clockwise around the lake) to the first stop sign. Go straight and up the hill to begin the ride.

To expand your mountain biking options even further, ask at the administration building for a copy of the snowmobile trail map. This adds about 30 miles of cycling in the area.

RIDE 55 *JOHN BUSACK CATTARAUGUS TRAIL*

Excellent views of the surrounding forests and mountains are the major attraction on this popular 37-mile loop. This part of New York state is often overlooked; the hills aren't as big, but the topography is similar to Vermont. The route passes through beautiful forests, predominantly red oak, white oak, and maple that create a riot of brilliant colors in the fall. The best time to catch the foliage is in early to mid-October.

This non-technical ride requires only minimal mountain biking skills. But its length and many climbs require good endurance. The route follows a mix of paved and unpaved roads. The unpaved roads are all hard-packed dirt, but some stretches only get seasonal maintenance. Watch for rough sections, especially in the spring.

General location: The loop starts and ends in Allegany, New York, and winds through forests to the surrounding towns to the north in Cattaraugus County.

Elevation change: The ride starts at 1,413' of elevation in the town of Allegany and reaches its highest point in Hinsdale (2,210'). There is about 2,700' of climbing, with individual climbs ranging from 500' to 800'.

Season: Fall is the best season for this ride. The daytime temperatures are very comfortable, averaging in the mid-60s. Summer can be muggy and the dirt roads in spring can get muddy. Expect snow between November and March. Avoid riding in deer hunting season, which starts in the late fall.

Services: All services available in Olean.

Hazards: Most of this ride is through farm country, so be on the lookout for traffic and dogs.

Rescue index: There are residences and farms all along the ride.

JOHN BUSACK CATTARAUGUS TRAIL

Land status: County roads and state-owned land.

Maps: County road maps are available at the Chamber of Commerce in Olean.

Finding the trail: Take NY 17 (Southern Tier Expressway) to Exit 24, which is 5 miles west of Olean, New York. Drive west on NY 417 for 1 mile to the first stop light and turn left. Drive about 1 block to the Fireman's Park on the left and park. The park is on Five Mile Road, which begins the ride.

Sources of additional information:

Chamber of Commerce
Exchange National Bank Building
North Union Street
Olean, New York 14760
(716) 372-4433

Hojo's House of Wheels
213 North Union Street
Olean, New York 14760
(716) 373-BIKE

Hojo's House of Wheels
9059 Main Street
Clarence, New York 14031
(716) 632-2631

RIDE 56 *HOLIDAY VALLEY*

This challenging ride goes through some of the most scenic areas of western New York. Even though the wilderness is long gone from this part of the state, the combination of forests, farms, and small towns makes for delightful cycling. There are excellent views of the surrounding mountains from the ridges and Little Rock City, and from the ski runs in Holiday Valley Resort. The maple, oak, and pine forests make for spectacular foliage in the fall. The area's scenery is often compared to Vermont.

The technical skills required are minimal, although there are plenty of optional ski and service trails at Holiday Valley which require more bike handling technique. Since there are many steep climbs, good endurance is a must for this out-and-back ride, which covers a variety of paved and unpaved roads over its 28-mile round-trip length. Half the unpaved roads only get seasonal maintenance, so they can be in rough shape, especially in the spring.

If getting dirty and muddy turns you on, stop at Holiday Valley Resort for a map and permission to ride their ski trails and service roads. These are actually logging roads, which are steep, rocky, and covered with deadfall.

General location: The ride starts and ends in the town of Ellicottville, New York, and winds through state lands and the town of Great Valley.

Elevation change: The lowest elevation on the ride is at Great Valley (1,477') and the highest is Little Valley (2,250'). There are 2 major climbs near Great Valley of about 800' each.

Season: The best time of year for this ride is autumn, because of the area's cool temperatures (the average high is in the mid-60s) and the spectacular fall foliage. Summer can be muggy and the dirt roads in spring are usually muddy because of snowmelt. Expect snow between November and March.

Services: All services available in Olean.

Hazards: Watch for traffic and the occasional loose dog.

Rescue index: There are residences and farms all along the ride.

Land status: County roads and state-owned land.

Maps: The USGS 7.5 minute topo maps are Salamanca and Ellicottville.

Finding the trail: From NY 17 (the Southern Tier Expressway) take Exit 23, US 219 North toward Ellicottville. From the Buffalo area take US 219 south

HOLIDAY VALLEY

toward Salamanca to Ellicottville. Park at the main lodge at Holiday Valley Ski Resort on US 219.

Sources of additional information:

Holiday Valley Ski Resort
Ellicottville, New York 14731
(716) 699-2345

Hojo's House of Wheels
213 North Union Street
Olean, New York 14760
(716) 373-BIKE

Hojo's House of Wheels
9059 Main Street
Clarence, New York 14031
(716) 632-2631

Notes on the trail: From the main lodge at Holiday Valley, pedal down Holiday Valley Road and cross over US 219 to the railroad tracks. Follow the tracks south to the town of Great Valley and turn right onto Mutton Hollow Road. Follow it to McCarthy Hollow Road. Turn right onto Hungry Hollow Road, then turn left onto Rock City Road. Continue on to Little Rock City, then turn around and return to Hungry Hollow Road and turn left. Turn right onto Whig Street. Continue to Mutton Hollow Road and turn right. Then retrace the route back to Holiday Valley.

Holiday Valley welcomes mountain bikers and holds a mountain bike race in the fall. Stop in for a map of the ski trails and service roads, and permission to mountain bike on their property.

Glossary

This short list of terms does not contain all the words used by mountain bike enthusiasts when discussing their sport. But it should be sufficient as an introduction to the lingua franca you'll hear on the trails.

ATB all-terrain bike; this, like "fat-tire bike," is another name for a mountain bike

ATV all-terrain vehicle; this usually refers to the loud, fume-spewing three- or four-wheeled motorized vehicles you will not enjoy meeting on the trail—except of course if you crash and have to hitch a ride out on one

bladed refers to a dirt road which has been smoothed out by the use of a wide blade on earth-moving equipment; "blading" gets rid of the teeth-chattering, much-cursed washboards found on so many dirt roads after heavy vehicle use

blaze a mark on a tree made by chipping away a piece of the bark, usually done to designate a trail; such trails are sometimes described as "blazed"

BLM Bureau of Land Management, an agency of the federal government

buffed used to describe a very smooth trail

clean while this can be used to describe what you and your bike *won't* be after following most trails, the term is most often used as a verb to denote the action of pedaling a tough section of trail successfully

deadfall a tangled mass of fallen trees or branches

diversion ditch a usually narrow, shallow ditch dug across or around a trail; funneling the water in this manner keeps it from destroying the trail

double-track the dual tracks made by a jeep or other vehicle, with grass or weeds or rocks between; the mountain biker can therefore ride in either of the tracks, but will find that whichever is chosen, no matter how many times he or

	she changes back and forth, the other track will appear to offer smoother travel
dugway	a steep, unpaved, switchbacked descent
feathering	using a light touch on the brake lever, hitting it lightly many times rather than very hard or locking the brake
four-wheel-drive	this refers to any vehicle with drive-wheel capability on all four wheels (a jeep, for instance, as compared with a two-wheel-drive passenger car), or to a rough road or trail which requires four-wheel-drive capability (or a *one*-wheel-drive mountain bike!) to traverse it
game trail	the usually narrow trail made by deer, elk, or other game
gated	everyone knows what a gate is, and how many variations exist upon this theme; well, if a trail is described as "gated" it simply has a gate across it; don't forget that the rule is if you find a gate closed, close it behind you; if you find one open, leave it that way
Giardia	shorthand for *Giardia lamblia,* and known as the "backpacker's bane" until we mountain bikers expropriated it; this is a waterborne parasite that begins its life cycle when swallowed, and one to four weeks later has its host (you) bloated, vomiting, shivering with chills and living in the bathroom; the disease can be avoided by "treating" (purifying) the water you acquire along the trail [see "Hitting the Trail"]
gnarly	a term thankfully used less and less these days, it refers to tough trails
hammer	to ride very hard
hardpack	used to describe a trail in which the dirt surface is packed down hard; such trails make for good and fast riding, and very painful landings; bikers most often use "hardpack" as both a noun and adjective, and "hardpacked" as an adjective only (the grammar lesson will help you when diagramming sentences in camp)
jeep road, jeep trail	a rough road or trail which requires four-wheel-drive capability (or a horse or mountain bike) to traverse it
kamikaze	while this once referred primarily to those Japanese fliers who quaffed a glass of sake, then flew off as human

bombs in suicide missions against U.S. naval vessels, it more recently has been applied to the idiot mountain bikers who far less honorably scream down hiking trails, endangering the physical and mental safety of the walking, biking, and equestrian traffic they meet; deck guns were necessary to stop the Japanese kamikaze pilots, but a bike pump or walking staff in the spokes is sufficient for the current-day kamikazes who threaten to get us all kicked off the trails

multi-purpose   a BLM designation of land which is open to multipurpose use; mountain biking is allowed

out-and-back   a ride in which you will return on the same trail you pedaled out; while this might sound far more boring than a loop route, many trails look very different when pedaled in the opposite direction

portage   to carry your bike on your person

quads   bikers use this term to refer both to the extensor muscle in the front of the thigh (which is separated into four parts), and to USGS maps; the expression "Nice quads!" refers always to the former, however, except in those instances when the speaker is an engineer

runoff   rainwater or snowmelt

signed   a signed trail is denoted by signs in place of blazes

single-track   a single track through grass or brush or over rocky terrain, often created by deer, elk, or backpackers; single-track riding is some of the best fun around

slickrock   the rock-hard, compacted sandstone which is *great* to ride and even prettier to look at; you'll appreciate it more if you think of it as a petrified sand dune or seabed, and if the rider before you hasn't left tire marks (through unnecessary skidding) or granola bar wrappers behind

snowmelt   runoff produced by the melting of snow

snowpack   unmelted snow accumulated over weeks or months of winter, or over years in high-mountain terrain

spur   a road or trail which intersects the main trail you're following

technical   terrain that is difficult to ride due not to its grade (steepness) but because of obstacles—rocks, logs, ledges, loose soil . . .

topo   short for topographical map, the kind that shows both linear distance *and* elevation gain and loss; "topo" is pronounced with both vowels long

trashed   a trail which has been destroyed (same term used no matter what has destroyed it . . . cattle, horses, or even mountain bikers riding when the ground was too wet)

two-wheel-drive   this refers to any vehicle with drive-wheel capability on only two wheels (a passenger car, for instance, compared with a jeep), or to an easy road or trail which a two-wheel-drive vehicle could traverse

water bar   earth, rock, or wooden structure which funnels water off trails

washboarded   a road with many ridges spaced closely together, like the ripples on a washboard; these make for very rough riding, and even worse driving in a car or jeep

wilderness area   land that is officially set aside by the Federal Government to remain *natural*—pure, pristine, and untrammeled by any vehicle, including mountain bikes; though mountain bikes had not been born in 1964 (when the U.S. Congress passed the Wilderness Act, establishing the National Wilderness Preservation system) they are considered a "form of mechanical transport" and are thereby excluded; in short, stay out

wind chill   a reference to the wind's cooling effect upon exposed flesh; for example, if the temperature is 10 degrees Fahrenheit and the wind is blowing at 20 miles per hour, the wind-chill effect (that is, the actual temperature to which your skin reacts) is *minus* 32 degrees; if you are riding in wet conditions things are even worse, for the wind-chill effect would then be *minus 74 degrees*!

windfall   anything (trees, limbs, brush, fellow bikers) blown down by the wind

Photo by Dave Hammond

When not hard at work on his next mountain bike trail guide or writing articles for *VeloNews, Dirt Rag,* or the *Baltimore Sun,* JOE SURKIEWICZ revels in conquering technical single-track trails, riding his road bike, and savoring the early films of Barbara Stanwyck. He lives in Baltimore, Maryland, with his wife Ann Lembo and their cat Wally.

The Mountain Bike Way to Knowledge is through William Nealy

No other great Zen master approaches William Nealy in style or originality. His handwritten text, signature cartoons, and off-beat sense of humor have made him a household name among bikers. His expertise, acquired through years of meditation (and some crash and burn), enables him to translate hard-learned reflexes and instinctive responses into his unique, easy-to-understand drawings. Anyone who wants to learn from the master (and even those who don't) will get a good laugh.

Mountain Bike!
A Manual of Beginning to Advanced Technique

The ultimate mountain bike book for the totally honed! Master the techniques of mountain biking and have a good laugh while logging miles with Nealy.

Soft cover, 172 pages, 7" by 10"
Cartoon illustrations
$12.95

The Mountain Bike Way of Knowledge

This is the first compendium of mountain bike "insider" knowledge ever published. Between the covers of this book are the secrets of wheelie turns, log jumps, bar hops, dog evasion techniques, and much more! Nealy shares his wisdom with beginner and expert alike in this self-help manual.

Soft cover, 128 pages, 8" by 5 1/2"
Cartoon illustrations
$6.95

From Menasha Ridge Press
1-800-247-9437

FALCONGUIDES *Perfect for every outdoor adventure!*

FISHING
Angler's Guide to Alaska
Angler's Guide to Minnesota
Angler's Guide to Montana
Beartooth Fishing Guide

FLOATING
Floater's Guide to Colorado
Floater's Guide to Missouri
Floater's Guide to Montana

HIKING
Hiker's Guide to Alaska
Hiker's Guide to Alberta
Hiker's Guide to Arizona
Hiker's Guide to California
Hiker's Guide to Colorado
Hiker's Guide to Hot Springs
   in the Pacific Northwest
Hiker's Guide to Idaho
Hiker's Guide to Missouri
Hiker's Guide to Montana
Hiker's Guide to Montana's
   Continental Divide Trail
Hiker's Guide to Nevada
Hiker's Guide to New Mexico
Hiker's Guide to Oregon
Hiker's Guide to Texas
Hiker's Guide to Utah
Hiker's Guide to Virginia
Hiker's Guide to Washington
Hiker's Guide to Wyoming
Hiking Softly, Hiking Safely
Trail Guide to Glacier National Park

MOUNTAIN BIKING
Mountain Biker's Guide to Arizona
Mountain Biker's Guide to
   Central Appalachia

Mountain Biker's Guide to
   Northern New England
Mountain Biker's Guide to
   Southern California

ROCKHOUNDING
Rockhound's Guide to Arizona
Rockhound's Guide to Montana

SCENIC DRIVING
Arizona Scenic Drives
Back Country Byways
California Scenic Drives
Oregon Scenic Drives
Scenic Byways
Scenic Byways II
Trail of the Great Bear
Traveler's Guide to the Oregon Trail

WILDLIFE VIEWING GUIDES
Arizona Wildlife Viewing Guide
California Wildlife Viewing Guide
Colorado Wildlife Viewing Guide
Idaho Wildlife Viewing Guide
Indiana Wildlife Viewing Guide
Montana Wildlife Viewing Guide
North Carolina Wildlife Viewing Guide
North Dakota Wildlife Viewing Guide
Oregon Wildlife Viewing Guide
Texas Wildlife Viewing Guide
Utah Wildlife Viewing Guide
Washington Wildlife Viewing Guide

PLUS—
Birder's Guide to Montana
Hunter's Guide to Montana
Recreation Guide to
   California National Forests
Recreation Guide to
   Washington National Forests

Falcon Press Publishing Co. • *Call toll-free 1-800-582-2665*